The International Education Leadership Companion

As a leader navigating the complexities of an international education community, you need a manual to help you address the unpredictable and rapidly evolving scenarios you face. Surround yourself with the team of experts inside the chapters of *The International Education Leadership Companion* as they present a practical resource for everyday leadership challenges. Blending a compilation of theory and practice, the lessons offered within these chapters are grounded in standards of leadership from internationally renowned international school educators. The book's advice is brought to life by authentic case studies to offer meaningful reflection opportunities that directly translate to your job at hand: successfully leading international education communities in a world characterized by volatility, constant change, and uncertainty. Whether you are a new leader stepping into your first international role or a seasoned professional looking to refine your approach, the insights within these pages offer both practical guidance and profound inspiration. Leadership can feel isolating, but it cannot be effectively done alone – immerse yourself in *The International Education Leadership Companion* and bring your trusted, experienced guides alongside you throughout the journey!

Catarina Song Chen is with the U.S. Department of State Office of Overseas Schools responsible for Strategic Initiatives and Partnerships and an award-winning school leader with over 25 years of experience in education.

Colin Brown is Superintendent of Escuela Internacional Sampedrana, accreditation lead evaluator, and presenter of best practice with over 25 years serving in education.

Lindsay Prendergast is an international education leader, leadership coach, and best-selling author with over 20 years serving in education.

Also Available from Routledge Eye On Education
(www.routledge.com/eyeoneducation)

Leadership Teams in America's Best Schools: Improving the Lives of All Students
Joseph F. Johnson, Jr., Cynthia L. Uline, Stanley Munro, Jr., and Francisco Escobedo

Making Community Schools a Reality: Harnessing Your Power as a School Leader through Collaboration
Emily L. Woods

Wholehearted School Leadership: Rewiring Our Schools for Courage, Justice, Learning, and Connection
Kathryn Fishman-Weaver

Data Analysis for Continuous School Improvement, 5th Edition
Victoria L. Bernhardt

Culturally Conscious Decision-Making for School Leaders: A Toolkit for Creating a More Equitable School Culture
Shauna McGee

Teacher Leadership Practice in High-Performing Schools: A Blueprint for Excellence
Jeremy D. Visone

Coaching Education Leaders: A Culturally Responsive Approach to Transforming Schools and Systems
Nancy B. Gutierrez, Michelle Jarney, and Michael Kim

Finding Your Path as a Woman in School Leadership: A Guide for Educators, Allies, and Advocates
Kim Cofino and Christina Botbyl

Becoming an International School Educator: Stories, Tips, and Insights from Teachers and Leaders
Edited by Dana Specker Watts and Jayson W. Richardson

Bringing Innovative Practices to Your School: Lessons from International Schools
Jayson Richardson

The International Education Leadership Companion

Lessons and Best Practices from Expert Leaders

Edited by
Catarina Song Chen, Colin Brown,
and Lindsay Prendergast

Designed cover image: © Getty Images

First published 2026
by Routledge
605 Third Avenue, New York, NY 10158

and by Routledge
4 Park Square, Milton Park, Abingdon, Oxon, OX14 4RN

Routledge is an imprint of the Taylor & Francis Group, an informa business

© 2026 selection and editorial matter, Catarina Song Chen, Colin Brown, and Lindsay Prendergast; individual chapters, the contributors

The right of Catarina Song Chen, Colin Brown, and Lindsay Prendergast to be identified as the authors of the editorial material, and of the authors for their individual chapters, has been asserted in accordance with sections 77 and 78 of the Copyright, Designs and Patents Act 1988.

All rights reserved. No part of this book may be reprinted or reproduced or utilized in any form or by any electronic, mechanical, or other means, now known or hereafter invented, including photocopying and recording, or in any information storage or retrieval system, without permission in writing from the publishers.

Trademark notice: Product or corporate names may be trademarks or registered trademarks, and are used only for identification and explanation without intent to infringe.

ISBN: 978-1-032-94729-7 (hbk)
ISBN: 978-1-032-94728-0 (pbk)
ISBN: 978-1-003-58145-1 (ebk)

DOI: 10.4324/9781003581451

Typeset in Optima
by KnowledgeWorks Global Ltd.

Contents

About the Editors and Contributors	vii
Preface	xii
Acknowledgments	xiv

1. **Introduction** — 1
   Lindsay Prendergast, Catarina Song Chen, and Colin Brown

2. **Rebuilding Education as We Know It and the Urgency of Now: Transforming Education to Meet a Transforming World** — 4
   Ulcca Joshi Hansen and Jim Hardin

3. **Leading Cultures of Dignity** — 25
   Rosalind Wiseman and Mark Ulfers

4. **Leading the Vision: A Human Learning Ecosystem for Our Times** — 49
   Kevin Bartlett and Jeremy Moore

5. **Leading the Streamlining Shift in Curriculum: What to Cut Out, Cut Back, Consolidate, and Create to Prepare Future-Ready Learners** — 64
   Heidi Hayes Jacobs and Catarina Song Chen

6. **Managing the Politics of the Board Room** — 87
   John Littleford and Catriona Moran

7. **Leading the Organizational Culture** — 102
   Ruth Allen and Patrice Dawkins-Jackson

Contents

8.	**Leading Change Begins with Trust** *Vicki Denmark, Colin Brown, and Lindsay Prendergast*	121
9.	**Guiding Teachers through Change** *Myron Dueck and Colin Brown*	140
10.	**Leading for a Flourishing Society** *Kam Chohan and Michael Johnston*	166
11.	**Leading with Resilience** *Bloodine Barthelus and Shauna Hobbs-Beckley*	183
12.	**Driving Leadership: A School Leader's Journey** *Shannon Hobbs-Beckley, Laura McBain, Ariel Raz, and Richard Boerner*	205
	Index	225

About the Editors and Contributors

Editors

Catarina Song Chen is the US Department of State REO for Strategic Initiatives and an award-winning school leader with over 15 years of experience as a Head of School in Brazil. She has served as the Vice President on the board of trustees for AMISA and serves as a board member and organizational leader for AAIE, AISH, and various other international education organizations.

Colin Brown, Ph.D., is an international education leader with 28+ years in teaching and administration across six countries. He is the founder of the CATES Educators' Conference and TAI-FAIR, founding Board Chair of EAPISA, and has led dozens of international school accreditation reviews for Cognia and WASC. Dr. Brown is a sought-after speaker on curriculum innovation, leadership, and professional growth.

Lindsay Prendergast, Ed.D., has served as a leadership coach, director of strategy for a non-profit, school leader and teacher for nearly 20 years. She is the co-author of the bestselling *Habits of Resilient Educators* series (Corwin, 2024–2025) and an international thought leader with many of the worlds' leading educational organizations.

Contributors

Ruth Allen, Ed.D., has spent nearly two decades as a head of school in Colombia. She earned her doctorate from the University of Bath,

About the Editors and Contributors

specializing in the establishment of institutional legitimacy in international schools. She firmly believes that learning and leadership thrive on trust, each reinforcing and sustaining the other.

Bloodine Barthelus, Ed.D., is an education leader with extensive experience in social-emotional learning (SEL) and school climate. As the former Senior Director of Practice at CASEL, she oversaw initiatives supporting SEL implementation across schools around the world. Previously, she led SEL and school climate efforts in DC Public Schools, developing districtwide SEL plans and professional learning. Dr. Barthelus holds a doctorate from the College of William and Mary, focusing her research on the relationship between student infractions and SEL.

Kevin Bartlett is a distinguished international education leader with extensive experience across five countries. As the Founding Director of the Common Ground Collaborative, he has co-designed accreditation systems and initiated the IB Primary Years Programme. Kevin's commitment to inclusive education and systemic transformation has earned him recognition, including International Superintendent of the Year and induction into the AAIE Hall of Fame.

Richard Boerner is an award-winning educator with over 30 years of experience in US and international schools. He has led three international schools across South Korea, Bangladesh, and Brazil. Recognized for his innovative leadership, Richard founded the Graded Learning Lab and received the 2022 AMISA International Education Leadership Award and the 2023 AAIE Dr. Keith Miller International Innovation Leadership Award.

Kam Chohan, Executive Director of the Educational Collaborative for International Schools, is a global education leader with expertise in DEI, leadership, and curriculum. Kam is known for her work with the UK Government's Behaviour Insights Team to apply the Nudge Theory to improve student outcomes on a national level. She is committed to fostering inclusive, future-focused learning environments worldwide and was honored with NEASC's 2022 Exemplary Service Award.

Patrice Dawkins-Jackson is the founder and CEO of The Blueprint Collective and former associate of networked improvement science at the

Carnegie Foundation. She previously served as an educator in Georgia, a U.S. Department of Education Teaching Ambassador Fellow, and director of organizational learning & development, focusing on equity and innovation.

Vicki Denmark, Ph.D., Dr. Denmark's professional career in education spans over 40 years. Throughout her career, she has held various roles, including classroom teacher, a professor, an executive leader in a large public school system, and in an international school improvement company. She is currently the CEO of her consulting company.

Myron Dueck is an educator and administrator with over 25 years of experience in Canada and New Zealand. He has developed innovative grading and assessment systems that empower students. Author of the bestsellers "Grading Smarter, Not Harder" and "Giving Students a Say," Myron advocates for student-centered learning and regularly shares his insights globally.

Jim Hardin, Ed.D., A former Peace Corps volunteer, Jim has taught and led schools in Japan, the UAE, Scotland, and Poland for 23 years, with another 12 years in US public education. He believes international schools have a duty to lead transformative change, championing human-centered learning, deep pedagogical innovation, and future-focused education.

Shannon Hobbs-Beckley is an education leader with over 28 years of experience in international and US schools. She has served as an administrator, professional learning coordinator, instructional coach, and classroom teacher. As a sought-after leadership and performance coach, she specializes in leadership, adult learning, and organizational development. She presents globally on these topics and also works with schools and individuals on their growth journeys.

Shauna Hobbs-Beckley, Ed.D., is an education leader with 30 years of experience in public and private education. She has held key roles in curriculum, assessment, and instructional leadership, both nationally and internationally. Committed to innovation and continuous learning, she shapes educational strategies and fosters inclusive, student-centered learning environments.

About the Editors and Contributors

Heidi Hayes Jacobs, Ed.D., focuses on upgrading curriculum mapping, modernizing school ecosystems, creating responsive learning spaces, and developing confident future-ready learners. Featured in numerous books, articles, podcasts, courses and software platforms, her models and practices are used by educators throughout the world.

Michael Johnston, Ed.D., is an education leader with extensive international experience in Mexico, Russia, Qatar, Singapore, Guatemala, and Germany. Dr. Johnston serves on the Board for the Association of International Education Leadership (AAIE). Committed to sustainability and community engagement, he fosters authentic learning experiences that connect students deeply to the world around them.

Ulcca Joshi Hansen, PhD, JD, is a futurist and author of the award-winning book "The Future of Smart." Her work interrogates the assumptions that shape our modern-day systems, and explores how to prepare individuals and communities for the opportunities presented by rapid social change. An internationally-recognized expert on human-centered design, Dr. Hansen works to design educational systems that align with what human development, neuroscience, and the realities of technological advancement tell us human beings will need to thrive. She holds a PhD from Oxford University and a JD from Harvard Law School.

John Littleford served as teacher, trustee, and head of school for over 25 years. For the past 30 years he has been a consultant to over 6000 independent and international schools. Littleford & Associates' clients also include corporations, foundations, universities, and other non-profit organizations.

Laura McBain is Managing Director at the Stanford d.school, where she leads professional education and partnerships. A designer, author, and global speaker, she focuses on equity, education, and innovation. Formerly with High Tech High, she helps organizations use design for transformation and is the author of *My Favorite Failure* on learning through setbacks.

Jeremy Moore, PhD, is an experienced international school leader and consultant with RG175. As a school Head, he has led strategic growth, campus expansions, accreditation, and team development in the Cayman Islands and South Africa. He has served on boards for Middle States Association of

Colleges and Schools, Common Ground Collaborative, and AMISA, advancing global education leadership.

Catriona Moran, Ed.D., is a distinguished educational leader with over three decades of international experience across Japan, Taiwan, and Vietnam. She has been named Principal of the Year by the National Association of Elementary School Principals and the U.S. State Department. She serves on the Board of Trustees for the East Asia Regional Council of Schools (EARCOS).

Ariel Raz is an education leader with extensive experience in experiential teaching practices. As Head of Learning Collaborations at the Stanford d. school, he designs learning experiences that inspire professionals to engage in creative work. Committed to innovation and continuous learning, Ariel shapes educational strategies and fosters inclusive, student-centered learning environments.

Mark Ulfers is the Director of the U.S. State Department Office of Overseas Schools, bringing 28 years of experience as an international school head. He led schools in Singapore, Cyprus, Taipei, Frankfurt, and Paris. A former AAIE Executive Director, he has also chaired EARCOS and co-founded the Academy of International School Heads.

Rosalind Wiseman is the best-selling author of nine books, including *Queen Bees and Wannabes*, the inspiration for *Mean Girls*, and *Masterminds & Wingmen*, named Best Parenting Book by Books for a Better Life. She serves as a senior leadership consultant for the U.S. State Department's Office of Overseas Schools, supporting 195+ schools globally. She also contributed to David Yeager's new book *10 to 25* on leading the next generation.

Preface

The challenges and opportunities facing international educational institutions today extend far beyond geographical boundaries, demanding a new breed of leaders who can navigate the nuanced complexities of global education. *The International Education Leadership Companion* is designed to support current and aspiring leaders by offering a comprehensive exploration of the dynamic realm of international educational leadership. In an era shaped by diverse cultural, political, and socioeconomic contexts, this book synthesizes the expertise of global education leaders who bring decades of experience guiding schools in dozens of countries with the insights of internationally renowned education experts across the field.

Each chapter is co-authored by a pair of experts: one who shares deep expertise as an experienced international school leader in the role of Director or Head of School, and one or more thought leaders who bring specialized knowledge as experts in the chapter's topic. This structure ensures that the book provides both practical, field-tested wisdom and research-backed strategies to equip leaders with the tools necessary to navigate the complexities of international education.

The book is organized into 12 chapters, each delving into a critical aspect of educational leadership. The chapters collectively paint a rich picture of the multifaceted nature of leadership in international schools. Readers will encounter discussions on innovative instructional leadership, inclusive learning environments, school governance and board relations, and the impact of emerging technologies. By blending authentic case studies with theoretical approaches framed by renowned experts, the book provides a unique window into the lived experiences of those at the forefront of international education leadership. The overarching narrative aims to stimulate critical dialogue and deepen our understanding of leadership in an international context, highlighting both commonalities and unique challenges within the field.

This book is intended for aspiring or new education leaders eager to accelerate their professional growth. By learning from real-world case studies situated in the context of research and established leadership frameworks, readers will gain valuable insights into navigating common leadership scenarios in K-12 schools. Whether stepping into leadership for the first time or refining their approach in a new international setting, readers will find strategies and perspectives to enhance their impact and prepare them for the evolving demands of global education leadership.

Through its blend of research and practical wisdom, *The International Education Leadership Companion* aspires to empower the next generation of leaders to shape educational institutions that thrive in an increasingly interconnected world.

Acknowledgments

The Editors would like to thank the incredible education leaders who contributed their time, wisdom, and expertise to this volume as a gift to the greater education community. We are tremendously appreciative of the insights of Kristen Moreland who supported the Editors in refining the words on these pages. And we are each forever grateful to our families who shoulder the burden of our overextended schedules with their support and encouragement.

Introduction

*Lindsay Prendergast,
Catarina Song Chen, and
Colin Brown*

International schools represent a vibrant and dynamic sector within global education, encompassing thousands of institutions that serve diverse communities across the world. While these schools vary in structure, curriculum, and governance, they share a unifying purpose: fostering global citizenship, bridging cultures, and preparing students for success in an interconnected world (Hayden & Thompson, 2013). Leading an international school requires a unique set of skills—balancing innovation with tradition, navigating cultural complexities, and building cohesive school communities that transcend geographic and national boundaries. It is a leadership challenge unlike any other, filled with both profound opportunities and demanding responsibilities (Bunnell, 2019).

The International Education Leadership Companion is designed to support and inspire current and aspiring leaders in international schools. This collection of perspectives from seasoned educators and renowned thought leaders offers a deep dive into the multifaceted nature of leadership within international education. Across its chapters, this book explores the essential dimensions of effective leadership, from shaping a compelling vision to fostering inclusion, managing change, and building resilient teams. The contributors to this volume share invaluable lessons drawn from their own experiences and deep expertise, providing both practical strategies and profound insights into the evolving landscape of international education leadership.

Readers will embark on a journey through the key pillars of international school leadership. As international school leaders face increasing uncertainty in a VUCA (Volatile, Uncertain, Complex, Ambiguous) world, the ability to lead with adaptability and resilience becomes paramount

(Morrison, 2018). Ulcca Joshi Hansen and Jim Hardin explore strategies for leading through a holistic, human-centered paradigm rooted in developmental science, equipping leaders with the tools to foster whole-child growth, authentic equity, and global citizenship. Bloodine Barthelus and Shauna Hobbs-Beckley turn the lens inward, emphasizing the importance of leader resilience and well-being, ensuring that those who guide school communities can sustain their passion and effectiveness over the long term. Finally, Rosalind Wiseman and Mark Ulfers examine leadership within the broader school community, emphasizing the critical role of culture, stakeholder engagement, and navigating external sociocultural influences.

Kevin Bartlett and Jeremy Moore delve into the importance of vision-driven leadership, illuminating how a clear and shared purpose fuels school success. John Littleford and Catriona Moran examine the critical partnership between school leaders and their school boards, emphasizing the power of trust and collaboration in governance (Walker & Riordan, 2010). Shannon Hobbs-Beckley, Laura McBain, Ariel Raz, and Rich Boerner highlight the urgency of leading innovation, framing how schools can shift from traditional models toward more meaningful, student-centered learning experiences.

The volume also tackles essential topics such as inclusion, growth, and learning design. Kam Chohan and Michael Johnston explore the complexities of school culture, unpacking the approaches that drive sustainable and positive impact on society. Heidi Hayes Jacobs and Catarina Song Chen provide insights into leading learning, offering frameworks that enable leaders to cultivate transformative educational experiences.

Change is a constant in international education, and leaders must be adept at managing transitions. Vicki Denmark and Colin Brown examine the nuances of leading change, offering guidance on navigating resistance and fostering long-term progress. Myron Dueck and Colin Brown focus on team leadership, outlining strategies to build strong, collaborative faculty cultures that drive school success. Meanwhile, Patrice Dawkins-Jackson and Ruth Allen discuss the pillars of cohesive resource management, demonstrating how strategic planning and design can optimize a school's impact.

The International Education Leadership Companion is more than a guidebook—it is a conversation among leaders, a space to reflect, learn, and grow. With the rapid expansion of international education and the increasing complexity of global schooling, this book serves as an essential resource for those who seek to lead with vision, innovation, and integrity. Whether you are a new leader stepping into your first international role or a seasoned professional looking to refine your approach, the insights within these pages offer both practical guidance and profound inspiration. We invite you to join this journey, engage with these voices, and chart your own path in the ever-evolving world of international education leadership.

References

Bunnell, T. (2019). *International schooling: The teacher's guide.* Emerald Publishing.

Hayden, M., & Thompson, J. (2013). *International schools: Principles and practice* (2nd ed.). Routledge.

Morrison, K. (2018). *Management theories for educational change* (2nd ed.). SAGE Publications.

Walker, A., & Riordan, G. (2010). Leading and managing international schools. *International Journal of Leadership in Education, 30*(1), 51–63. https://doi.org/10.1080/13632430903509766

2

Rebuilding Education as We Know It and the Urgency of Now

Transforming Education to Meet a Transforming World

Ulcca Joshi Hansen and Jim Hardin

We stand at a crossroads in education. Familiar systems and structures now seem inadequate, even obsolete, in the face of rapid societal changes. The COVID-19 pandemic, the rise of artificial intelligence, and a growing awareness of system injustices have all converged to expose the limitations of our traditional education model. While this convergence has created disruption, it also presents a profound opportunity to rethink what education should be and how it can serve our children and communities in this new era.

International schools are uniquely positioned to lead this transformation. With their resources, autonomy, and diverse communities, they have the opportunity and obligation to reimagine education. Freed from public education constraints, these schools can redefine what education can be. This moment demands more than incremental reform; it calls for rethinking our purpose, priorities, and practices. International schools must lead the way in creating a new paradigm for education—one that is profoundly human-centered and capable of addressing the complexities of a world that is increasingly volatile, uncertain, complex, and ambiguous (VUCA) (TechTarget.com, January 2025).

The Current Landscape of International Education

Over the past several decades, international schools have often mirrored the dominant trends in education, particularly those rooted in Western paradigms. While these schools frequently serve privileged populations and enjoy substantial resources, their fundamental approach to teaching and learning remains grounded in the Cartesian-Newtonian worldview, shaping education systems globally. This model, emphasizing standardization, quantification, and control, has undoubtedly provided structure and predictability in educational design. Yet, it has also led to unintended consequences, particularly in a VUCA world.

The strengths of this legacy are clear: international schools excel in preparing students for measurable academic success, often reflected in stellar exam performance and placement in selective universities. Accreditation frameworks like WASC (Western Association for Schools and Colleges), NEASC (New England Association of Schools and Colleges), and CIS (Council of International Schools) reinforce a shared language of accountability, fostering consistency and comparability across diverse educational contexts. Standards-based assessments, curriculum mapping tools, backward-planning frameworks, and pedagogical models elevating best practices have driven ways of working in international schools that prioritize consistency, accountability, and measurable outcomes.

However, these strengths can obscure significant limitations. The dominance of mechanistic, left-hemisphere approaches to learning—focused on categorization, abstraction, and standardized outcomes—leaves little room for the holistic, relational, and contextual ways of knowing the complexity of the real world. The rigid systems designed to rank and sort students often fail to nurture the full range of human potential, including creativity, empathy, and adaptability. This factory-model approach is increasingly misaligned with the needs of today's students, not to mention future generations.

International schools are at a pivotal moment. As the world becomes increasingly complex and interconnected, traditional measures of success are no longer enough. The demands of a VUCA world make it urgent for students to develop a broader range of capabilities, including resilience, ethical decision-making, and a sense of purpose. Yet, international schools often remain tied to legacy systems, predictability, and control over adaptability and innovation.

These schools are uniquely positioned to break free from legacy constraints. With their autonomy, substantial resources, and multicultural communities, international schools can lead a shift toward a new education paradigm that reflects the interconnectedness of modern challenges. Their multicultural and multilingual environments provide fertile ground for fostering global citizenship and helping students understand their role in a shared, interdependent world. Reimagining success demands redefining it—not as a narrow pursuit of academic or economic achievement, but as a holistic process that empowers students to thrive in uncertainty and contribute meaningfully to society.

Reimagining success requires moving beyond incremental adjustments to systems and curricula. Schools must rethink the structures, norms, and assumptions that shape education. A human-centered model goes beyond adding social-emotional learning programs or embedding competencies like creativity and critical thinking into existing frameworks. It demands transforming systems—aligning governance, professional development, teaching practices, and community engagement to support whole-child development.

At their best, international schools have already demonstrated glimpses of the future. When systems align around shared values and priorities, schools transcend institutions of learning to become ecosystems where belonging, purpose, and innovation flourish. This is both a challenge and an opportunity for international schools: to fully leverage their strengths and reimagine a model of education that reflects the complexities of the world students will inherit.

Understanding Our Present Education System through Two Worldviews

To understand both the limitations of our current educational system and the possibilities for transformation, we must first examine two fundamental ways of seeing and being in the world that have shaped human societies across time and continue to influence our approaches to education today.

The dominant worldview in Western society for the past several centuries, often referred to as the Cartesian-Newtonian worldview, emerged from the scientific revolution and Enlightenment thinking (Hansen, 2007). This perspective has profoundly shaped our educational institutions and practices. It:

- Emphasizes rationality, objectivity, and a mechanistic view of the world
- Values categorization, quantification, and the pursuit of universal truths
- Sees the individual as separate from nature and community
- Prioritizes linear thinking and predictable outcomes
- Focuses on standardization and measurement
- Views knowledge as discrete, objective, and transferable

This worldview gave rise to many of our dominant economic, political, and social systems, including the factory/industrial model of education, with its emphasis on standardization, measurement, and hierarchical sorting of students. While this worldview has enabled us to make significant advances in scientific understanding and technological capability, it has also created educational systems that increasingly fail to meet the needs of today's learners and society.

In contrast, an older way of seeing the world exists—one that has historically driven human societies and continues to inform indigenous cultures globally. This holistic-indigenous worldview (Hansen, 2021):

- Emphasizes interconnectedness, wholeness, and respect for the natural world
- Values intuition, creativity, and multiple ways of knowing
- Recognizes knowledge as emerging from experience and relationship
- Sees humans as inseparable from nature and community
- Embraces complexity and uncertainty
- Values collective wisdom and shared learning

This worldview has historically grounded human societies as they lived in deep awareness of their dependence on and relationship with the natural world. While this perspective was largely marginalized during the rise of industrial society, its wisdom is increasingly relevant to addressing contemporary challenges.

The Brain's Two Ways of Knowing

These contrasting worldviews find a fascinating parallel in human brain structure and function. The brain's hemispheric division offers profound insights into how humans engage with the world and, by extension, how we might better approach education.

To be clear, this insight into hemispheric distinctions is not about the disproven idea that "left-brained" people are analytic, or that "right-brained" people are creative. Both hemispheres of the brain are involved in everything we do, including high-level activities such as reasoning, imagining, and creating. However, the hemispheres do engage differently with the world, working both individually and in concert, which allows human beings to do two critical things simultaneously.

On the one hand, humans have learned to make use of the world, manipulate our surroundings, locate discrete entities, and figure out their behaviors and their utility. In order to do that, the brain creates a simplified version of reality—something like a map. A map isn't reality, but for many purposes, it works better than the real thing because the real thing is simply too complex to survey and analyze every time we need to, say, drive to the beach. To navigate the world, we conjure abstract, narrower versions of it; we create categories, maps, rubrics, and comparisons. This is the work of our left hemisphere.

On the other hand, we exist in the world as embodied beings, moving through space, flooded with sensory input, interacting with others, interpreting clues about how to engage—in short, having experiences that don't fit into neat categories; that immerse us, surround us, move through us. This embodied way of experiencing the world is associated with the right hemisphere. It's an intuitive, body-based, and timeless way of being. To take just one example of the dual experience that's happening in us all the time, our left hemisphere allows us to recognize the little person sitting across from us in the airport as belonging to those categories known as "family" and "child," someone who must not be ignored or left to fend for themselves. Our right hemisphere elicits the complex emotions of caretaking, disciplining, cuddling, and playing. Our right hemisphere allows us to not only know the world but to experience it in a visceral way.

In more concrete terms, the left hemisphere pulls things out of context to identify features and give them names, while the right tends to see things in context—to experience connections between things as much as the things themselves. The left tends to make things abstract, while the right makes things vivid and concrete. The left seeks to know what to do and what things mean, seeking certainty and control, while the right is attuned to how things feel and how they simply are, embracing ambiguity and uncertainty (McGilchrist, 2012).

Everything we know about human evolution and the health of individuals, communities, and society suggests that our experience, while informed and strengthened by left-hemisphere capabilities, should be governed by right-hemisphere awareness of connection, wholeness, and embodiment. Yet our educational systems, reflecting the dominant Cartesian-Newtonian worldview, have increasingly privileged left-hemisphere approaches.

Our Current Context: Three Critical Forces

Against this background of competing worldviews and complementary brain functions, three intersecting forces make educational transformation at this moment in time not just desirable but imperative.

1. The VUCA World Reality

Today's students face a world characterized by volatility, uncertainty, complexity, and ambiguity (VUCA). The human brain is not wired to thrive under any one of these conditions; the convergence of them in the world today points to the need for young people to develop a very different set of capabilities than those most valued in the existing education system.

This reality fundamentally challenges our traditional educational approaches, which were designed for a more predictable world. The COVID-19 pandemic provided a stark example of VUCA in action; schools and societies faced rapidly changing circumstances, conflicting information, complex systemic challenges, and profound uncertainty about the future. This experience highlighted the inadequacy of educational systems focused primarily on content transmission and standardized outcomes.

The VUCA world demands capabilities far beyond traditional academic skills. Key among them:

The ability to manage and work within ambiguity: Without this ability, our brains and bodies are prone to remain in a perpetual state of fight or flight, leading to behaviors that are unhealthy for individuals and communities. This means young people must develop the ability to navigate situations and challenges with no clear answers; hold multiple perspectives simultaneously; and adapt to evolving circumstances.

Understanding our interdependence with each other and the natural world and being able to consider the ethical implications of choices for other people and systems: The modern world is dominated by systems, products, and narratives that celebrate individual achievement, individual needs, and individual well-being. Education reflects this individualistic culture, emphasizing individual work, individual grades, and the ranking and sorting of students. Yet, if challenges such as the COVID pandemic, climate change, mass migration, and financial crises have shown us anything, it is the ways in which our global ecosystem connects our lives in large and small ways. Young people must learn to recognize systemic connections, develop sustainable perspectives, and engage in values-based decision-making that incorporates considerations of values, ethics, and the consequences of choices.

Self-knowledge and learning agility: In a rapidly changing world, young people must constantly evolve and improve their knowledge and skills. Given the many opportunities they will have to reinvent and find a place for themselves in a changing world, having a strong sense of identity and purpose and the ability to be self-reflective and meta-cognitive about their own growth and learning will be crucial. As artificial intelligence and technology continue to evolve, young people will need to continuously learn how best to manage these tools and apply discernment and ethical judgment in their use.

These capabilities, which align with both the holistic-indigenous worldview and our understanding of extended cognition, cannot be developed through traditional, siloed academic subjects or measured through standardized tests.

Instead, they emerge through the development of uniquely human capabilities that AI and technologies, as non-biologically based intelligence, will be unable to replicate in meaningful ways.

2. The AI Revolution and Our Uniquely Human Capabilities

The rapid advancement of artificial intelligence adds urgency to our need to reimagine education. AI increasingly demonstrates mastery of left-hemispheric tasks, precisely those skills our current educational system prioritizes:

- Rapid information processing
- Pattern recognition in defined domains
- Logical analysis and deduction
- Rule-based decision-making
- Memory and recall
- Standardized problem-solving

Rather than competing with AI in these domains, education must develop young people's ability to be what Ethan Mollick terms "co-intelligent" with AI (2024). This means developing the distinctly human cognitive abilities that align with right-hemispheric function and extend beyond what AI can replicate. These capabilities reflect how human intelligence works as an integrated system that extends beyond the brain to include body, environment, and social relationships (Paul, 2021).

Embodied Cognition: Unlike AI, human thinking is inseparable from physical experience. This includes:

- The role of movement in learning and memory formation
- Gesture's importance in understanding and explaining concepts
- The bidirectional relationship between physical states and cognitive performance
- The integration of sensory experience in meaning-making
- The embodied nature of emotional intelligence and empathy

Situated Cognition: Human thinking is deeply influenced by physical and social contexts:

- Environmental cues shape thought patterns and behavior
- Physical settings affect cognitive performance and creativity
- Social contexts influence problem-solving approaches
- Learning transfers differently across various situations
- Cultural contexts shape meaning and understanding

Distributed Cognition: Human intelligence extends beyond individual minds:

- Knowledge is created and maintained across networks of people
- Tools and technologies become extensions of cognitive capacity
- Multiple perspectives enhance problem-solving capability
- Collective wisdom emerges from group interaction
- Innovation often occurs at the intersection of different knowledge domains

These forms of cognition represent uniquely human capabilities that AI cannot fully replicate because they involve the complete integration of physical, environmental, and social dimensions of experience. They align with the holistic-indigenous emphasis on interconnectedness and embodied knowing, supporting the development of capabilities needed in a VUCA world.

3. *Human Development in Our Contemporary Context*

Research in neuroscience, human development, and learning science increasingly supports what the holistic-indigenous worldview has long recognized: children and young people are not small adults, and our traditional educational structures profoundly misalign with their developmental needs.

Early childhood and elementary education should prioritize right-hemispheric capacities through play-based, embodied, and social learning, ideally outdoors in the natural world. This is the period during which children learn to navigate the world in their physical bodies through active play, a foundational aspect of their later cognitive development and learning capacity.

Brain development in early childhood is highly dependent on social relationships with caregivers, siblings, peers, and extended family. At this age, emotional connections, interactions, and conversations shape children's brains. As they enter elementary school, children's growing understanding of the world and their relationship to it helps foster connections between ideas, beings, and systems.

We must design systems that reflect the reality that human development and learning during the first eight to ten years of life are jagged and highly individual. Children develop a vast range of skills necessary for functional adulthood—from sensory processing and core strength to social skills and numeracy. Development across these areas does not happen uniformly; depending on a child's family, circumstances, personality, interests, experiences, and context, they will develop across this range in different orders and at different paces. This variation is not problematic except when our education system designates some areas of development more important than others in the name of "school readiness," pathologizing perfectly normal developmental progressions.

Adolescence, extending from puberty through about age 25, has been historically misunderstood and undervalued. As young people's brains open up after the hormonal changes of puberty, they are primed to develop in ways that correlate strongly with success in early adulthood. This is a period when young people need opportunities to engage deeply in thinking and learning that feels purposeful and relevant, as they seek to answer the driving question: "Who do I want to be in the world?"

During this period, two elements are critical for healthy brain development and personal growth: relationships with adults and peers that enable young people to feel part of their wider community, and opportunities to engage with ideas and experiences that connect knowledge with their past experiences, emotions, and concerns about the future. How adolescents think, more than what they specifically think about, is what grows their brains over time. Ideally, young people would have opportunities to explore areas of curiosity and interest deeply, engaging in real-world learning, including internships and apprenticeships.

The Future Is Now: Embracing a Human-Centered Approach

In examining contemporary educational approaches, three distinct orientations emerge: conventional, whole child/innovative reform, and human-centered/liberatory (HIL). While conventional schools remain wedded to the industrial model, and whole-child programs attempt to patch its shortcomings through targeted initiatives, HIL schools represent a fundamental reimagining of education that aligns with both human developmental needs and the demands of our rapidly evolving world.

HIL education moves beyond mechanical, decontextualized learning to embrace an approach that reflects the complexity and interconnectedness of modern challenges. In true right-hemispheric, both/and fashion, these schools don't eliminate direct instruction or teacher-guided learning. Instead, educators view teaching methods as tools, choosing among them based on the situation and student needs. Some students need more structured guidance than others, and some subjects benefit from teacher-delivered lessons or expert presentations.

Figure 2.1 Educational orientations
Source: Hansen (2021).

These schools work effectively with the widest range of learners in terms of cognitive profiles. By integrating close relationships and socio-emotional work throughout their approach, they effectively reflect trauma-informed and healing-centered practices. This enables them to engage productively with young people who have affective, socio-emotional, attentional, and other developmental differences, as well as those who have experienced trauma or adverse childhood experiences.

Rather than framing learning differences as weaknesses to be remediated, HIL schools take the full measure of a student's capabilities in shaping their work. While they ensure students develop fundamental skills needed for life and learning, they determine which skills are truly "basic" on an individual basis and approach skill development flexibly. The amount of variation in learner outcomes generally increases with age—elementary students engage with a consistent set of learning experiences, while high school students pursue specific learning paths matching their interests and aspirations.

Assessment in HIL schools relies minimally on standardized testing, emphasizing instead teacher observations, student self-assessments, authentic work products, portfolios, and exhibitions. Each of these reinforces the focus on the process and progression of learning. If a student prefers to listen to a story via audiobook while others read hard copies, they're usually allowed to. The focus remains on engagement with learning rather than specific modalities.

Strong relationships ensure every student is known and their particular needs are addressed in everyday work. If this means finding ways to provide food, transportation, or accommodate work or family responsibilities, the school helps with that. This consideration strengthens each student's sense of belonging and enables truly personalized learning.

The shift from an equity framework to a liberatory framework is especially significant. Rather than pursuing uniform outcomes, HIL education empowers students to define and pursue their own paths to success. It recognizes that outcomes will look different for different learners, whether they have significant cognitive challenges, are interested in skilled trades, or are twice-exceptional learners needing more academic stimulation alongside support for learning differences.

This approach represents not just a new way of teaching, but a new way of understanding human potential and our collective future. As international schools, often privileged with resources and motivated learners, we have both the opportunity and responsibility to lead this essential evolution in education. The challenges ahead require more than incremental change—they demand a fundamental reimagining of education that nurtures our common humanity and our capacity to create positive change together.

Embracing a Human-Centered Model at the American School in Japan

As one of the oldest and most well-regarded international schools in the world, The American School in Japan (ASIJ) has long excelled in fostering academic excellence and global citizenship. However, as the world becomes increasingly complex, interconnected, and uncertain, traditional models alone are no longer sufficient. Real adaptive change, especially at an institution with ASIJ's rich history of success, takes deliberate effort. Over the last few years, there has been significant progress, and today, ASIJ is poised on the edge of transformative change. Central to this journey has been three key commitments that have allowed us to shift from a legacy of excellence toward a vision of human-centered, future-focused education. These commitments reflect our evolving understanding of what it means to prepare students for success and impactful lives in an ever-changing world.

Commitment 1: Embracing a Vision-Centered Approach to Strategy

In 2017, it was clear that the school's history of excellence was both its greatest strength and challenge. ASIJ had long defined success through traditional metrics: strong academic outcomes, impressive college placements, and a reputation as a leader among international schools. While these measures reflected past achievements, they did not align with the future we wanted to build. Rather than focusing on incremental, short-term goals, the team anchored their work in a longer-term vision tied to a mission renewed during the 2017–2018 school year.

This shift required a reimagining of what strategy means for ASIJ. Instead of creating a fixed improvement plan, a Strategic Design Framework (SDF) was developed, a living document shaped by the community that reflects shared aspirations. Over time, this framework evolved into *Vision 2030,* an outward-facing eBook that defines where the school is going and why. For example, every major initiative—from curriculum redesign to professional development—is filtered through the lens of *Vision 2030,* ensuring coherence and purpose across the school. In moving away from static, goal-bound approaches, ASIJ embraced a vision-centered strategy reflecting the complexity and interconnectedness of our mission and values. By aligning every decision with this vision, leaders prioritized adaptability and purpose over compliance and static benchmarks. *Vision 2030* became the compass for meeting emerging challenges with clarity and coherence.

Vision 2030 challenges AISJ to move beyond traditional success metrics, allowing the school to redefine success through the development of student agency, adaptability, and discovery of purpose. In anchoring strategy to mission, ASIJ embraced the interconnected and purpose-driven principles Ulcca Joshi Hansen describes as essential for creating meaningful, human-centered education systems.

Commitment 2: Human-Centered Learning through KVC and Deep Learning

Know, Value, Care: Building a Culture of Belonging

At its best, ASIJ has always been a school where students felt known, valued, and genuinely cared for. Long before *Know, Value, Care* (KVC) became a formal part of our mission, these principles were embodied by teachers and coaches whose impact endures. The community recognized that these three words—*Know, Value, Care*—carried intentional logic and depth. First, a student must feel known as a learner and someone with unique strengths, needs, identities, and aspirations. Then, they must feel valued and respected as individuals whose presence enriches the community. Finally, they must experience a culture of care that nurtures their growth and allows them to become their authentic selves. When a student experiences KVC, they are transformed by the belief that who they are matters, what they can achieve is limitless, and they are part of a community committed to their success.

Embracing KVC meant more than adopting a slogan or adding it to posters. It required a commitment to reviewing and renewing ASIJ's systems, norms, practices, and policies—the elements that often shape a school's culture in invisible ways. Slowly but surely, KVC began to infuse all aspects of school life, becoming a lens through which everything was viewed—from social-emotional learning (SEL) practices to counseling services and advisory programs, from classroom interactions to our faculty onboarding, appraisal, and professional learning systems—and it proved especially vital during the disruptions of the COVID-19 pandemic. KVC reminded everyone that educating students goes beyond academics; it means fostering their social-emotional health, sense of belonging, and ethical development as connected members of a larger world. By grounding the community in this foundational commitment, ASIJ strengthened its culture of belonging, ensuring every student could find their place and thrive within the community.

Deep Learning: Engage the World, Change the World

After grounding everyone in *Know, Value Care*, ASIJ focused on reimagining how students learn and engage the world. To bridge the gap between the vision and classroom practices, leaders adopted Michael Fullan's competency-based Deep Learning model (2018), becoming one of the first international schools to join the New Pedagogies for Deep Learning (NPDL) network. This model's emphasis on six global competencies—Mindset, Global Citizenship, Communication, Collaboration, Creativity, and Critical Thinking—offered a path to move beyond compliance-driven standards and empower students to take greater agency over their learning. At its heart, Deep Learning requires a profound shift from "teacher-directed" to "teacher-framed, student-led" learning, where educators provide structure and frame learning experiences. Still, students actively explore, question, and apply their knowledge to real-world contexts. Unlike traditional standards-based learning, which often privileges specific cognitive skills, Deep Learning values a broader range of human capacities. It reflects the human-centered principles that Ulcca Hansen describes—recognizing that rigorous education must also be relational, adaptable, and deeply connected to students' development as individuals. For ASIJ, this shift represented a significant evolution, as it challenged the school to move beyond measures of success rooted in control and predictability toward a model that prepares students to thrive in an increasingly volatile, uncertain, complex, and ambiguous (VUCA) world.

Deep Learning also represents a fundamental shift in defining educational equity and inclusion. As Ulcca Hansen describes, traditional systems often privilege learners with strong verbal or logical reasoning skills while marginalizing those whose strengths lie in creativity, empathy, or adaptability. A competency-based approach like Deep Learning levels the playing field by valuing a broader range of human capacities and creating pathways for all students to thrive. In a world increasingly shaped by artificial intelligence, this model focuses on developing distinctly human skills that machines cannot replicate: the ability to think critically, collaborate meaningfully, and make ethical decisions in the face of complexity. By nurturing these capacities, Deep Learning doesn't just prepare students for success; it empowers them to lead purposeful, impactful lives. As Paulo Freire reminds us in *Pedagogy of the Oppressed* (2018), "Education must empower learners to engage the world and change the world." At ASIJ, Deep Learning has become the way of ensuring students can do just that.

Commitment 3: Systems Thinking for Adaptive Change

Shifting to a human-centered approach requires more than adopting an ethos like *Know, Value, Care* or a pedagogical model like Deep Learning. It demands a transformation of every system within the school to align with and support a shared strategic vision. At ASIJ, these systems—spanning governance, admissions, advancement, counseling, and more—are seen as interdependent and deeply integrated. Drawing on Michael Fullan and Joanne Quinn's *Coherence Framework* (2016), leaders recognized the importance of establishing a collective purpose that unifies efforts and fosters collaboration across teams and divisions. At the same time, Heifetz, Linsky, and Grashow's *The Principles of Adaptive Leadership* (2009) guided the school in tackling the more profound cultural transformations necessary for meaningful change. As Heifetz and his co-authors describe, adaptive challenges require mobilizing people to confront norms, values, beliefs, and habits, creating an environment of continuous learning and adaptation. Much like a rowing team in perfect unison, each system must pull its oar in harmony with others to develop a sense of glide, a state of flow where the school moves forward effortlessly toward its common destination. Below are the key systems that AISJ reimagined to ensure they fully align with *Vision 2030*, each contributing while reinforcing the whole.

Key Systems Driving Vision 2030

- *Divisions:* Empowering each division—ELC, ES, MS, and HS—to lead the critical work of aligning teaching, learning, and community practices with *Vision 2030*, ensuring that KVC and Deep Learning principles are embedded in all initiatives to foster innovation, inclusion, and the holistic development of every student.
- *Student Support:* Embracing a holistic, inclusive model powered by Universal Design for Learning (UDL) and tailored interventions, ASIJ ensures every student feels known, valued, and cared for, fostering growth and belonging within a supportive community aligned with *Vision 2030*.
- *Board of Directors:* Providing mission-driven leadership through strategic oversight, resource stewardship, and policy development that aligns with *Vision 2030*, fostering a culture of transparency, innovation, and collaboration.
- *Recruitment and Retention:* Attracting teachers seeking a professional environment that challenges them to deliver a transformative, human-centered education in their context while retaining those who embody ASIJ's values and aspirations and are deeply committed to advancing *Vision 2030*.
- *Appraisal and Professional Development:* Fostering a professional culture where purpose is clearly defined, and we are accountable for it, where we work together to challenge defaults, improve systems, and grow through professional learning programs and appraisal systems rooted in *Vision 2030*.
- *Counseling:* Modeling professional excellence, ASIJ's counselors deliver comprehensive social-emotional, academic, and college counseling while supporting advisory programs, fostering inclusion and equity, and assisting families in times of crisis—all aligned with KVC principles and *Vision 2030*'s commitment to human-centered education.
- *Safeguarding:* Fostering a holistic, human-centered commitment to emotional and physical safety, focused on belonging and

inclusion through transparent policies, proactive risk mitigation, and an unwavering focus on student well-being aligned with KVC principles.
- *Advisory and House Programs:* Creating essential spaces for connection and belonging, these initiatives foster meaningful relationships, promote leadership and collaboration, and strengthen students' social-emotional growth, building a vibrant, supportive community aligned with ASIJ's values and *Vision 2030*.
- *Admission and Enrollment Management:* Selecting mission-fit families who align with ASIJ's future-focused, human-centered vision of education—balancing KVC with the rigor of Deep Learning—and integrating them into a vibrant community where expectations are high, and values are shared.
- *Advancement:* Strengthening relationships with alumni, parents, and donors to foster a culture of philanthropy, secure resources for transformative programs, and align community support with *Vision 2030's* innovative goals.
- *Marketing and Communications:* Amplifying ASIJ's vision and values through strategic storytelling, multimedia innovation, and digital platforms that deepen engagement, elevate the school's global profile, and align with *Vision 2030*.
- *Technology:* Leveraging innovative tools and practices to amplify learning, foster digital citizenship, and provide students with future-ready skills while ensuring equity, well-being, and alignment with *Vision 2030's* human-centered goals.
- *Signature Programs:* Offering transformative experiences that extend learning beyond classroom walls—including those provided by our Deep Learning Seminar program, Japan Center, and Partnerships program—and exemplifying ASIJ's commitment to walking the talk of *Vision 2030* by fostering innovation, real-world engagement, and a human-centered approach to education.
- *Parent Engagement:* Strengthening the home-school partnership through dynamic, multimodal programs—such as the ASIJ 2030 Series, Mustang Connections, and KVC Parent Partners Series—that deepen parents' understanding of *Vision 2030,* foster two-way communication, and empower families to navigate the challenges of parenting in complex times.

- *Human Resources:* Fostering a culture that embodies KVC principles, supporting employee well-being and professional growth, assisting families with childcare housing, and navigating local and national regulations to ensure a strong sense of belonging and community.
- *Co-Curriculars:* Providing opportunities in athletics, performing arts, or clubs and activities that encourage students to engage beyond the classroom, discover passions, build teamwork and leadership skills, and develop competencies aligned with ASIJ's *Vision 2030*.

Achieving alignment across these systems is challenging, but the results are transformational when successful. In *The Boys in the Boat* (2013), Daniel James Brown captures the phenomenon of a rowing team entering a state of flow—a moment when every oar moves in perfect synchrony, creating an effortless and unstoppable motion across the water. At ASIJ, this is the vision held for our school's systems: interdependent, synchronized, and entirely focused on advancing *Vision 2030*. By fostering this level of coherence and interdependence, AISJ ensures that every decision, action, and system contributes to a future where students, educators, and the broader community thrive.

The Path Forward

The challenges we face as a society are complex and interconnected. Climate change, social inequality, and political polarization cannot be solved through incremental changes to existing systems or by applying more technology. They require a fundamentally different way of thinking and being in the world, and this transformation must begin in education. The path forward lies in reimagining education holistically, aligning every part of a school's vision, systems, and practices with the values of human-centered learning.

We can no longer afford to focus primarily on what can be standardized and measured through conventional assessments. Instead, education leaders must cultivate various skills and dispositions to enable young people to thrive in a complex, ever-changing world. This requires schools to prioritize adaptability and coherence—ensuring that systems like ASIJ work interdependently to foster learning, belonging, and purpose. The convergence of our growing understanding of human development, the challenges of a VUCA world, and the rise of artificial intelligence make this shift desirable and imperative.

Human-centered/liberatory education offers a path that aligns with our time's demands and our most profound understanding of human development and learning. It provides a framework for nurturing the uniquely human capabilities that will be crucial in the decades ahead while honoring each learner's inherent dignity and potential. As ASIJ's journey illustrates, achieving this vision is not just about adopting new strategies but also about building a culture of belonging and coherence across every system within a school.

For international schools, this moment presents both an opportunity and a responsibility. With our resources, motivated learners, and relative autonomy, we are uniquely positioned to lead this educational transformation. The subsequent chapters of this book will explore in detail how we can reimagine leadership, community engagement, and pedagogy to create learning environments that genuinely serve the needs of young people and our collective future.

The future of education is not about tweaking the existing system; it's about embracing a fundamentally different vision of what education can and should be. The time for this transformation is now, and schools that embrace it—like ASIJ—will prepare students to thrive and empower them to lead and create a better world.

References

Brown, D. J. (2013). *The boys in the boat: Nine Americans and their epic quest for gold at the 1936 Berlin Olympics*. Viking.

Freire, P. (2018). In M. B. Ramos (Ed.), *Pedagogy of the oppressed*. Bloomsbury Academic. (Original work published 1970).

Fullan, M. (2018). *Deep learning: Engage the world, change the world*. Corwin.

Fullan, M., & Quinn, J. (2016). *Coherence: The right drivers in action for schools, districts, and systems*. Corwin.

Hansen, U. J. (2007). *Holistic education*. Oxford University. https://ora.ox.ac.uk/objects/uuid:6a51f6c8-3821-4fc5-b329-728b02921e47/files/mca12e3873133cb38fe3b531625c9edfd

Hansen, U. J. (2021). *The future of smart.* Capucia Publishing.

Heifetz, R. A., Linsky, M., & Grashow, A. (2009). *The practice of adaptive leadership: Tools and tactics for changing your organization and the world.* Harvard Business Press.

McGilchrist, I. (2012). *The master and his emissary: The divided brain and the making of the Western world* (Reprint ed.). Yale University Press.

Mollick, E. (2024). *Co-intelligence: The power of collective wisdom.* Portfolio.

Paul, A. M. (2021). *The extended mind: The power of thinking outside the brain.* Mariner Books.

TechTarget. (n.d.). VUCA (volatility, uncertainty, complexity, and ambiguity). TechTarget. Retrieved January 21, 2025, from https://www.techtarget.com/whatis/definition/VUCA-volatility-uncertainty-complexity-and-ambiguity

Leading Cultures of Dignity

Rosalind Wiseman and Mark Ulfers

Preface

Rosalind Wiseman is an advisor to international schools and regional overseas schools associations. Mark Ulfers is the director of the Office of Overseas Schools, US Department of State. Since 2016, when Mark was the Head of School at the American School of Paris (ASP) and Rosalind was first hired to consult with ASP's middle and high school, their collaboration has been one of on-going learning with a singular goal: to use decades of experience to support international schools and the families they serve with common sense, research, and lessons learned about how schools of belonging are led and come into being. While some of the issues that began their thought partnership in 2016 are as present and important today, the challenges facing international schools to nurture well-being and a sense of belonging in our school communities have only increased in complexity as have the "hows" of meeting the needs of young people.

Today, we are even more convinced that the key to a thriving international school is to create, adopt, and then "live" school with a set of agreed upon Essential Agreements that are based on a set of principles that guide the expectations and actions for how everyone in the school community will be treated. However, creating Essential Agreements is not as easy as having good intentions and bringing together a group of people in a school community to agree on how we should treat each other. It requires intentional work based on a commitment to the research and practice of how adults manage their communication with young people, the voices of and our knowledge of child and adolescent development, and then integrating both into a school's design of learning and culture building.

DOI: 10.4324/9781003581451-3

In this chapter we will lay out what we believe that work needs to be through: (1) acknowledging the complexities of international schools' context; (2) understanding adult mindsets; (3) appreciating young people's social needs; and (4) specific strategies and tools to support adults and young people to work together to build school culture.

We also see these agreements as an investment in youth development. And ... they are so much more. They are the compass that keeps a school leader pointed in the right direction in spite of the constant power dynamics, cultural complexities, and inevitable competing interests and challenges they must navigate and facilitate every day.

Introduction

The mission of international schools is to join their students on a positive educational journey; one where a young person develops positive self-perception, universal values of critical thinking, curiosity in the face of uncertainty, resilience in response to adversity, responsibility to themselves and others, and connection to and facility with a greater global community.

When asked what makes them feel connected to a school, students consistently point to one thing: relationships. Positive, meaningful relationships—with teachers, peers, and mentors—are the foundation of belonging. Research confirms this. A study[1] of over 14,000 youth found that students who build strong relationships are more engaged, more motivated, and more likely to contribute positively to their school communities. And yet, in that same study, less than half of students reported having consistent, positive relationships with either their peers or the adults in their school.

"A student should not need to choose between doing well and being well," is an often used phrase that is all too accurate. As an example, adolescent students responding to the "ChallengeSuccess" survey from the Stanford University School of Education (https://challengesuccess.org/) provide a sobering view:

- 90% are sleep deprived
- 75% report exhaustion, difficulty sleeping, and headaches because of stress
- 77% report engaging in at least one academically dishonest behavior in the last month

- 63% report workload is a major source of stress
- Nearly 50% put forth effort but rarely or never find school interesting or enjoyable
- Nearly 30% report that almost none of their homework is useful to their learning
- Only 42% feel they can really be themselves at their schools and only 40% feel like a part of the school community.

At the same time, there are two seemingly opposing "truths" in international schools. We are what we proudly proclaim: communities made up of people holding many passports from cultures around the world. Our students and their families enrich our schools by bringing diverse customs, experiences, and perspectives into the school community. And it is also true that the same cultural richness can predict misunderstandings and conflict. Our students may experience bullying and other forms of social aggression based on xenophobia, learning differences, and other identities. Parents can become angry about perceived signs of disrespect of their cultures or be hesitant to talk to each other because they make assumptions about national differences and approaches to parenting. And educators and administrators who are tasked with intervening in these conflicts often feel inadequate and unprepared to respond effectively.

Any school is a community of people and therefore of relationships, emotions, conflicts, and assumptions about young people. In addition, for today's schools, no matter how much technology advances and changes how we educate, managing ourselves in groups and creating a sense of belonging for everyone in our community is key to a school where parents want to bring their children, faculty want to teach, and students can learn.

The idea is to articulate a school's values explicitly and intentionally or young people and adults will create them implicitly, and therefore are vulnerable to negative power dynamics undermining what we say our international schools stand for. For better or worse, they will become the unspoken power dynamics of the school community, making a school community vulnerable to the wrong norms for supporting youth and creating a school culture that undermines the very values of an international school.

With this complex dynamic as our foundation, the most effective tool for building a thriving international school culture is a set of explicit

Essential Agreements; a shared and practiced set of commitments created and maintained by a representative group of students, administrators, educators, staff, and parents that define the values and expectations of a school community. These agreements benefit everyone as they serve both as an investment in youth development and shape the foundation of how a school functions, guiding the relationships of all community members.

Any Essential Agreements will be tested; it's one of the most important reasons they exist. They are the steady ground under our feet when we feel unstable or unbalanced and we don't know what to do or where to go.

It is hard work for a school leader to shepherd a culture of belonging within the community. It takes everyone's attention to build a unifying culture because it runs deep, embedded into everything a school thinks and does. Considering that in one study (Search Institute, 2022) only half of youth surveyed reported strong relationships with educators, it may also be true that school leaders really do not know how to bring a school community to a place where happiness and success are a result of positive relationships and belonging.

A psychologically safe school is one where teachers and students might not even be aware of speaking up, challenging ideas or decisions simply because to do so seems so natural. It is taken for granted that each voice is appreciated. There is a seamless blending of trust and respect. Both sides know they have learned from each other. The teacher might thank the student for calling out important content or perspectives. The student and teacher walk away knowing they can rely on each other. And who knows, the student-teacher conversation could result in new ways of thinking and doing at the school, giving rise to a new project, policy or a better way to engage students in their learning. The interpersonal skill of speaking up is how schools of belonging work. All voices are invited and the Essential Agreements celebrate such a culture of belonging.

With this as our background, let's dive in with two examples where these dynamics come to life.

A Service Trip Goes Terribly Wrong...

An international school in Western Europe organized a service-learning trip to the southern tip of the Kalahari Desert, South Africa. The purpose of the trip was clear: to provide local students with English instruction to help them matriculate to university and, in the process, to give students from the overseas school an opportunity to act as ambassadors for international education, representing the values of service, cultural exchange, and responsibility. Yet, despite the carefully laid plans and the well-intentioned mission of the trip, a small group of students disregarded the school's expectations. They smoked, purchased alcohol, and trespassed, putting themselves and others at risk. Their behavior not only threatened their own safety but also undermined the relationships the school had built with the local community. What was meant to be a meaningful experience collapsed, leaving administrators and faculty questioning how a few students could have acted so selfishly, disregarding everything they had been taught about being a member of an international school. These students knew better. Why were they willing to take these risks that could hurt so many people in so many ways?

An Exam Goes Terribly Wrong…

At another international school, a eleventh-grade science exam was administered that every tenth grader in the country was mandated to take. Shortly after the test was taken, the administration discovered that the exam's answers had been leaked on a social media platform the day before. Every student in the grade had known about it, most had taken advantage of the leak, and not a single student had come forward to report it. By the time the administrators found out, some students had been singled out (falsely) as being the ones who reported the cheating and the rumor was now flying around the school. The administrators and faculty were deeply disappointed, embarrassed, and worried. This school was already in the political crosshairs of the ruling government's educational ministry who had mandated the exam in the first place. They couldn't afford to look like the school was tolerating the students' behavior. They adored their students; how could these young people let themselves down and damage the reputation of the school? Faculty and administrators were left grappling with the same fundamental question as those dealing with the failed service-learning trip: Why did students make these choices? They knew the school's values. They knew academic dishonesty carried serious consequences. Why was that not enough to motivate even one student to act with integrity? And the big question … what should the consequences be?

The Silent Social Contract—It Does Not Work

When a student joins a school they enter into a social contract; a set of, usually, unspoken agreements about being a member of the school community. Suffice to say, these two examples, while common, are behaviors that violate any school contract. And it is also true that every school leader has, at some point, found themselves bewildered by student choices, asking, *Why would they ever think this was okay?* or *How could they do something so reckless knowing the potential harm to themselves, their peers, or the school community?* These questions, however, are often asked from a place of reaction and frustration rather than genuine inquiry. The truth is, when educators ask these questions, they usually believe they already know the answer: that adolescents are impulsive, risk-taking, hormone-driven, and unable to fully control their impulses because, after all, "their brains aren't fully developed until they're 25."

But if we pause and reflect for a moment, we see that this assumption doesn't fully explain student behavior. The same students, with the same brains, who make reckless, thoughtless, and self-serving choices are also capable of profound self-discipline, complex problem-solving, and long-term planning. They write thoughtful essays for AP Literature, design intricate chemistry projects, and dedicate months to planning service-learning initiatives. In moments of social conflict, they can also be incredibly strategic, calculating ways to elevate their own social status, undermine their peers, or keep something hidden from the school administration and/or their parents. Clearly, it is not that students *cannot* engage in reasoning and decision-making. The question, then, is not simply why they make bad choices but *how* we, as educators, understand how to communicate and share power with them so we create an environment where they are motivated to make ethical, responsible decisions and commit to the social contract we ask them to agree to when they join our school community. Simply, it is the difference between compliance and commitment.

Toward a Community Contract for Belonging

This challenge requires us to ask: What does it take for students to understand and be intrinsically motivated to engage with the values we believe are core to the international school community? How do we prepare the adults who are responsible for guiding young people's development to best support them along their journey knowing that part of young people's development is to make mistakes, push boundaries and test norms? And lastly, how do we hold adults in our community accountable to the same standards we hold our students?

Whether we like it or not, we are in a relationship with young people where we are constantly giving each other information and guidance about our working relationship. We need to know if our actions are working for them. And young people feel a greater sense of belonging and well-being in their schools when they have a voice in how school "does" school. Whether we admit it or not, they are the experts of what it is like to be a student in our schools. From the disciplinary process, to how students are using AI, to cell phone policies, to why students can be reluctant to ask adults for help, they are the experts on the school experience because they are having the experience. Time and time again, we have seen when students can tell administrators what it is like to be them, administrators see things that they never would have otherwise.

To go back to our cheating example, those 11th graders were the only ones who knew why they cheated, why they didn't come forward, and how a school leader could best communicate to them. The students knew what they were doing was wrong, they knew they could have been caught, and if they were that their teachers would be disappointed in them. Can we admit that the most common response educators say in these moments, *"We are so disappointed in you. You should be disappointed in yourself. Academic dishonesty can carry with you for the rest of your life"* is usually the least effective? In this case, what happened was four students from the grade were chosen to meet with an administrative team to understand what the motivations to cheat actually were and to strategize together the best way for the Head of School to meet with the grade and design the meeting so students would be more likely to engage and take it seriously.

Bringing Belonging to Life

While there are significant and well documented benefits to attending international schools, there are inherent complexities. Chief among them is the rate of which families and faculty "turnover" at the school. High turnover rates tend to centralize social power to home-country national students, especially if the native language is not English, and is the social language of the school. Home-country nationals know the social norms of the home culture and school while new or not-native students understandably do not, and must navigate learning them while trying to build new friendships.

The turnover rate also impacts parents' social dynamics in ways similar to their children's. Parents also want to fit into their new home culture, or even if they don't, they want their children to be successful in making friends. So, for many parents, while the invaluable benefits of one's children being exposed to different cultures is clear, it is often weighed against the challenges and sometimes guilt of moving children to another school; especially when they are happy in their old school.

For young people who stay in the same school, the social dynamics are complex as well. Students can be hesitant to stand up for each other because they understand the cost is high; for both home country students and guest students. It can be hard to invest in a new student because you know the heartbreak of a new friend leaving, you can feel trapped in the group you are in; especially if your family is part of a tight knit social group, and it can feel too hard to stand up for a new student outside of the group. The common social dilemmas young people face about going out, breaking rules, staying out too late, leaving friend groups, making new ones, are significantly more complicated in this social ecosystem.

Definitions matter. Places of belonging define things. As an example, students, parents, teachers, and administrators define bullying and the thresholds for such behavior in different ways. So often no one bothers to consider the context of bullying (or other behaviors of rudeness or being mean) and on top of it all discipline seems the immediate consequence rather than a good dose of empathic listening and designing disciplinary consequences that actually meet their goal; of teaching the aggressors the intrinsic motivation to stop and signaling to the student body that the adults are trusted care-takers of their emotional and physical safety. If we want policies and protocols to inform places of belonging, free of fear or threat, then many voices, especially those of young people, are essential to bring understanding and commitment.

Here are some other insights students have shared with us:

Students want to see the relevance of their education. Our students understand how complex our world's problems are and understandably believe their education should prepare them for it. When they complain about their course work, it is a reasonable request to their educators to align their teaching content with skills and information that their students can apply, or if not, to explain how it will be relevant later.

Students want acknowledgement of the educational systems' contradictions. In our schools and in our mission statements, we tell students that their education is about creativity, curiosity, and independent thought. And yet they are evaluated through rigid, standardized measures. They are increasingly frustrated at the contradiction of the higher mission of learning (creativity, critical thinking, higher purpose) against the transactional demands of the educational system and expectations of their adults in their lives who demand and measure them against these standards. [MU1]

Students don't need a deciding vote, but they do want to know their voice is taken seriously. We know many schools are trying to incorporate student voice into their decision making but it's important to be careful so as to not come across as performative (something this generation is incredibly suspicious of). When students feel that their input is not taken seriously, their frustration can lead to disengagement, cynicism, and a reluctance to participate in shaping school culture. One of the reasons why this is happening so much is the relentless responsibilities the average administrator and educator must accomplish everyday. So even when we do ask for students' opinions, unless we have a formalized system to consistently communicate with those students, we rarely go back and explain how we made the decision we ultimately arrived at. Which makes them think that the only reason why we asked their opinion is to look like we care when we actually don't.

From the Educator's Perspective

Teachers feel that this generation of students is just "different." Teachers report having a harder time connecting with students, struggling to convince students to join groups or accept a "new" person in their group, or voice an opinion that they are not sure is correct academically or will meet the approval of their peers.

Administrators and faculty report feeling less trust from parents. Not only does this make it harder to develop relationships quickly, it is also easier to assume interactions will go poorly. Administrators go through their day knowing that a seemingly "small" conflict always has the potential to grow quickly into a large one while keeping their commitment to the larger purpose, vision and mission of the school.

Those are the challenges in our context. And yes it can feel overwhelming but they are there whether we admit them or not so better to see them so we can do something about it.

Raising Our Communication Game: How Adults Can Better Engage with Young People

Creating caring and respectful relationships across the school community is everyone's work—from home, school, and through experiences within the wider community of people and places. And so often the adults are wringing their hands about disconnected youth, mental health worries, and risk-taking behavior without first truly investigating the issues with students. As adults, we jump right over them seeking solutions. What a missed opportunity to really understand!

One of the biggest reasons schools struggle to create meaningful relationships with youth and to codify Essential Agreements that describe a place of belonging is the assumption that teachers and administrators already know how to talk to young people. But even the most experienced educators struggle with communication. Talking to young people in a way that actually works isn't something you just get. It's a skill—one that requires constant self-reflection, support, and practice. And in the moments when it matters most, it takes a lot of effort to put that skill into action.

This is not about coddling students. It's not about being nice. It's not about giving up authority. It's about being an effective communicator with a group of people who require a specific, developmentally appropriate approach to communication in order for it to be productive.

David Yeager, in *10-25: The Science of Motivating Young People*, describes the problem clearly. When interacting with young people, adults tend to fall into one of two roles: the "Enforcer" or the "Protector." The "Enforcer" relies on dominance, demanding compliance through fear, control, and possibly shame. The "Protector," on the other hand, avoids conflict and lowers expectations in the name of preserving a relationship. They're so afraid of pushing too hard that they don't push at all. While there can be positive motivations in both the Enforcer (the Enforcer wants the child to hold themselves to high standards) and Protector (want to support the emotional needs of the child) neither approach works. In both cases, the adult loses credibility, and the young person stops engaging.

The alternative, Yeager argues, is adopting a Mentor Mindset—one that holds young people to "high expectations while providing high support." The difference is simple but powerful: when you tell a young person that you believe they can meet high standards, they're more likely to rise to the challenge. Being respected is motivating. And when we communicate in a way that challenges them while taking them seriously, we create a school culture where every young person—not just the loudest or most seemingly confident—has the opportunity to succeed.

Young People Want to Be Taken Seriously

More than anything, young people are trying to figure out how to be valued by their peers and the adults in their lives. Research has shown that when adolescents are motivated by social rewards—whether that's earning the respect of their peers, being seen as helpful, or proving themselves in a group setting—they can show the same level of critical thinking, decision-making, and long-term planning as adults.

Psychologists like Erik Erikson have argued for decades that adolescence is about becoming an independent social actor—someone who contributes to a larger community. The result is that young people are highly attuned to status. They are constantly scanning their environment for cues about who matters, who holds power, and how they are being perceived.

Here's where this becomes a problem.

When a young person feels like an adult doesn't take them seriously, they shut down. Before they can hear feedback—before they can see it as something meant to help them grow—they need to feel respected. If they feel like the adult talking to them thinks they're incompetent, immature, or not worth listening to, they disengage. It doesn't matter how logical, fair, or reasonable the adult is being. If a young person doesn't believe you take them seriously, they won't take you seriously either.

And this is where even the best-intentioned educators get stuck. You think you're being clear. You think you're being supportive. But then the young person completely shuts down, gets defensive, or doesn't respect you and even tries to manipulate you. Yeager describes this as one of the biggest reasons young people disconnect from adults. Even when we think we're being encouraging, young people often interpret it as something else. We assume they understand where we're coming from, but they don't. And once that misunderstanding takes root, the conversation is already over.

The Adolescent Predicament: The Impossible Choice between Social Survival and Long-Term Well-Being

For better or worse, adolescence is about learning how to be valuable to a group. Young people need to feel like they—and the things they care about—matter to the people who hold power in their lives. But that same drive puts them in an impossible position. Yeager calls this the Adolescent Predicament—the mismatch between a young person's need for status and respect and the amount of status or respect they actually feel they have. It forces young people into no-win situations. Do they make a choice that helps them socially but might hurt them in the long run? Or do they make a choice that's better for their future but damages their social standing in the present or their acceptance in their group?

We see this play out in schools all the time.

Why do students break rules on a school trip? Why do they cheat on a test? Why don't they step in when they see a peer doing something wrong? It's not because they don't know better. It's because they are constantly calculating risk. They know what the "right" thing to do is. But doing the right thing jeopardizes their social status, because it very well might be a threat to their social survival. And most adults struggle to see this ever present dynamic, even when they should be able to remember their own adolescence. But the truth is, few do, so our approach seems unrealistic because it is unrealistic.

More than twenty years ago, in *Queen Bees & Wannabes*, Rosalind described adolescence as feeling like being stuck in a life raft in the middle of the ocean. There's only so much food and water. You need to prove to the others in the raft that you are valuable to the group's survival, not a liability. That pressure never goes away. Every social decision a young person makes is filtered through that fear of being thrown overboard. If we want young people to listen to us, we need to see them in that lifeboat and then ask and then give them what they need to row strongly to navigate the choppy waters they're up against.

What Happens When We Get This Wrong

When we don't recognize the realities of the Mentor Mindset, the Adolescent Predicament, or young people's need for earned prestige, we default to communication patterns that don't work.

We get stuck in Enforcer or Protector Mindsets, either coming across as controlling and authoritarian or too lenient to hold students accountable. We assume that young people's "prefrontal cortex impairment" means they aren't capable of contributing meaningfully to school culture. And we design learning environments based on what we think should motivate them, instead of what actually does.

And when those strategies don't work? Instead of adjusting, we double down.

In professional development trainings, we asked educators in five international schools to give examples of what their colleagues say to students when they can see young people disengage or behave in ways a teacher feels they need to give direction. Here's what they came up with:

"I have your best interests at heart."

"Are you making good choices?"

"You need to let it go."

"This conversation is over."

"Calm down, relax, take a breath."

"You are making this a bigger deal than it needs to be."

"You just don't understand yet."

"Now is not the time for this."

"Are we done here?"

"Follow the rules, they are there for a reason."

"Who has the most qualifications here?"

Every single one of these statements shuts down the conversation before it can begin.

When a young person hears "You just don't understand yet," they think, *Well, then why should I even try?" or, "Oh yes I do–you're the person who doesn't understand!" When we tell them to "let it go," we are dismissing what they care about. When we say, "Follow the rules, they are there for a reason," we are denying them the opportunity to think critically about why those rules exist in the first place or reflecting for ourselves that there is a possibility that some rules are ineffective, part of the problem, or exist for the convenience of the school rather than the welfare or learning of the child.

Young people want to be challenged. They want to be respected. They want to be taken seriously. And when we stop dismissing them, when we stop seeing them as prefrontal cortex-impaired liabilities, and when we actually invite them to be our thought partners, they step up.

This isn't about giving up authority. It's about using our authority to see how to work with them in the way that works best for them. It's tough for school leaders to authentically share power with young people. Just think of the social capital you give a young person when they are taken seriously, are involved in decisions, solve problems within a web of fellow student and adult support, and then are allowed to lead. Sharing power with students thoughtfully creates a culture of belonging where young people's ideas are taken seriously in collaboration with caring adults. It is complex and complicated; one that requires ongoing work. And it is the best way for a school leader to develop new leaders and role model ethical leadership for everyone in the community.

Keep in mind the survey results and the voices of young people. Only 40% of responding youth reported they can be themselves while at school or that they feel a true part of the community. We want our young people engaged because young people don't just want to survive the raft. They want to learn how to guide it.

Bringing Dignity into Our Language: Rethinking Respect in Schools

We hope you have noticed how often the word respect came up in the last two sections of this chapter. Making the mentor mindset shift isn't just about communication strategies. It also demands that we rethink what we mean when we use the word respect—a word that is so embedded in school culture that we rarely stop to examine how it actually plays out in the lives of young people.

Schools love to talk about respect. It's everywhere—on posters in hallways, in mission statements, in school handbooks, in the daily language of teachers and administrators. Adults constantly tell students to "show respect," to "treat others with respect" or, when disciplining them, to reflect on how they were being "disrespectful." But here's what we don't like to admit: the way respect is used in schools is often inconsistent, performative, manipulated, and even weaponized to reinforce power rather than relationships.

Think back to when you were growing up. Who did you respect? Was it a teacher, a coach, a family member, a neighbor? And why? Chances are, you respected them not because of their title or authority, but because of how they treated you. They challenged you, held you accountable without humiliating you, and saw something in you that maybe even you hadn't seen yet. You didn't respect them because of their position; you respected them because of the way they used the power that came with that position. What they showed you wasn't about respect at all. It was about dignity.

Now think about the moments when you were told to respect someone you absolutely didn't respect. Maybe it was an adult who abused their authority, treated you unfairly, or demanded compliance without earning your trust. That's the thing about respect: it can be forced. It can be wielded like a weapon. It can be demanded without being deserved.

Young people recognize this dynamic instantly. It's why they say, "I'm not going to give you my respect until you earn it." And honestly? They're right.

Respect, in its original Latin root re-spectare, means "to see again." It's something that is observed, recognized, and built over time based on actions. Yet in schools, we use it very differently. We tell students to respect people whether they deserve it or not. We tell them to be kind and polite to a classmate who has been mean to them. We tell them to respect a teacher, even if that teacher has never shown them respect in return. Without realizing it, we are teaching students that respect is about obedience, deference, and silence in the face of power.

Dignity is something entirely different. Dignity is not earned. Dignity is not conditional. Dignity is the fundamental recognition that every human being has worth, no matter their behavior, no matter their mistakes, no matter how much they disagree with you. Dignity is what makes someone feel seen. It is what allows people to exist in spaces without fear of being ignored, humiliated, or dismissed. When we lead with dignity, everything changes. Conversations shift. Conflicts de-escalate. Accountability becomes possible in ways that respect alone can never achieve.

This distinction matters. If you compete to demand respect, it becomes a race to the bottom. The power struggle intensifies. Everyone digs in deeper. No one listens. But if you compete to demand dignity, it becomes a race to the top. It creates the space for people to be challenged without feeling diminished, to take responsibility without feeling humiliated, to admit mistakes without losing their sense of self.

Students, as we mentioned earlier, are particularly attuned to these power dynamics. They know when they're being dismissed. They know when they're being asked to comply instead of contribute. And they know when the expectations placed on them are not being met by the adults in the room. Respect, to them, is about effort on both sides of the teaching relationship. Dignity is about knowing that, regardless of who you are, your experiences and your voice matter.

Essential Agreements Translate Dignity and Respect

Understanding how these two words work together is the foundation of creating Essential Agreements in schools. Young people want two things: to be seen, which is dignity, and to earn their place in a group, which is respect. When we demand dignity, we affirm a person's inherent worth. When we offer respect, we acknowledge their actions and contributions. Treating someone with respect might look the same as treating them with dignity, but the experience of it is entirely different. One can feel like submission; the other feels like empowerment.

Hard conversations, accountability, and the creation of Essential Agreements all depend on this distinction. When a school community leads with dignity, those difficult moments become manageable instead of destructive. Students feel safe enough to be honest. Educators feel confident enough to hold their ground without resorting to control tactics. And schools become places where young people don't just follow rules—they take ownership of the culture they help create.

Principles to Design Essential Agreements

We have finally arrived where we can begin to build our Essential Agreements. We have described the context, the challenges, the crucial importance of using respect and dignity in our language, and offered a different approach to reframe those challenges. Our last building block for Essential Agreements is using a principle based practice to guide our thoughts and actions to bring our community together. Think of these as your co-created norms to also support the participants to have constructive conversations as you build the Essential Agreements together.

To build essential agreements we believe these five principles are paramount to guide the process.

1. No one knows everything, together we know a lot.
2. Listening is being prepared to be changed by what you hear.
3. Validate. Don't relate.
4. Easy on people, hard on ideas.
5. Take ownership when it's hard.

We want to show you some examples of bringing the principles to life;

No One Knows Everything, Together We Know a Lot

In the Art of Gathering,[2] Priya Parker challenges us to be intentional and mindful as we bring people together for any event; let alone something as profoundly important as creating Essential Agreements for a community. So it's not enough to be satisfied with having a parent and a student or even a board member at the table because if we aren't intentional we will default to the people we usually turn to; a member of the PTA Exec committee or Student Council.

Our principle, **No one knows everything, together we know a lot,** helps us design against that default decision making. To that end, here are some questions to help bring this principle to life.

1. *Who do we usually ask to participate in conversations about the school?*
2. *Who will increase our knowledge of what it is like to be a member of our school community?*
3. *Who will challenge our thinking and say what needs to be said?*
4. *How will we invite them to participate?*
5. *Could they be reluctant to contribute freely in our group? How will we ask them?*
6. *How will we acknowledge their contribution?*

> **Listening is being prepared to be changed by what you hear.** This principle is profoundly important as the group comes together to do its work. This definition of listening doesn't mean you have to agree but it does mean you commit to entering into conversations understanding that you could learn something or see something a different way. A commitment to listening like this addresses the challenge of inevitable power dynamics between people in the group from some speaking over others or being silenced. For example, some adults don't have experience sitting around a table with young people and taking their concerns and experiences seriously. Staff can feel reluctant to share experiences they have with parents about their children's behavior because they are worried about possible repercussions.
>
> **Easy on people, hard on ideas.** We live in a world that is upside down, where we are hard on people and easy on ideas. Meaning, people are easily vilified for an unpopular opinion or blamed for making mistakes. Even if they aren't, we fear it so much that many of us are stopped from contributing for fear of judgment. Easy on people, hard on ideas means when a group comes together to do the hard work of creating Essential Agreements, we will give people the benefit of the doubt and work together to give our best efforts towards solving the problem we face.

Validate Don't Relate

When people in positions of power work with others who have less power, they can attempt to connect by saying something that comes across as "I'm just like you." It's usually a well-intentioned effort to connect but it can backfire easily. It happens all the time with young people when an adult says, *"I was your age once, I know what it was like."* Or, *"I know these seem like big problems now, but once you get older, you will forget about them//they won't matter."* Our suggestion is a reframe like, "I don't know what it is like growing up today, so I'm looking forward to learning from you as we put these Essential Agreements together" is invaluable to the work. When the group is sitting around the table, this is a good principle to remind people to remember; especially when they are getting to know each other. People with less social power will contribute when they believe their opinions and experiences are taken as seriously as others.

Take Ownership When It's Hard

Haven't you heard someone in a school say, *"We do all of these programs here, but we can't control the 'messages' our students receive at home. Parents don't have the same values as we do at school."* And that's it. People look around at each other, nod in affirmation, and then it feels like there is nothing to be done about this intractable mixed message problem that none of us has any control over.

We would like to take a step back to reflect on what statements like these communicate.

Children can't learn positive social behavior if they see that behavior inconsistently. In fact, research shows that young people need one adult who is consistently supportive and holds them accountable to support their emotional and psychological development.

But the other message that statement conveys is that our parents' values are (1) bad and (2) in opposition to ours—which are good.

Not a great way to approach parents as our partners and we can't build Essential Agreements with this as an unchecked belief in our community. What we have found time and time again is that the vast majority of problems with parents have come from a moment where they felt that they (themselves, their children, and/or their culture) were not being treated with dignity and then a conflict grew between the adults in the community intensified from there; sometimes way out of proportion to the problem that started the disagreement.

Therefore, school leaders need to be proactive and counter that sentiment with the following in their own words,

> We know there will be parents who may not agree entirely with everything we do here. As long as dignity is our foundation, recognizing the essential worth of everyone in our community, we are not forcing anyone to change their values and we are upholding the mission of this school. And even if other adults in our students' lives contradict what we believe are our fundamental commitments to each other, what we teach and how we teach profoundly matters to our students' moral and ethical development. That's why we are working on these Essential Agreements and that's why we will keep working on them.

Now we have shared with you what we believe are the most important principles to guide our thoughts and actions as we intentionally bring members of a school community together to create Essential Agreements. With these principles to guide our intentions, what follows is an example of what Essential Agreements can look like.

Essential Agreements Language

Treating each other with dignity is our foundation: We recognize that conflicts happen in a community and to honor each other's essential worth and experiences we commit to always "go to the source" and talk it out when concerns exist.

Always a caring adult: We first listen and pay close attention to young people. We take every opportunity to help youth in our midst know they are valued. We are warm, encouraging, and commit to the skills of being an adult worthy of a young person's trust. Think of being with a young person who has just done a confusing thing, and say, "I am guessing it may be stressful to talk to me about what happened (or why we are here). Do you want to talk about that first before we talk about what took place?"

The elegance of a question: Our first instinct is to ask a well-placed question that challenges young people and people in the community to think with us. Our questions communicate our need to understand, especially what is going on within young people in our care. Our focus is to communicate, to take young people seriously and not to dishearten. To build confidence and trust with a young person who, let's say, has made a bad decision, why not lift the entire conversation by saying, "Can you help me understand how we got here?" Or how about this, "I'm guessing you have an understandable reason why this happened, if you can tell me what that reason is, it helps me figure out what is fair to do here. I still may have to make a decision about discipline here but at least I can do it with your perspective in mind."

- **Providing support and setting limits:** Our community members help guide each other through the good and tough times. We stand up for young people and are partners for ensuring well-defined internationally minded attitudes and behavioral boundaries within and beyond the school campus. We are united in being consistent with shared expectations to ensure safety and security of each child all within our community.

- **Recognize the specific motivational drives of young people:** Adults make decisions about young people based on what they think should motivate them not what actually does. To guard against this, we must always check ourselves if we are falling into that trap and ask young people for feedback.

- **Collaborating with young people as partners in learning:** We see young people as partners for teaching and learning and critical to creating a culture of belonging. We will take their ideas and perspectives seriously, involve them in decisions that affect their lives, will solve problems together and expect young people to take action and lead.

- **The Home and School Partnership:** While we recognize that the home and school partnership can be complicated, we must keep each other well-informed, mutually supportive, secure and focused on ensuring a positive, productive teaching and learning climate and age-appropriate supervision when away from school as well. When we feel that this partnership is out of alignment, we commit to realigning our agreements according to the principles we have said will guide our actions.

- **Inquiry over Assumption:** We recognize that any of us can be in a situation where we hear something as fact when it may not be. In that moment, we commit to learning more and yet acknowledge that sometimes people who know the facts may not be able to tell us everything without violating someone else' privacy.

We will elevate each other: If we hear that someone in our community is struggling, we will focus ourselves towards offering support, not speaking badly of that person. Maybe this is an opportunity for an elegant question that reminds us to support each other. This is the moment to possibly say, *"That must be really hard for that child. What can we do to support them?"*

It's Worth the Work: Our community-building work at our schools is never done; we never stop learning from each other and working together to continually improve how we support the growth and development of responsible, happy and healthy youth.

Conclusion

Schools are one of the few constants in an increasingly complex and interconnected world. They are where young people learn what it means to be part of a community—for better or worse. Our hope is that this chapter has made clear how invaluable Essential Agreements are in providing every member of a school with a shared ethical framework. More than just guiding principles, these agreements are what give a school its integrity. They are what allow a community to navigate conflict, uphold its values, and withstand challenges to its authority.

No matter the shifting political winds and social landscapes that schools must navigate, Essential Agreements serve as the ballast that keeps the ship steady in the storm. They define what everyone within the community can and must expect of each other. Essential Agreements are the one thing within our control to safeguard the well-being of every student, educator, and parent in our community. And when they are created with intention and truly lived, they ensure that schools remain what they are meant to be: places where young people can learn, grow, and thrive.

This chapter tells a story about the difficult work of building a community where everyone knows they belong. We know it is possible to find the way to this ideal, but not without everyone's voices.

Think of the school where the students cheated and used the answers to the exam. After meeting and getting guidance from a small group of students, the head of school who went before all the students and said,

> Instead of telling you that I'm disappointed with you, I'm disappointed in myself because I didn't realize how we were setting you up. I didn't appreciate how much you would feel that not using the answers would put you at a disadvantage against other students. I am going to listen and hopefully you will have enough confidence to tell me. I didn't listen before about how this test impacted you; I certainly did not listen to you when you called out the contradictions between the high stakes testing and the school saying we want you to be learning through inquiry; I did not understand the pressure this creates in you. I need to understand how we got here so we can all take ownership of what happened so it doesn't happen again.

For Your Consideration: As you reflect on this chapter, you have explored the complexities of international school contexts—environments shaped by diverse cultural perspectives, transient populations, and varying educational expectations. Understanding these dynamics is essential for shaping a school culture that is both cohesive and adaptable. You have also examined the role of adult mindsets, recognizing how deeply ingrained beliefs, past experiences, and professional identities influence the ways educators engage with change, collaboration, and student voice. Without acknowledging these perspectives, attempts to shift culture may be met with resistance rather than shared ownership. At the same time, we have delved into the social needs of young people, highlighting how a sense of belonging, autonomy, and purpose fuels their engagement and well-being. The challenge for leaders is to bridge these understandings—supporting both adults and students in meaningful ways—by implementing strategies such as structured dialogue, shared decision-making models, and reflective practices that cultivate trust and agency.

Now, the question is: How will you apply these insights to your leadership? Building school culture is not a passive process—it requires intentional design, thoughtful facilitation, and a willingness to navigate tensions. Your role is not simply to react to or manage the complexities but to embrace them as opportunities for growth and innovation. By fostering environments where adults and young people co-create the school experience—anchored by Essential Agreements—you help cultivate a culture that is not only inclusive and dynamic but also deeply rooted in shared values and collective purpose.

Building upon your learning from this chapter as well as Chapter 1, the chapters ahead will invite you to deepen your understanding of international education's unique challenges and opportunities, equipping you with additional insights and strategies to lead with empathy, and commit to building a school community that truly reflects the diverse voices within it.

Notes

1. https://searchinstitute.org/developmental-assets-profile
2. https://www.priyaparker.com/book-art-of-gathering

Reference

Search Institute. (2022). *Developmental assets profile*. Search Institute. https://link.springer.com/chapter/10.1007/978-3-031-07853-8_13

Leading the Vision
A Human Learning Ecosystem for Our Times

Kevin Bartlett and Jeremy Moore

 **Preface**

As former school leaders, we, the authors, shared one exceptional experience when we co-led the process of inspiring and developing the ideas and practices of a learning ecosystem at Cayman International School. Kevin Bartlett, acting as a consulting partner, brought the concepts and DNA of the Ecosystem to life, and Jeremy Moore, the School Director, guided the conversations, professional learning and programming, and multi-year implementation. A careful course was plotted, including the merger of reaccreditation, strategic planning, and development of a learning ecosystem, to ensure connectivity and continuity for the future-focused vision of the organization. More than just a strategic plan, a manifesto, entitled 'CIS Paradigms' was created as a site-based guide to the learning ecosystem at CIS. The development of common language was undeniable, and every educator knew the definition of learning. The school embraced key learning principles and moved forward from principles to practice. The new level of clarity of the shared vision for the organization was inspiring, and it unequivocally impacted learning in positive ways for students, educators and parents. This chapter reflects the theory and practice that guided this journey and is grounded in the work of the organization Kevin founded and leads, *The Common Ground Collaborative*.

The Big Idea: A Human Learning Ecosystem for Our Times

Current models of education are no longer fit for purpose. They simply don't reach all learners and provide them with life-worthy learning in systemic, equitable ways. We propose a new model. A model that asks the right questions and provides coherent, connected responses. A model that provides a shared, global learning language for all learning stakeholders. A model that engages learners with the universals, the human common ground, asking compelling questions that address content that matters. A model for teaching based on shared principles and practices that provide cultural patterns. A model for qualitative assessment that emphasizes learners providing substantive evidence in support of their own performance and progress. A model for global learning and teaching that transcends the boundaries of culture, nationality, and discipline.

It's notoriously hard to work *on* school while *in* school. School life simply gets in the way. We hope that it will be helpful to school leaders in any context, whether new to leadership or more experienced, to step outside the metaphorical noise and re-imagine their school as being one connected learning ecosystem, framed by the 'right' questions, toward which all stakeholders strive in collective, collaborative ways.

In our own school contexts, we realized that, as we worked on systems-building and leading toward our school's vision, we were engaging in the construction of a common language and shared beliefs and values. We were, in effect, building culture. Since we were engaging all learning stakeholders in this work, we were also building community. We were building the necessary human context for a global learning ecosystem. We were building a human learning ecosystem for our times. We think our times demand this of us.

Global education is at a pivotal point in its evolution, a moment that demands a transformative re-imagining of 'the learning business', requiring a radical shift from over-complex, siloed organizations to simpler, coherent learning ecosystems. With such an obvious need, why do we see so little deep, sustained change? We suggest that those who are leading schools toward a new vision are often constrained by compliance and confounded by complexity. Since everything is connected, 'changing everything' may afflict us with the 'paralysis of enormity'. We may feel that, as leaders, we should have all the answers. We propose that it is better for leaders to come with the questions and lead their communities to consensus of a vision that we can all live by to inspire the future we imagine. We propose a mindset of fearless inquiry, and we suggest five key questions that can frame one connected, coherent learning ecosystem, which we define as 'a practical design for modern, equitable learning that actually matters'. These questions, and our practical answers to them, illustrated by examples of successes from the field, frame not only this chapter but also provide a practical pathway for leaders to transform their own organizations.

Begin with Vision

In schools, education that is truly transformative is not realized by accident. Visionary leadership serves as the compass that guides a school. It is the ability to see beyond the present and imagine a future where the organization is living its highest potential. The success of a school is dependent upon the level of clarity and commitment to its purpose, the extent to which its beliefs are understood and upheld, the development of a shared vision, an effective roadmap for learning and progress, and the capacity of its leaders and community to foster a culture that embodies its ideals. As school leaders, it is common for us to feel like we should have all the answers. We propose that inquiry is a better mindset, bringing important questions to our communities and collaborating with and among all stakeholders to build consensus on answers we can all live by.

It's interesting to begin with questions of ourselves. Here are some starters you might try:

- Why lead?
- Why should anyone be led by me?
- What am I leading toward?

Having posed those fundamental leadership questions, we'll offer an answer to the final one. We suggest leading toward a future of greater simplicity and system. We propose leading a school in the process of designing one complete, connected learning ecosystem. Along the way, we suggest that leaders intentionally build one great school, with one culture, one curriculum, one community.

When leading the journey toward a future of simplicity, here are five questions that offer clarity and can frame one coherent learning ecosystem.

1. What *is* learning?
2. What's *worth* learning?
3. How does *everyone* access learning?
4. How do we create learning *cultures*?
5. How do we provide *evidence* of learning?

A school's answers to these questions provide a practical pathway to transformative educational experiences and realizing its preferred future.

The Why

This chapter focuses on the work of *The Common Ground Collaborative* (CGC) (n.d.) and is driven by the clear and present need for school transformation. Where there should be connections, we see gaps. Gaps between what teachers want to do for their students and the ways in which they are obliged to spend their time. Gaps between mountains of standards and the available time. Gaps between parents and schools, between disciplines, between departments. Gaps between what we promise and what we deliver. Gaps between what we assess and what students need to learn to thrive and contribute within their complex, challenging world. 'Engagement gaps' between learners and the classroom. Ultimately, we see a critical gap between millions of children and any halfway decent kind of education.

The goal of *The Common Ground Collaborative* is to help schools close gaps and build connections, to reinvent 'school' as one coherent learning ecosystem; a learning culture in which all learning stakeholders thrive. We strive to bring simplicity and system to the learning business. We want deep learning to reach all children and communities. In the words of Simon Sinek, we are playing 'the infinite game' (2021), which is why we will never fully 'get there' and why we will never stop. Our simple mission is: Becoming Human.

From Why to How to What

Given our commitment to finding simplicity, it's fitting that our own approach is simple. Equally, given our commitment to deep learning framed by inquiry, it is also fitting that we begin with a compelling question: In designing a learning ecosystem for our times, what questions should we ask ourselves?

This question launched an extended professional inquiry that resulted in the CGC learning ecosystem, a unified 'theory of everything', a practical design for modern, equitable learning that matters. We have created an approach that reduces stress and increases learning for all learning stakeholders. It is an approach that achieves our mission.

A Learning Ecosystem for Our Times

The Ecosystem is framed by five Questions that drive five 'elements':

DEFINE: What IS learning?

DESIGN: What's WORTH learning?

DIVERSIFY: How do all learners ACCESS learning equitably?

DELIVER: How do we create shared learning CULTURES?

DEMONSTRATE: How do learners provide EVIDENCE of their own learning?

These '5Ds' will frame the remainder of this chapter.

Define: What *Is* Learning?

If we want to make learning happen, we begin by defining the actual process of learning. Consider this school's approach:

Building Learning Experts

On the journey toward a shared definition, we worked backward from the behaviors of experts based on the commonsense notion that an expert has probably learned well. We determined that experts have a deep understanding of the ideas of their domain and the relationships among them, and that they are highly competent in the skills of their domain. We were also committed to the importance of developing expert human beings with strong, positive values and dispositions.

This definition addresses the learning of ideas, skills, and personal traits, translated into the a 'Three Cs' statement (CGC, 2025):

> Learning is the process of the consolidation and extension of Conceptual understanding, Competency, and Character.

The reason for separating out these forms of learning was not just to give us a simple definition, or a handy alliteration. We knew we needed to think differently about building learner capacity in conceptual, competency, and character learning because the *pedagogy* required to build each of these capacities is different.

The DNA of Learning

We built a methodology that is simple enough for applicability in multiple contexts yet complex enough to drive deep learning. We also developed the simple language that frames all learning goals in the CGC model, as follows (Table 4.1)

In real learning contexts, these three continuous learning strands are constantly interacting in the context of illustrative content that matters. These connected processes, spiraling through an individual's learning lifetime, evoke a powerful metaphor of the Three Cs as a living construct: a triple helix, or the DNA of learning. It's a bold claim, but the metaphor works to explain what's happening when we're learning. It helps us remember to plan, teach, and assess what matters. It brings teacher clarity and builds collective teacher efficacy.

Critically, the Three Cs definition also provides a common learning language that is simple enough and clear enough to frame the learning conversations of all learning stakeholders: learners, teachers, leaders, parents, governors, and other community partners so that we can begin to bridge the gulf in understanding that frequently blights efforts at true stakeholder engagement and collaboration. We think this holds true anywhere in the world. In the words of W. Edwards

Table 4.1 The CGC learning process

Type of Learning	Pedagogy	Learning Goal Sentence Stem
Conceptual	Connect-Construct-Contribute	We understand that …
Competency	Deconstruct-Identify-Practice	We are able to …
Character	Consider-Act-Reflect	We become more …

Deming (2012), 'If you can't describe what you're doing as a process, you don't know what you're doing'. We think that a common definition of the learning process matters. We believe it provides a global learning language for our times.

To extend our earlier metaphor, DNA does not live in a vacuum. It shapes a body. So, another question presents itself. 'What body of knowledge is important for these learners, right here, right now?' As we set out to identify learning that really matters, we framed our Design question.

Design: What's Worth Learning?

Here's a multi-faceted response:

It's Worth Learning to Be Experts

The CGC learning ecosystem develops learning experts, among children and adults. Experts have a deep conceptual understanding of ideas that matter, high levels of competency in key skills, and strong, positive moral character.

It's Worth Learning about Our Human Common Ground

We live in an age of divisions, where adherence to a group and mistrust of other groups is cultivated for reasons of profit and power.

It is more important than ever to find our human common ground. As our primary content organizer in CGC, we identified Six Human Commonalities. They provide 'The Why' behind the disciplines and are framed by pairings of universal concepts, amplified by 'We all' statements expressing our common ground.

The Commonalities support:

- Disciplinary learning that preserves the essence of the disciplines.
- Interdisciplinary learning, where learning draws from more than one discipline to enhance connections.
- Transdisciplinary learning, where ideas and outcomes transcend disciplinary boundaries, sitting above disciplines.

It's Worth Learning with the End in Mind

The Human Commonalities provide the potential to address our 'What's Worth Learning?' question from another powerful perspective. They help us address the big 'So what?' when it comes to 'receiving an education'. What does an expert learner walk away with? What transportable gifts? What capacities will help them succeed as individuals and as contributing members of the human community? What are the 'transferable goals' they will apply in the range of contexts that earners will encounter outside school?

Since real-world capacities will naturally draw from multiple disciplines, and since the Human Commonalities are transdisciplinary by nature, they are the natural source for authentic life-worthy outcomes for applicable transfer goals. In line with our focus on simplicity, the CGC has identified a manageable number of 6 transfer goals, one per Commonality, that collectively provide a 'Portrait of a Learner'. Here's just one example (Table 4.2)

These culminating capacities are built over time through one connected learning continuum and, in another fascinating benefit, through co-curricular pathways. We begin to shift from 'school and after-school activities' to achieving our end goals through a connected system of curricular and co-curricular learning. The Portrait also provides opportunities for evidence-based and learner-curated assessment: a key element in a balanced, principle-driven assessment system.

It's Worth Learning to Make Connections

If we are to focus on the Portrait as the end in mind, then we need to organize our curriculum to provide 'pathways to the Portrait'. The Human Commonalities provide the vertical organizers for a Learning Matrix

Table 4.2 From commonalities to capacities

A Portrait of a Learner	
The Human Commonalities	The Portrait of a Learner
PURPOSE and BALANCE	A Balanced Person
We all seek meaning and purpose in our existence and strive toward achieving balance in our lives.	Can independently pursue their passions, apply their values, and balance their resources to achieve a sustained sense of personal well-being and purpose.

comprising powerful Learning Modules organized for connection and coherence. They are designed to connect vertically from one year to the next and horizontally across the learning design in broad developmental bands.

Thereafter, Learning Modules are planned to a logical pattern that reflects our commitment to causal thinking. We always start with 'The Why', unpacking the focus and purpose of the Module by providing a powerful, Compelling Question, e.g., *So What's Real News?* and a narrative Story that explains to the reader the broad scope of the Module and why the content matters.

We then unpack 'The What', in terms of Conceptual, Competency, and Character Learning Goals. Using 'backward design' thinking, learned from Understanding by Design, the brilliant brainchild of Grant Wiggins and Jay McTighe (2005), we then plan 'The Evidence', a flexible choice of performance-based assessments that provide feedback for students to improve their learning and for teachers to inform our practice.

We then plan 'The How' as a set of Framing Questions and a Learning Sequence that responds to those questions while providing learners with opportunities to master the learning goals and tackle the assessments with confidence. Finally, we retrace our learning journey with our learners in 'The Reflection', which involves a range of creative ways for learners to relive, consider and consolidate their learning.

It's Worth Achieving Both Learning Coverage and Learning Uncoverage

Most schools still feel that they need to cover the standards while they have the desire to provide opportunities for 'uncovering' essential questions and big ideas. In CGC, we have been mindful of the need to provide both coverage and 'uncoverage' (a term from Wiggins and McTighe) and have been careful to build key disciplinary standards into our Modules. We check for spiraling coverage of these standards while using inquiry methodologies to bring learning alive for our learners. It's a tricky balance but worth it.

It's Worth Learning What We Want to Learn

As one facet of 'uncoverage', one of our primary methodologies incorporates approaches to inquiry-based learning. When it comes to inquiry, we provide a simple logical toolkit that includes a practical guide to forms of inquiry, with the differences in the 'forms' being largely determined by different degrees of learner independence. If and when schools wish to explore more 'open' inquiry, then we support that shift in a number of ways. This means that there are times when learners are invited to select and pursue their own lines of inquiry. Here's our opening invitation to them, 'What would you fight to learn?'

We believe that it's worth learning about our human common ground, that it's worth learning to become experts in important knowledge domains, and that it's worth learning how to build our expertise in the context of substantive content that really matters. It's worth working toward life-worthy, transdisciplinary transfer goals, which we have presented in The Portrait of a Learner. Ultimately, it's worth learning how to exercise our agency and work with urgency to act on the pressing global challenges and opportunities that face humanity, right here, right now. That's what's worth learning, and why. We think all of that matters. We think it provides a curriculum design for our times.

Diversify: How Does Everyone Access Learning?

There is insufficient space in this article to do justice to the importance and complexity of issues of diversity, equity, inclusion, and justice. Perhaps all we can do here is stress that the CGC has been committed from the outset to equity of access to learning for all learners, and access to equal opportunity for all community stakeholders.

To achieve this, we support schools in building a connected flow of 'purpose-policy-practice' decisions and actions so that the school's mission is reflected in its policies and enacted in its practices. We have synthesized all this thinking into an overarching Policy Framework, called Building Belonging, which we use with schools to bring consensus on supporting all forms of diversity in clear and consistent ways.

Becoming Better Schools

The benefits of inclusive education to individual children, their families, and the school community are incalculable. Inclusive schools, we believe, are better schools. They transform lives, while we learn to be smarter. As we build the capacities of our neurodiverse students, we build our own capacity, becoming more intelligent as an organization. We learn to be kinder, more generous, more open, more empathetic. All of this permeates the culture of inclusive schools. When we are inclusive, not by admissions or recruitment accident, but on purpose, we change. When we are deliberately diverse, we become inclusive not just as a matter of policy or program, but as a matter of identity. We get better, in all senses of the word. Equity matters. It is our duty to provide an inclusive organizational model for our times.

Deliver: How Do We Build Learning Cultures?

As research suggests, the factor that has the biggest impact on the quality of learning is the quality of teaching (Hattie, 2009). This should not come as a surprise. What is surprising is that the search for consistent quality of learning, and therefore consistent quality of teaching, seems to be such a long and winding road. The usual markers on that road seem to focus on developing 'standards' for teachers and then 'evaluating' teachers against those standards. It's all very compliance-oriented and rule-bound. Even the language around it smacks of the factory floor. In what other profession are we the 'supervisors' of our colleagues?

In CGC, we take a very different approach. Schools are not factories. They are living, organic learning cultures. Necessarily, then, if we are to create great schools we need to focus, first, on the school as a culture.

Cultures share a language, and by defining learning and framing it simply, we have offered the opportunity of a shared learning language shared by all learning stakeholders. Cultures share norms and values. We believe that great school cultures are framed by a few shared principles, not constrained by multiple rules and regulations.

We define a principle as 'a shared truth that brings order and freedom to a system'. We are more likely to follow a 'shared truth' than to attempt to comply, for example, with the mind-boggling number of 'teaching standards' that seem to over-populate teacher evaluation systems.

So, where do our Learning Principles come from? We believe that a well-crafted, co-created set of Learning Principles will be a practical synthesis of our shared learning experiences and the most reliable research. As always in CGC, we also believe in simplicity over complexity, so we generally work hard to synthesize our collective wisdom into 4–5 Learning Principles. We do so by reaching deep into the hearts and memories of community members, recalling 'learning stories' that have shaped them as learners, and translating those into Learning Principles, taking care to also integrate research into what works best to make learning happen.

Of course, a set of Learning Principles has no value on its own–just another wall adornment to nail up by the Mission Statement. The real learning impact comes when Learning Principles are translated into Learning Practices, then into the necessary Teaching Practices to support the learning. From here, a school creates Leading Practices to support the teaching. It's basic if/then logic. If we are living this principle, then here's what we'll see our learners doing, here's what our teachers will be doing in support, here's what our leaders will be doing, and here's how parents can provide informed, practical support, and here's how our Board can support this long-term culture-building strategy.

We have used this thinking to design a complete alternative to 'traditional teacher evaluation' systems, for the simple reason that they don't work. At least, if the goal is to improve student learning, they do not deliver sufficient tangible, sustained learning impact to justify the expenditure in teacher and leader energy.

In brief, we have replaced these ineffective systems with The Collective Growth System (CGS). For each 'principle' we develop a 'cultural continuum' that describes impacts the learner experiences in learning cultures that Transact, Transition, Transform or Transcend. From these continua, schools select one collective impact goal on which everyone works in collaboration. If, as Hattie and others confirm, collective teacher efficacy has such a high learning impact, it makes sense to build teacher efficacy collectively.

So, that's the simple idea. Drucker (2008) suggested that, when it comes to organizational change, 'Culture eats strategy for breakfast'. We need to build learning cultures. As Wheatley (2006) reminds us, 'It's only a culture if everybody buys in'. As leaders, we need to build a school-wide learning culture, sharing a common learning language shaped by a few deeply held shared learning principles that drive practices for learners, teachers, leaders, parents, and governors. If everybody buys in, then those practices are what we do when nobody's watching, so we are replacing supervision with shared vision. Our agreed practices provide the focus for continuous growth as learners, teachers, leaders, parents, and governors. These are simple patterns to help us lead and manage complex organizations. This work matters. We think it provides a learning culture for our times.

Demonstrate: How Do We Provide Evidence of Learning?

If there is an element of the learning business that is crying out for transformation, it is in our approaches to assessment, recording, and reporting. Assessment, rather like genres in literacy, has different purposes, audiences, media, and tools. In deciding where we should focus our attention in CGC, we have opted to focus primarily on assessment *for* and *as* learning. Schools may well feel the need for quantitative 'testing' approaches for various reasons. We prefer to complement those systems with qualitative, learner-centered, evidence-based assessment approaches with students as active agents in gathering, analyzing, and communicating evidence of their own learning, guided by teachers.

To achieve this goal, we have joined forces with Jay McTighe, co-founder of the deeply influential Understanding by Design (UbD) 'movement', to co-create *A Balanced Assessment System (BAS)*. The system is framed by five assessment principles that bring coherence, consistency, and continuity to assessment policies and practices.

Our early collaborations show great promise as we synthesize the most powerful innovations of both UbD and CGC in support of purposeful assessment. We are optimistic that our work will support schools in easing the stifling effect of an over-reliance on low-learning, high-stakes testing.

Closing the Learning Circle

Our Three Cs Self-Assessment Tool is one example of learner-driven, evidence-based qualitative assessment. It invites learners to comment on their own growth in conceptual, competency, and character learning, presenting their own learning evidence. This form of assessment closes the circle that began when we identified learning goals for each of the Three Cs. We think that a qualitative, evidence-based, learner-centered approach to assessment matters. We think it provides an assessment model for our times.

From Theory to Application

Can the principles and practices of a coherent learning ecosystem be actualized? The answer is 'yes', and these have been manifested in various ways in a multitude of school settings. The rhetoric about education reform is rife with untested theory and hyperbole, and contains lofty, out-of-touch assertions that are often unreasonable in their application to daily life in schools. As educational leaders, we have experienced the application of a learning ecosystem and the transformative nature of these principles coming to life in schools. There is a notable set of examples and anecdotes that illustrate the positive metamorphosis that results from effective leadership toward a shared vision.

References

Bartlett, K., & Low, D. (n.d.). *The learning playbook.* Common Ground Collaborative. https://www.commongroundcollaborative.org

Common Ground Collaborative (CGC). (n.d.). *The CGC learning ecosystem.* https://www.commongroundcollaborative.org

Deming, W. E. (2012). *The essential Deming: Leadership principles from the father of quality.* McGraw-Hill Professional.

Drucker, P. (2008). *The essential Drucker: The best of sixty years of Peter Drucker's essential writings on management.* Harvard Business Review Press.

Fullan, M. (2001). *Leading in a culture of change.* John Wiley & Sons.

Hattie, J. (2009). *Visible learning: A synthesis of over 800 meta-analyses relating to achievement.* Routledge.

McTighe, J., & Wiggins, G. (2005). *Understanding by design*. Association for Supervision and Curriculum Development (ASCD.

Sinek, S. (2021). *The infinite game*. Portfolio/Penguin.

Wheatley, M. J. (2006). *Leadership and the new science: Discovering order in a chaotic world*. Berrett-Koehler Publishers.

5 Leading the Streamlining Shift in Curriculum

What to Cut Out, Cut Back, Consolidate, and Create to Prepare Future-Ready Learners

Heidi Hayes Jacobs and
Catarina Song Chen

Each morning international school leaders wake up and head out the door to wrestle with the day's challenges and create fresh possibilities for their students. Given the vast array of settings, families, learners, teachers, languages, and resources in international schools, it would seem unlikely that there are common guarantees for these leaders to consider. But there are guarantees in education to face if we wish to grow curriculum and learning experiences to best prepare our learners.

Guarantees Leaders Can Count on

1. ***Knowledge will keep growing every day in every field.*** Tools for accessing information and shaping products will certainly increase in effectiveness, speed, and accessibility. There is no doubt that modern learners will need updated content, proficiencies, and learning experiences to prepare them for a future that is also guaranteed to be different from today. They need to be directly involved as agents in their own learning. The leader asks, "How will we keep up?"

2. ***Contemporary learners will need to develop the proficiencies to fulfill new roles.*** International school leaders often facilitate discussions about the attributes and the roles needed by their students to face future challenges. This practice reflects the findings in the report on Jobs and the Future of Work published by the World Economic Forum (2020) which identifies actual professional and work titles, that is, **roles,** versus broad descriptors of skills. Rather than simply generic roles (i.e., critical thinker, problem-solver), the will to step up and plan for the future and develop these new roles is evident in international schools. Teachers aspire to develop innovative designers, climate activists, media critics, documentary filmmakers, global ambassadors, computer programmers, mindful citizens, and community researchers (Jacobs & Alcock, 2017). We see these roles described in examples of a school's Portrait of a Graduate and in mission statements in international schools throughout the world. Yet, the challenge is not only developing demonstrations of learning that correspond to these future-oriented roles but also finding the space to do so. The leader asks, "How can I ask my teachers to develop these roles with all of the demands on them?"

3. ***International school professionals wish to develop promising curriculum projects to lift and enliven learners.*** There is no dearth of ideas in our schools. When perusing the mission statements and Portraits of a Graduate from a range of international schools, there is striking consensus that international educators certainly want to move forward and support their students in this commitment to future forward learning by providing a global perspective. Yet, international school professionals often feel restricted.

The desire to grow learning and meet these desired aspirations is a lofty one, because there is a dilemma confronting international school communities. As education leader and researcher Michael Johnston notes,

> It's a familiar sight at many of the international schools I've worked at: students and teachers become passionate about an issue, implement a well-intentioned but less than systemic plan and ultimately the initiative loses steam or does not produce the desired results.
>
> (2022, p. 23)

The dilemma is then the need to complete curricular programs as prescribed, to meet assessment requirements, and at the same time assist each student in a classroom. This proves insurmountable when nothing is "taken off the plate" for teachers. It is a confounding problem that international leaders must address head-on or accept that the problem will not only persist, it will worsen. The leader reflects, "This is overwhelming for them and me."

A Call to Action

International school leaders must streamline the curriculum to lead learning into the future and engage students as partners in learning. Choices need to be made about the curriculum at each school setting based on its learners and the setting as to:

- What to cut out
- What to cut back
- What to consolidate
- What to create

To assist leaders in making these choices, this chapter lays out a five-step curriculum review process adapted for international schools. Readers will walk through each step with coaching points and references to specific international schools that have worked through their own reviews. The chapter concludes by describing what happens when schools have room to innovate both on the everyday classroom level and school-wide projects. Authentic examples are shared from international schools directly engaged in preparing their students to become future-ready.

The Need to Streamline

Curriculum will become increasingly cumbersome if schools keep adding content demands every year without pausing, reflecting and analyzing, and making cogent choices. What happens to our goal of modernizing learning when the reality of keeping up is so demanding? The pressures of a jam-packed curriculum are extremely detrimental to the education profession and adversely affect learners. When leaders feel the burden of trying to meet every program demand, there is pressure put on teachers to "cover content," which is the nemesis of learning. When teachers feel frenzied, this feeling is likely passed onto their students resulting in diminished learning. In their study on the worldwide trend toward teacher burnout, Agyapong et al. (2022) found that the overwhelming workload demands on teachers is one of the most frequently cited factors in anxiety and depression among faculty members contributing to teachers leaving the profession.

With more curriculum demands, major program standardized tests, and looming deadlines, coverage increases as teachers must "get students ready" which often translates as "must get students memorizing." Students can mentally drop out or drive themselves into knots with such tense demands. Sometimes, a school might create a very special project, but this is, in fact, an admirable outlier that can be perceived as a well-intended gesture toward the modern.

There Must Be Space in the Curriculum to Provide the Conditions for Innovation

Even as the demands on leaders and teachers can take their toll, there is great interest from prospective parents to have their children experience a dynamic curriculum. International private schools are growing and at the same time, they are diversifying their offerings to appeal to families of various financial levels. Adam Gray-Smith, a researcher with ISC Research (International School Consultancy), notes in the EdWeek MarketBrief, *International Private Schools Are Growing, and Diversifying Their Curriculum Offerings* (Caffey, March 14, 2024) that this global expansion is occurring with a corresponding expansion in the range of curriculum offerings, moving away from a strict adherence to either United Kingdom, United States, Cambridge, International Baccalaureate, or Advanced Placement, the five key curricula that "dominate the international schools market," which are taught by 77% of all international schools.

To be clear, international schools are seeking to offer a range of curriculum experiences. As Gray-Sim explains, "it is very rare that one school offers just one curriculum" and that two-thirds of international schools offer a hybrid, which in this case means including regulations in different countries requiring state, provincial, district, or national requirements. Thus, even with these realistic challenges, there is also a desire for enhanced possibilities for responsive learning experiences. The motivation for making this shift is underscored in the ISC Research Report, Global Market Overview: "When it comes to curriculum selection, our field research suggests a prevailing desire among international schools for flexible curricula. Such flexibility allows schools to tailor content to the needs of their location, student community and overarching vision and ethos" (2023, p. 74).

Leading Learning Requires Administrators to Facilitate Efforts to Make Realistic Choices about What Matters Most in Program Planning

What is needed is for learning leaders to make a shift so that there is room to create a responsive modern curriculum. There is a need to proportionally adjust to the growth of knowledge. The impact will lighten the load on teachers and perhaps even prompt joy. Certainly, there are questions on how to address many respected preexisting, purchased programs of study. These programs are thoughtfully constructed and attempt to guide school personnel in the teaching of important intellectual and character-building learning experiences. Nevertheless, the over-packed curriculum problem exists whether the source is an excellent program designed by an organization, a publisher, or designed internally by staff. A leader can attempt to ignore the problem, but it will come back to haunt every year. There is simply too much curriculum, and a short school year coupled with the looming need for bringing in the new knowledge being developed every day.

What Is Streamlining the Curriculum?

The concept of streamlining describes making deliberate choices in the curriculum to make "learning easier to access, understand and use," thus making it more "effective, purposeful, timely and effective" (Jacobs & Zmuda, 2023, pp. 5–6). The Online Etymology Dictionary (n.d.) notes the origin of the word coming from the field of hydraulics in the early 1900s meaning "free from turbulence" and business to simplify or eliminate unnecessary work-related tasks to improve efficiency.

Streamlining the Curriculum: What to Cut Back? Consolidate? Create?

As leaders, you are empowering faculty to make curriculum choices with transparency and hope. Hope because the goal is to deepen the best in current practice, shed what is not necessary, and make room to create possibilities for learners. Streamlining is intrinsically motivating to professionals. Ultimately, the purpose of streamlining is to open the possibilities for joyful, exhilarating, relevant learning for our students. Students become partners in the curriculum planning. The focus throughout our chapter is on actions that leaders can take to streamline and engage students directly in their learning journey.

Leading the Shift: Setting the Stage for Streamlining in an International School

This occurs when leadership nurtures a shift in a school's approach to curriculum decisions. Moving past rigid, compliance-driven decisions, a faculty comes together to make sense of curriculum for their specific student population. It is a collaborative approach which is necessary for a review process. The implication is that formal programs are to be respected but permission is needed to collaboratively determine priorities.

Setting the stage for streamlining is often easier when school faculty members have participated in curriculum design and mapping initiatives. Many international school educators have had professional development experience with models such as *Understanding by Design* or *Concept Based-Curriculum* and are familiar with the careful choices in unit planning. When international schools have worked with mapping curriculum using software platforms, they can look at both cross course and vertical views of the curriculum. Given that each international school has unique contexts regarding the locality, national education requirements, political environments, and the transiency of student and teacher populations, it seems particularly important to have a realistic and streamlined curriculum that can be adapted and communicated with ease.

Central to establishing readiness is to encourage your faculty to consider the meaning of streamlining. To streamline is not to simply cut things out or cut back. As Dreyfuss said, "People are made safer, more efficient, more comfortable – or just plain happier" (pp. 25–26). Leading the shift in streamlining requires that a school leader openly declare that as a faculty you are going to take on an editorial stance. You are going to make sense of the many demands and sift through what is essential for your learners guided by clear editorial criteria. For example, leaders will directly ask faculty members to point out areas in the curriculum that have perpetually concerned them in terms of being unwieldy or overpacked. Set the stage by acknowledging the classical and critical need for both formal internal coherence to the needs of your specific learners and external alignment to the standards throughout a school curriculum.

Internal coherence: The axiom for developing internal coherence is setting criteria based on the best interest of a specific student population with its unique needs, aspirations, resources, and characteristics. Whether a curriculum was fully developed by an individual teacher or team or whether the basis is a textbook or purchased program reverence, streamlining can be applied to any curriculum source. Of note is that often we have seen that teachers may not feel they have permission to adjust programs or materials even when good sense suggests it is necessary. Any resource, whether a dynamic textbook, an online set of modules, or a fully developed program, needs to be adapted for a specific setting. These programs were not designed just for a specific group of children in a specific location, rather they are designed for any and all students and are placed in the hands of the onsite educators to make adaptations. As a leader, it is critical to consistently convey that responsive learning ensures that learning experiences need to be geared directly to your specific students.

External alignment to standards: The need to align curriculum and assessment directly to agreed-upon standards established by professional organizations (AERO standards, for ex.) or from a fully developed program (for example, Approaches to Learning (ATLs) from the International Baccalaureate). There are international schools that are obliged to align curriculum and assessment to host country national standards. Regardless, the standards are not the curriculum, they are proficiencies. They usually do not indicate when to teach, what to teach, or how to assess. Standards provide a K-12 spiraling set of proficiencies that are to be embedded in the curriculum and demonstrated by learners.

Leaders who are clear that their faculty operates with insight to both the need for internal, vertical articulation and communication coupled with the power of embedding standards into their classroom planning can confidently move forward with streamlining. Learning leaders can leverage the need for greater coherence as a school-wide motivator for streamlining.

> At the Community for Learning, a PreK-12 international school based in Santa Domingo in the Dominican Republic, the head of school, Carla Meyrink, could see the build-up of packed curriculum and the need to streamline. "I needed an approach that would revitalize our faculty and give them a purpose to reinvest in the curriculum." She encouraged her curriculum coach, to set the stage by beginning vertically in English Language Arts. Nicole began by working with teachers in grades 7–12 with input from students to create a "story" of what a child would experience on their journey, 7–12. It was clear that there was too much repetition and too much on the student's plate. They were ready to begin to make choices about what to cut back on, what to consolidate, and what to create.

Shifting to an editorial stance: When learning leaders ask, "What do we cut out? What do we cut back? What do we consolidate? What do we create?" they are empowering and leading their faculties, their leadership networks, and their organizational affiliates to make choices. A streamlining review requires that the leader clarifies that as the faculty will be taking on an editorial stance, it will require deliberate and open discussion in the review process to establish editorial criteria for making curriculum choices as described below in the 5-Step Streamlining Curriculum Review Process.

Leaders declare process credibility: Faculties need to be reassured that this review is credible. That is, they need to feel confident that action will be taken to address any problems that have emerged. Establishing in advance in writing what the limitations of making changes may be is wise given that there are clearly certain programmatic and political demands that international schools must respect. For example, an end-of-the-year examination required by an organization or a national government will stay in place.

Five Step Streamlining Curriculum Review Process – International School Adaptation

Step 1: Identify the curriculum area needing review

Identifying a priority area in need of streamlining review whether a course, grade level subject, or unit of study. The curriculum scope for review could be a one-year course, for example, year 3 math or freshman biology, or it might be a specific unit of study, such as Ancient Civilizations, year 6. The review could be on a vertical subject over several years, for example, social studies year 5 to year 8. In making the case for a review, there are tell-tale signs reflected by teachers: "I never finish this course;" "My last month of school is packed with jamming everything in;" "Our kids rush through this unit and never get the skills;" "There is just too much expected for me to cover and for the students to memorize:" "My students are bewildered and have stopped participating," "All I am doing is lecturing to cover the material, I am not engaging the kids in interactions." It is highly recommended that teachers directly seek student input whether in surveys, interviews, or discussion groups about their concerns regarding their learning. As previously stated, students need to be agents of their own learning.

Also previously noted, international schools often rely on programmes requiring adherence to a thoughtfully designed sequence of concepts. The reason why these curriculum reviews are particularly necessary is to be open and insightful about adaptations. The priority area can be proposed by any faculty member, department, or group of teachers. When leadership and teachers have reviewed the proposed areas, consensus is reached as to what should be reviewed and the order of importance. To be clear, there can be simultaneous reviews pending on the faculty involved as well as reviews that are spaced out over time.

The American International School of Budapest has been actively conducting streamlining work. Tami Canale, Director of Teaching and Learning, 6–12 explains what prompted their reviews:

> "Our initial motivation (~2017) was the fact that we just could not teach everything that the standards frameworks were asking us to. We needed a way to agree on what was most important, and Ainsworth's book gave us a framework to do that. Fortunately, we began this work before COVID, and it was very helpful during the pandemic for teachers to already know what the essentials were when they were having to make decisions about prioritizing limited time. Our latest motivation is focused on student needs: the worldwide mental health crisis, preparing students for exponential growth and change (VUCA learning), response to AI in education".

Step 2: Determine who should be on the review team

We recommend opening a range of perspectives by deliberately including various participants besides those immediately affected. It is very easy for a faculty department or group to get "stuck" in their collective patterns when reviewing curriculum. In other words, if it is a second grade reading course needing review, it might be wise to include a first and third-grade teacher in the review session and certainly a reading specialist on the faculty. If there are questions about the vertical sequence of a content area such as social studies or science, not only should members of that department be asked to review the sequence but a few members of the English department who might add a different perspective on how writing is being included in the curriculum. Whether it is the arts or physical education or an elective like Psychology, inviting other viewpoints brings perspective when making the choices on what matters most.

There certainly can be opportunities for whole-school reviews as underscored by David Chadwell, Associate Head of Teaching and Learning at Saigon South International School, who notes that the faculty was responding to the "wondering of what was to be taught post-COVID." There was a pervasive sense that curriculum needed clarifying and priority standards needed to be clearly articulated.

> Prior to COVID, we knew we had to articulate the curriculum, but post-COVID, we knew and felt that there were priorities and just going backward didn't make sense. There was a desire to understand and fix areas of disconnection and misunderstandings and gaps within departments, across the divisions, and throughout the school. There was inefficiency with teachers trying to understand what was being taught before and after their courses and continually going in circles to create something, multiple restarting of conversations, and misunderstandings of what was going on across the school. This was the opportunity for Power Standards and an articulated streamlined, guaranteed, and viable curriculum. It was very much teacher desire and structurally teaching and learning office.
>
> Everyone was involved, really. All teachers were talking about the standards that they were teaching which eventually led to, "Are these the Power Standards for your unit and course?" And then, "Are there gaps within the course? Across the department?" There were also middle-level leaders (Intellectual Development Leaders based on our mission) who led and facilitated divisional conversation and collaboration across the school. The EC-12 Learning Coordinator, Associate Head of School for Teaching and Learning, and SBGR Implementation Specialist were pivotal in guiding and "holding" the work." It was very much a teacher desire.

Step 3: Establish the criteria for the review

It is necessary to establish specific criteria for the review as a group. Whether it is job-like or vertical teams, small groups of teachers and division and department chairs should begin a discussion about the four fundamental questions that will guide the process.

In Figure 5.1, adapted from Jacobs and Zmuda, Streamlining the Curriculum, the four questions are described to begin discussions with faculty as applied to a middle school history course. Leaders can ask for examples of each question in small groups to ensure that there is a collective understanding of the questions.

Leading the Streamlining Shift in Curriculum

Five Step Curriculum Review Process

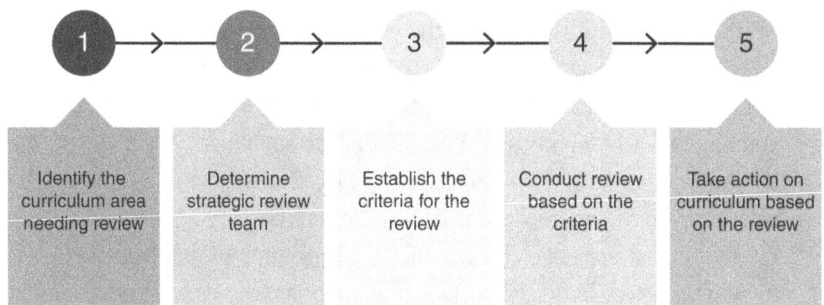

Figure 5.1 Five step curriculum review process
Source: Jacobs, H.H. and Zmuda, A. Streamlining the curriculum: Using the Storyboarding Approach to frame compelling student journeys. ASCD: Alexandria, VA. 2023.

Establishing Editorial Criteria around Four Key Questions: Example High School History Course

An example of the positive results of a review where teachers were deliberately seeking connections and opportunities for interdisciplinary consolidation at the American School of Budapest was a significant improvement in the quality of the curriculum across subjects, as Tami Canali reflects:

> Understanding how concepts live across the curriculum and having those cross-curricular conversations among teachers has led to a more complete picture of student learning for all teachers. For example, when we were reviewing the grade 9 curriculum across English, social studies, science, math, PE, and advisory, the math and PE teachers realized that they could work together to help students see their personal fitness data in PE class applied in a real way in math class, and they created an interdisciplinary project as a result of this one conversation.

75

Step 4: Conduct the review process using the editorial criteria

We have found that to launch the review, it can be instructive to ask the lead faculty who are actually teaching the target course to "tell the story of" the course and explain why the current units or layout exist. They can address what the intention of the course is for students, that is, what is hoped that students will develop and understand because of the course. Perhaps the key standards and aspirations are identified. At this point, the discussion can turn to what is preventing the intended outcome. The reasons for bringing the course or series of courses up for review become clear in a give and take discussion. At this point, the review process is a natural next step. To be clear, many international schools have great faith in their existing curriculum and are motivated to review to deepen and make clearer connections for learners. At the American School of Barcelona (ASB), elementary principal, Kristen MacConnell, has been leading her faculty in a streamlining process that focuses on consolidation.

> As with many international schools, there are requirements from the host country's national education ministries. At ASB, students in grades 1–5 must take 150 minutes of Spanish Literacy, and 150 minutes of Catalan Literacy (if they are Spanish passport holders), and 90 minutes of Social Studies (Sociales) in a 6-day cycle. The school has been conducting a formal vertical review to meet the requirement through careful integration so that students develop their literacy skills across English, Spanish, and Catalan while also applying their literacy skills in the Sociales and Science curriculum. As Kristen notes," Our teachers are motivated to make meaningful space in their demanding schedules for natural connections in the curriculum. We guide our streamlining process by identifying interesting inquiry driven questions, conceptual understandings and the transdisciplinary skills most important for our learners to reach our Portrait of a Future Ready Fifth Grader by the time they head to middle school.

Step 5: Take action on the curriculum review and share openly with colleagues

Streamlining is the aim of the review process to provide more time and space to go deeply into the curriculum and make room for upgrades and new possibilities. There is often a wave of good feeling when teachers are treated like professionals and can have an impact on the lives of their students. The actions to be taken most naturally correspond to the initial impetus for the review in the first place. Curriculum documents are commitments to be shared by professionals in a school.

- If, for example, an English department in a middle school has elected to cut out a novel in sixth grade and spend more time on a short chapter book series, then the agreed upon novel will be eliminated from the curriculum.
- If a history department has determined it is better to focus on agreed upon key historical figures in more depth in the study of Ancient China in their upper school versus attempting to cover multiple names and dates, then the curriculum will be revised.
- If, in years 2 and 3, an elementary math program wishes to consolidate the units on measurement and currency with their ongoing numeracy units on fundamental addition, subtraction, multiplication, and division because they see the possibility for applications, they will do so directly in the curriculum.

Actions should be formally documented on the curriculum platform used throughout the school whether it is Google document, a spreadsheet, or curriculum mapping software. Figure 5.2 below provides leaders with a tool to coach international schoolteachers through the process of streamlining.

Editorial Question	Establish Criteria for Review	Conduct Review and Generate Possible Actions
What to cut out? Make room for deeper investigation and development of key concepts and skills.	Cut out points to highlight what matters most, given time constraints and the specific learners, and decide what to let go. • Situation conditions—such as a shortened academic calendar, staggered classroom schedules, alternative onsite attendance, and increased online learning demand—will influence decisions.	When making decisions about cutting a unit, identify crucial standards and foreground them when designing learning experiences. • Bundling standards that naturally cluster together helps sort out which standards are crucial, and which are not.

Figure 5.2 Establishing editorial criteria around four key questions: example high school history course

Source: Jacobs, H.H. and Zmuda, A. Streamlining the curriculum: Using the Storyboarding Approach to frame compelling student journeys. ASCD: Alexandria, VA. 2023.

(Figure 5.2 Continued)

Editorial Question	Establish Criteria for Review	Conduct Review and Generate Possible Actions

 **What to cut back?**
 	
Foreground important cognitive and technical skills, content that is central to the big idea, and key demonstrations of learning.
	Review the thumbnail story of the curriculum through the year to determine the placement of units.
	
	• Cut back by distinguishing the most crucial from less crucial elements.
	• Consider cuts in skills, content, and assessments as you determine criteria.
		Determining skill, content, and assessment cuts requires setting clear priorities about what is essential for learners.
		
		• **Skills:** Elevate skills that are integral to a given discipline, as well as subskills tied to Future Forward Learning Goals.
		• **Content:** Confront the tendency to cover content.
		  • Distinguish content that directly supports and is central to the Future Forward Learning Goals and storyline.
		  • Given the larger aims and goals of the unit, cut nonessential materials, information, facts, and subtopics.
		• **Assessment:** Evidence of learning is bedrock to the design of learning experiences.
		• Determine as a faculty which formative and summative assessments, as well as which demonstrations of learning, are the most revealing across grade levels and vertically.
		• If there are cuts in the curriculum, then there will be corresponding cuts in the assessments

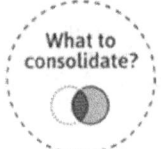 **What to consolidate?** Combine elements to make a more effective coherent whole.	Search for related and clear connections within a unit or among units, then combine them when possible. • Review the scope and sequence of a year's units to see where to merge units of study.	Consolidation can occur within an existing unit by pulling together concepts or materials that overlap. • Designing interdisciplinary units of study can be fruitful when consolidating content, whether within a course or among subjects and courses.

(Figure 5.2 Continued)

Editorial Question	Establish Criteria for Review	Conduct Review and Generate Possible Actions
What to create? Provide fresh perspectives for learners, bringing in multiple subject areas as lenses through which to consider common topics, problems, issues, and themes.	Relevance means generating new curriculum units or projects that are responsive to learners. • Viewing content through the lenses of multiple subject areas can provide fresh perspectives. • Consider including phenomena-based learning that supports inquiry into emergent problems and issues in students' lives. • What is key is the immediacy of the situation under consideration, whether it's personal, local, or global.	Learners can examine current and relevant topics, problems, issues, case studies, and themes either as individual units or as a series of units. • Create engaging and timely learning experiences that are personal, local, or global. • Replace a more dated unit with a fresher one. A unit might focus on a breakthrough in science, a historical research find, a new work of literature, a seasonal change in a tree on the elementary school playground, or a local issue under debate.

(Figure 5.2 Continued)

Editorial Criteria Review and Actions

After a school has reviewed and vetted its curriculum choices, there is a shared commitment and knowledge about what the students in a school will be experiencing. The foundation for learning is stronger. Communication about what matters most has been the focus of PLCs, curriculum reviews, and department meetings. There is now more space and will for innovation.

We asked David Chadwell to elaborate on the impact of the streamlining review at Saigon South International School. He notes:

> Clarity of understanding. Some tried to hold on to too many standards because they "liked" them and realized the need to focus more as further iterations continued. It allowed for department conversations, reflections, and examinations. And for cross-divisional conversations. This strengthened both teacher leaders and overall collaboration across the school.

As Eloise Milligan, curriculum director at Shaler School District in Pennsylvania, notes, "I have never seen anything like this impact a faculty's sense of purpose and commitment. They are pumped and ready to move forward because the curriculum layout makes sense."

Leaders Post-Streamlining: Curricular Space to Innovate and to Engage Students

The Leader Asks, "Now We Have Space to Innovate, Where Do We Begin?"

With curricular breathing room, leaders and teachers can step up and respond with innovation. The root word of innovation is nova which in Latin means "to give birth." In a school setting, innovative curriculum can be scaled to be implemented school-wide, interdepartmental, individual grade, multi-grade, individual classroom, groups of students, or for an individual student. With the space to be responsive, innovative design can be directly injected into the ongoing daily curriculum to revitalize and motivate learners. When there is space, there can also be outstanding school-wide projects outside the usual program and concurrently fresh opportunities on the classroom level that enliven the ongoing curriculum. Encouraging students on personal quests to burrow into a problem and develop a solution can be integrated into the design of a course if there is room to do so. This is at the heart of future-ready preparation. In either the daily ongoing curricular or school-based project context, students are directly engaged as partners in their own growth through these curricular actions. Streamlining provides the conditions for nurturing innovations when learners are directly engaged as partners versus a passive step back to the antiquated coverage approach of the curriculum.

The Leader Asks, "How Can We Learn from Colleagues to Help Our Own School?"

It is important to study and celebrate the remarkable accomplishments of colleagues in the international school community on their innovative projects and to learn from them. Studying successful projects is a powerful way to inspire similar efforts. Of particular interest is how the leaders in these schools created the conditions for innovation and in particular how they managed the dilemma of a demanding school curricular program. Further, do they see that the power of the innovative project permeates the rest of the school program?

We asked these questions of the leaders at the schools that were awarded the International School Award organized by ISC research in 2024. The awards shed light on inspired initiatives rooted around intercultural understanding and are connected to the UN Sustainable Development Goals (SDGs) to share their insights about the conditions for innovation.

At DPS International, Gurgaon, India, we see their remarkable program as an outstanding example of streamlining curriculum through consolidation. Given the program, the entire experience highlights the value of structured innovation within the school environment, empowering students while aligning with broader educational goals. Rima Singh, head of school shares the power of their innovation at DPS International School (DPSI), Gurgaon, India.

> The Student Task Force Programme is designed to foster student agency, leadership, and alignment with the UN Sustainable Development Goals (SDGs). Middle Years Programme (MYP) students, particularly those in MYP 4 and 5 (ages 15–16), formed groups based on personal interests. Middle Years Programme (MYP) students, particularly those in MYP 4 and 5 (ages 15–16), formed groups based on personal interests. Each group worked under the mentorship of a teacher and focused on impactful projects, such as:
>
> - First Aider: Peer first-aid training (SDG: 3, 4)
> - Biodiversity Crusaders: Environmental initiatives like micro-gardens and recycling (SDG: 15, 11, 4)
> - Financial Literacy Experts: Financial education workshops and guest speaker events (SDG: 8, 4)

- Artisans Supporters: Supporting local artisans through markets and donations to local schools (SDG: 1, 8, 4)
- Wellness Squad: Promoting healthy lifestyles (SDG: 3, 4)
- Tech for Good: E-waste recycling and AI education (SDG: 11, 4)
- Social Media Force: Safe social media usage and school promotion (SDG: 11, 4)
- Star Gazers: Astronomy education (SDG: 4): These efforts resulted in tangible outcomes like new skills for students, environmental awareness, financial support for local schools, and meaningful community engagement.

The project succeeded due to scheduled school time specifically allocated for task force activities. This structured time allowed students to plan and execute their action plans without disrupting other academic priorities. Additionally, each group was assigned a mentor to guide their work, proposals were reviewed and approved by the school leadership fostering ownership and accountability. Mentors ensured the availability of resources, such as meeting spaces, collaboration tools, and connections to external organizations.

The success of the task force model has permeated the school's broader culture. It has fostered enhanced student agency, integration of SDGs, skills development, and community partnerships. Collaboration with NGOs and local artisans has strengthened ties between the school and the broader community.

We note that the program is at every grade level and developmentally responsive to each grade level and thoughtfully integrated into the program. It was key that the schedule was adapted to give space and to ensure integrity and aims of involving students to develop and navigate their plans under the guidance of mentors. This requires cutting back on certain tasks and specific times to be upgraded with the commitment to this outstanding program. It is heartening that the results of the innovation have not taken away from the ongoing school curriculum but, rather it has strengthened the broader culture.

With a desire to foster global citizenship and empower students to make meaningful, positive change in the world, The SALT International School in Gyeonggi-do, South Korea, designed the "Students in Action" (SIA) initiative. The focus is on helping students engage with real-world global issues, develop leadership skills, and foster community-based service projects that address the United Nations Sustainable Development Goals (SDGs). The principal, Justin Park, describes this student-facing aims and achievements:

> SIA involved students from diverse age groups, ranging from middle to high school (grades 6–12), who had an interest in global issues, leadership, and service. Students participated across various disciplines, including social studies, environmental science, and community service. These young leaders were guided by our passionate faculty who worked with them to create impactful projects, from fundraising for health care and education in Rwanda through the Love Rwanda initiative, to local environmental clean-up efforts through the Plogging program. The resulting performance from SIA was remarkable. The Love Rwanda initiative raised funds for healthcare and education, directly benefiting children in rural Rwanda. Meanwhile, the Green Youth and Plogging programs allowed students to engage in local environmental awareness campaigns. The students presented their initiatives at high-profile events, including the National Assembly of Korea and the Governor's Deputy Office in Ulaanbaatar, Mongolia, where they received accolades and praise for their dedication to global citizenship.

We asked Justin to explain how the school streamlined to create the necessary space for operationalizing such a bold innovation. He explained:

> To make room for transformative, real-world projects like Students in Action (SIA), SALT International School introduced the SALT Problem/Project-Based Learning (SPBL) course, where students are introduced to project ideas early in their academic journey. This course encourages students to explore and develop solutions to

real-world challenges, preparing them for future leadership roles. SPBL allows students to apply academic knowledge to practical situations, encouraging a hands-on, collaborative approach to learning. In addition to this, we worked flexibly with the school timetable, ensuring that students had dedicated time to engage with these projects without disrupting the progression of core subjects. We adjusted our schedule around key school events, spirit days, and extracurricular activities to create space for project work. For example, we aligned breaks and special activities like Plogging with academic periods, so students could participate in both educational and service-oriented projects without overburdening their schedule. These adjustments were made without jeopardizing subject integrity or course progression. Through careful planning, we ensured that students maintained focus on their academic goals while gaining valuable experience outside the classroom. The integration of SPBL into our program not only helped streamline the process of balancing academics with impactful community work but also reinforced the importance of flexibility and adaptability in education. Yes, innovation permeates our ongoing program of studies. The success of SIA has inspired our faculty to incorporate more project-based, hands-on learning across the curriculum. Through our journey with SIA, we've learned the importance of creating conditions that empower students to explore, lead, and solve real-world challenges. One of the key lessons is the value of collaboration. Encouraging cross-departmental collaboration between teachers, counselors, and community leaders fosters a holistic learning environment. Additionally, we learned that even when time is scarce, investing in meaningful, student-driven projects can yield extraordinary results."

It is equally important to recognize that streamlining can be an impetus for purposeful innovative curriculum action on a daily basis. It excites a faculty because it is geared to directly solve ongoing teaching and learning problems. For example, a Year Two teacher who has consolidated his math program and is now creating more authentic and engaging applications is building off the streamlining approach. A Physics teacher in an upper school ensures that each quarter her students design and carry out an "active and applied" physics experiment in their immediate school or home environment. In short, we do not want to encourage a special project over the need for daily and ongoing originality in lesson planning and unit design. They can be mutually beneficial. Thus, the focus on innovation need not lead to a major school project that goes beyond the parameters of a classical school curriculum, but it can lead to the upgrading and uplifting of a school culture and approach to daily instruction. A thorough review of the curriculum based on unpacking and prioritizing standards can lift a school faculty.

Next Steps

As educators, we cannot have it both ways. It is not feasible to just keep adding more and more curriculum while not taking something off the table or consolidating what's on the table or creating a new table. If we wish to develop powerful and motivating learning opportunities that reflect the world in which students live and are geared to prepare them to be future-ready, we need to deliberately streamline the existing curriculum and programs of study. Certainly, teachers feel bewildered by the demands, and too often our students are flummoxed.

Creating the conditions for developing Future-Ready learners and shaping learning experiences responsive to their needs requires a formal commitment to innovation accompanied by a commitment to streamlining. These are mutually dependent actions.

We see that international schools on every continent have developed thoughtful mission statements, graphic displays, and lofty aims for their graduate portrait. If there is a genuine commitment to encourage students to display initiative and imaginative approaches, then there should be a corresponding need to have their teachers do the same in their planning. Learning leaders in international schools can set up the opportunity to make these approaches come alive when they conduct streamlining reviews to provide the space and inspiration for innovation. Our five-step review process is a model for leaders to consider. There are certainly multiple approaches one might consider, but we encourage a natural review process where the entire school community is involved. Streamlining is not simply a quick audit or a checklist; it is the deliberate attempt to revise and upgrade a curriculum that is workable and reflective of the needs of a specific group of students in a specific international school. Streamlining is a process that directly reshapes and recharges. Future-Ready learners require a Future-Ready curriculum.

References

Agyapong, B., Obuobi-Donkor, G., Burback, L., & Yifeng, W. (2022). Stress, burnout, anxiety, and depression among teachers: A scoping review. *International Journal of Environmental Research and Public Health, 19*(17), 10706. https://www.ncbi.nlm.nih.gov/pmc/articles/PMC9518388/

Ainsworth, L. (2010). *Rigorous curriculum design: How to create curricular units of study that align standards, instruction, and assessment.* Lead and Learn Press.

Coffey, T. (2024, March 14). International private schools are growing and diversifying their curriculum offerings. EdWeek Market Brief. https://marketbrief.edweek.org

Gray-Smith, A. (2023). Whitie paper: What data tells us about the international schools market. *ISC research report: Global market overview.* ISC Research Report.

Jacobs, H., & Alcock, M. (2017). Bold moves for schools: How we create remarkable learning environments. ASCD.

Jacobs, H., & Zmuda, A. (2023). *Streamlining the curriculum: Using the storyboarding approach to frame compelling learning journeys.* ASCD.

Johnston, M. (2022). Community of care and support for students. In C. S. Chen, L. Prendergast, & W. Ting (Eds.), *Stories from across the globe: Leadership lessons from 13 international school leaders* (p. 22). School Rubric.

The Online Etymology Dictionary. (n.d.). Streamline. Online Etymology Dictionary. https://www.etymonline.com

World Economic Forum. (2020). Jobs and the future of work: Identifying new roles for a changing world. https://www.weforum.org/reports/jobs-and-the-future-of-work

Managing the Politics of the Board Room

John Littleford and Catriona Moran

Imagine a school board where communication flows freely, decisions are made strategically, and every member understands their role in shaping the future of the institution. What if every board meeting was not a place of dysfunction but a space for collaboration, trust, and vision? The challenge for international school boards is finding this balance. This chapter invites you to explore the complexities of board governance—from navigating the tricky terrain of board-member relationships to ensuring that leadership transitions and crises are handled with skill and foresight. Ready to discover how the unseen mechanics of governance can transform a school's future? Let's dive in.

Building an Effective, Working Board

The board of an international school has only three jobs:

1. Overseeing mission integrity which includes governance and strategic planning
2. Fiscal oversight
3. The hiring, guiding, and when necessary, removing the director

The best way to ensure that the goals of the board, the director, and their definition of the school's mission are aligned is to start with the right composition of the board. Schools need to recruit and retain wise, strategically thinking board members and reduce their turnover.

DOI: 10.4324/9781003581451-6

Board Institutional Memory

> The executive committee of an international school board hired a consultant to benchmark the compensation of its long-term, valued director with the goal of extending the contract. The consultant's role was to guide them in designing an attractive compensation package that was competitive and fair.
>
> The Chair said, "I am leaving the country for a new post so we must finalize this contract extension and the next steps in our recently approved strategic plan." The Vice Chair and Treasurer then announced that they, too, were leaving within months for new positions. Out of nine board members, the three most influential ones were leaving.

Board institutional memory refers to the collective knowledge and experiences that provide an understanding of the history and culture of an organization. Across decades of partnering with boards of both independent and international schools, without question, the loss of board institutional memory has proven to present the single biggest challenge to the health and progress of the institution. Yet very few schools address this challenge because it often means changing the bylaws or possibly the articles of incorporation as well.

Institutional memory and board stability are critical to a director's ability to develop the capital to make the right decisions at the right time by following a moral compass as well as political instincts. Sometimes, directors find it difficult to reach that balance.

For many boards, the causes of the loss of institutional memory are the following: a small board elected by the parent body with high board turnover, highly politicized election practices, and parent board members who play to the audience of good friends, colleagues, and neighbors rather than having the commitment to ensure the integrity of the mission.

Unfortunately, short-term board members tend to lead to short-term board chairs, which in turn leads to short-term directors.

Post-pandemic, the expatriate population has shrunk worldwide, but employment transfers are still very common, perpetuating a root cause of board transiency. This consultant has many international client directors who have a new board chair yearly.

At a recent board governance workshop, there were 22 board members in the room. The director was in his fifth year. I asked which board members served six years ago when the current director was chosen. Only three were there. Thus, most of the institutional memory was gone.

Boards of for-profit schools, family-owned schools, and "chains" of schools have very different governance structures and practices. The stability of these schools is based on the CEO of the company, the owner, or the designated (regional or national) CEO appointed by the corporate leader.

Privately owned chains also have internal political fights, buyouts, and share splits, all of which can force out the founders and bring in new owners. These can cause as much dysfunction as parent-elected and parent-dominated boards.

Role of the Governance, Policy, and Nominating Committee on Trustees

This is the most important committee of any board. Many schools do not even have such a committee. Others pay little attention to it. The chair of this committee is or should be the second most powerful person on the board. The members of this committee should be three to five of the most respected members of the board.

This committee has very specific functions; if all of them were performed well, there would be no need for term limits. Term limits move off board members whom the board leadership cannot bring itself to dismiss, but they also move off valued members.

Role 1: Cultivate a pool of prospects: The director, the committee chair, and other board members on the governance committee might recommend prospects. Those who are being cultivated should not know they are being considered. If the board is parent-elected, these are people whom the committee may encourage to run in upcoming elections.

Role 2: Assess potential candidates: The committee is responsible for ensuring that the candidates (and their spouses or partners) are not one-issue, agenda-focused prospects who will tend to micromanage.

Role 3: Invite new members: This includes a visit by the chair and governance chair to ask the potential candidate three questions:

- Can you give us the time?
- Can you give us the money (if there is an expectation of annual giving)?
- Do you realize you are giving up the ability to influence your own child's educational experience while you gain influence over the school's mission?

> While leading an international school orientation, three new board members were present. I asked each of them why they wanted to serve. Two gave typical answers. The third said, "I have time on my hands, so I can be in the building, wander the halls, pick up the vibes, and even visit classrooms to get a sense of the quality of the teaching."
>
> When challenged, he said, "We evaluate the head, do we not? To do so, we must know the quality of teaching of those he has hired and supervised. And I think I would make a great board chair because I have the time to do this job, which the current chair does not. She is a full-time professional."
>
> The Board leadership was unconcerned because this Board Member "tends to exaggerate." Unfortunately, this person created three years of utter dysfunction at the board level, resulting in the premature departure of some valued members and the early departure of a truly valued director.

Role 4: Board orientation: Though of critical importance, this role is all too often done inadequately. One thing that is most commonly observed to be missing in orientation is a review of the recent and midterm past, asking themselves the question, "Was there anything in hindsight that the board did wrong and should have done differently?" Those who forget the lessons of history are doomed to repeat them.

Role 5: Governance training: The committee upholds the responsibility of overseeing the annual governance training of all board members.

Role 6: Board evaluation: This comprises the evaluation of the chair, the evaluation of any board member whose term is coming up for renewal, and the evaluation of the full board.

Role 7: Addressing member behavior: The committee is responsible for warning a board member of misbehavior or inappropriate behavior.

Role 8: Member removal: The committee is, therefore, also responsible for removing a board member for continued rule-breaking despite warnings.

> A board chair reported that he had to remove two of the nine parent-elected Board Members. He said, "Every board member must sign a statement of confidentiality and a statement of no conflict of interest annually. Two leaked out at a cocktail party a confidential agreement to buy a neighboring property, and that leak caused an uproar among the locals, so we lost that opportunity."

Board Composition

Boards need at least one CEO or retired CEO on the board, but the membership of most international school boards is almost 100% professional. Professionals do not work for boards themselves and do not regularly hire and fire employees. Like directors of international schools, the CEOs of large privately and publicly held companies do, and they have more of a tendency to have a broader understanding of issues faced by the board.

Boards with too many attorneys are often risk-averse. Boards that are dominated by accounting professionals tend to micromanage the budget. Boards that are heavy with entrepreneurs tend to make riskier decisions. Boards need a mix but beware of the educator joining a board. Professionals who are educators or human resource managers can sometimes confuse their roles.

New board members especially want change. As a consultant, when boards tell me they want "new blood" on the board, I say, "You do not want blood on the floor!" Healthy boards are the ones in which the newer members sit quietly at first and learn the ropes, the rules, and the culture of the boardroom.

Choosing a Chair

After the conclusion of a director search, it is advisable to have the chair of the search committee become the next board chair to ensure that the director has advocates still on the board who chose him or her.

When choosing a chair, beware of the person who wants the job too much. Ideally, the Committee on Trustees/Nominating Committee should have to persuade the preferred prospect to take on the position.

Good chairs are also compassionate, empathetic, and, when necessary, have the courage to protect the director from constituent attacks, which often happen when the director is simply doing the job he or she is being paid to do.

Strategic Versus Operational Focus

When asking boards to rate on a scale of 1 to 10 how strategic (10) or operational (1) they are on a regular basis, the average grade worldwide is 5. Boards appear to know when they are micromanaging the head and administration, but they do it anyway and cannot seem to help themselves.

> On the sidelines of the rugby field, the head of school watched the Friday night game with pride as her son was playing exceptionally well. A board member, also a parent of one of the players, approached her and began a conversation about a recent disciplinary action taken by the principal. "Do you think those suspensions were really justified this week?"

In close-knit educational communities, such overlapping roles and casual encounters are common and expected. In these moments, leaders must skillfully navigate their dual roles, gently steering board members away from operational matters and reinforcing the distinction between governance and management responsibilities.

One of the key challenges for the director of an international school is to ensure that board members are engaged in strategic matters while respecting the boundaries of operational management. Clear delineation between governance and administration is crucial. This separation is maintained through regular board training, which should be conducted with every new board member and repeated annually with the entire board. The National Association of Independent Schools (NAIS) Principles of Good Practice emphasize the necessity of such training, underscoring that the board's primary focus should be on long-range strategic planning rather than day-to-day operations.

In a closely connected school community, even a rugby game or social gathering isn't immune to casual conversations about school suspensions! This sideline chat reminds us that the director's job is to skillfully juggle multiple roles, ensuring board members stay focused on strategic goals. Fortunately, in this case, effective board training occurred, and the director could calmly say, "Now, you know this isn't something I will discuss with you. Your son is playing well tonight." By maintaining clear boundaries and fostering open communication, the director ensures everyone is on the same page—whether on the field or in the boardroom.

What Types of Boards Are Usually Dysfunctional?

The answer is simple: the presence of parents on site daily who are communicating with parent board members at school, in the parking lot, or at social events outside of school. These parents are also in constant contact with and share gossip with teachers and staff as well as fellow parents.

Other kinds of dysfunctional boards are those who are elected, those who behave reactively to crises, those who are averse to change or urging too much change, and those who do not know how to nurture their director.

The Director and the Board's Partnership Dynamics

Key Partnerships

The first key partnership is that of the director and board chair. The "no surprises" rule means that the chair is the biggest public supporter and the most honest private critic of the director. Honesty, vulnerability, and trust take time to develop and are the cornerstones of a healthy board and, hence, of a school.

The second key collaboration at the board level is between the director and each board member. A director needs to have a personal and political relationship with every board member and ask them these three questions in person at least twice a year.

- How am I doing as the director? (though this is not a formal evaluation)
- How are you doing as a board member?
- How are your children doing?

This final question is an important one, and while the director does not want a board member exerting pressure on behalf of his/her own child, the political reality is that a director should be familiar with how a board member's children are faring.

The third partnership is that of the board chair with each board member. Consider the example of a board chair who shared that he had called for the renewal of the director's contract and lost the request by only two votes. The chair had not realized how some disgruntlement had built up around his partnership with the director. The chair misread the politics of the board room, and the director left.

About 80% of governance problems occur when the chair and the director do not have a close relationship, and about 20% of board governance issues occur when the chair and head get along too well. In the latter case, the rest of the board is put off, even envious, of the director-chair partnership.

Given the trends in international schools reflecting that it is most commonly the third chair in a director's tenure who fires them, a simple reflection question prompts attention to mitigating this challenge: "How many of you could successfully manage three marriages?"

The Politics of Change

Besides the loss of institutional memory on the board, the other reason for the sudden departures of directors is undertaking the type or pace of change.

Many boards ask directors immediately upon acceptance of the job to move on certain risky or sensitive issues or to launch a strategic planning process. These may make the faculty feel insecure, and the faculty in turn undermines the director with the parents and the board.

It just takes a new director with no political capital and no real honeymoon period to dismiss one key (or perceived key) employee, and the rest of the staff begins to unify in opposition and question the new outsider.

An internal successor is often more successful than an external hire mainly because the internal candidate knows the culture and knows what change the culture will accept and how soon.

> A board asked its director in her first 18 months to move out the long-serving Lower School Head whom the board deemed incompetent. The director asked for more time to do her own assessment of the individual's performance. The board, having felt shut out of decision-making by a long-term previous director, wanted to reassert its power. Fearing for her own job and against her better judgment, she let the person go. A few months later, the board fired the director in part because the faculty was very angry about the sudden dismissal of this popular administrator.

There must always be an entry plan and a transition plan for a new director, and there must be at least one "honeymoon" year of little change and building of political goodwill. Rapid director turnover leads to constant searches. The cycle of leadership transition undermines the school's reputation, financial health, and mission consistency.

Leading during a Crisis

In times of crisis, the partnership between the director and the board is crucial, with the board chair and director needing to be "on speed dial." Every school leader faces crises, and how we navigate these moments defines our leadership and often our survival as director. A strong director-board relationship and a solid crisis communication plan are essential for guiding the school through challenging situations.

Schools learned this very quickly during the COVID-19 pandemic. They discovered that trust is hard to earn, harder to keep, and can quickly dissolve if people feel left in the dark. Clear, coordinated communication is vital.

Good leaders are visible to their communities. During crises, the director and the board must be visible and aligned in their messaging to keep the community informed and reassured. While the board is not responsible for writing messages or creating playbooks—those duties belong to the senior leadership team and staff—it plays a critical role in providing oversight, offering guidance, reviewing processes, and securing resources to ensure the school is well-prepared and responsive during crises. Boards comprise experienced directors from various industries, leadership roles, and backgrounds; tapping into this expertise, when appropriate, is valuable.

In a crisis, leaders must remain focused on students' and staff's immediate needs rather than becoming distracted by media-driven narratives. Sticking to facts and maintaining control of the narrative is essential. Regular updates addressing rumors and misinformation help restore stability and foster trust and unity.

During long-term, high-impact crises like COVID-19, reporting can feel like a job in itself. Frequent board updates on program continuity, enrollment, responses to government mandates, and internal and external communications are necessary. While much of this work may be conducted by the communications department, the director's involvement in decision-making and overseeing the tone and timbre of the communication is crucial. Every word matters, and even internal communications can quickly become public, so all messages must be clear, concise, and consistent. While this work is time-consuming, it's critical for the board and executive leadership, strengthens collaboration, and helps the communications team stay alert to impacts across the community.

A key focus during and after a crisis should be the recovery of students, staff, and the community. By prioritizing recovery, leaders can help their communities heal more quickly and prevent division. After the immediate crisis is under control, reflect and evaluate the school's response with the board. Review protocols and identify areas for improvement to be even better prepared for future challenges.

Effective crisis management is about staying true to the school's values, maintaining open communication, and focusing on the community's well-being. By following these principles, school leaders can navigate even the most challenging crises and emerge stronger, having built resilience and trust within their school.

Running an Effective Board Meeting

Assuming a new director role presents numerous challenges, and running a first board meeting can be particularly daunting. Recently, a director with a distinguished career in a proprietary international school, where the owner was the sole board member, faced the challenge of leading board meetings in a school with a 13-member board. He asked, "What do I need to know about boards, and how do I run a board meeting?"

Board meetings, usually monthly, require careful planning, preparation, and execution. Collaborate with the board chair to craft a clear and focused agenda, prioritizing critical issues and allocating appropriate time for each item. The importance of distributing the agenda and supporting documents in advance and giving board members sufficient time to review and prepare cannot be overemphasized.

Robert's Rules of Order is a widely used manual of parliamentary procedure that provides guidelines for conducting meetings and making decisions as a group. Chapman House Rules are another set of guidelines that may be used. If the board uses these procedures, the director must become familiar with them in advance.

Start and end the meeting promptly to respect everyone's time. Facilitate discussions to ensure all voices are heard, working with the board chair to keep conversations on track and avoid tangents—present information clearly and concisely, emphasizing key points and implications, including presentations by other educational leaders.

Listen attentively to board members' input, valuing their perspectives and expertise. Be open about challenges and setbacks to foster a culture of trust and collaboration. Aim for consensus in decision-making, ensuring all board members feel their views have been considered.

Finally, make sure that you have accurate and timely documentation of meeting minutes, capture key discussions, decisions, and action items, follow up on assigned tasks and action items, and provide updates on progress in subsequent meetings.

Occasionally, a conflict will arise at the board meeting, and it is critical to maintain a professional tone and decorum throughout. When conflicts occur, stay calm and address them constructively, focusing on resolution and maintaining a positive working relationship among board members. As the head of the school, remember that you are a paid employee of the school and the board members are volunteers. Including student presentations at board meetings can also serve as a powerful reminder of the school's mission and vision.

Protocols for Head Evaluation

The second most important committee on any board is the Head Support Committee, which oversees the head's annual evaluation, compensation changes, and the renewal of the contract. Many boards do not have such a committee. The board has only one employee: the head/director. Nurturing that relationship is one of the board's three crucial functions and unfortunately, the one most often poorly managed.

> A director was midway through his initial three-year contract. The board chair said that his evaluation was positive and that his contract would be extended. The chair called back to say, "Some board members feel that we need a modified 360 approach for your evaluation, and a committee will be interviewing your eight direct reports."
>
> Several days later, the director was told that now his contract would not be extended. Reflecting on the question of whether he was aware of discontent among his leadership team, he said, "No." When asked if anyone on the leadership team had been considered formally or informally as potential candidates for his job, he said, "Yes, two."

When a board conducts an external search, and either lets internal candidate(s) be a part of the search and then rejects them or does not consider them at all, there is potential for bad feelings that come back to bite the incoming director.

In the corporate world, a form of 360-degree evaluation is common. No corporate CEO has board members whose children are influenced by the CEO's employees. However, directors do have parent board members whose children are influenced by the director's employees, such as the teachers. It is not an analogous situation to a corporate setting.

Unless the director is long-term and fully in control, the practice is very threatening to directors in their first one to eight years.

> A board chair reported that their director's contract was coming up for renewal, and at the most recent board meeting, a new board member gave each board member a polished document entitled "Head of School Evaluation." It was his compilation of feedback from a range of students, faculty, parents, and staff that he had interviewed to help advise the board on whether the director's contract should be renewed.
>
> The entire board eventually voted to remove this board member. However, the entire process was so divisive that the director departed eighteen months later anyway.

How should a director be evaluated? It does not require long checklists, "instruments," a 15-item job description, or a personality inventory. It includes these simple steps:

1. An evaluation/compensation committee of the board is appointed. It usually includes the chair, the finance chair, and perhaps the vice chair, immediate past chair, or likely next chair. The committee should consult with the director about its makeup.
2. The committee meets with the director late in the second semester, during the end of school break, or early in the first semester to set no more than three to five mutually agreed-upon goals tied to the school's own strategic planning needs.
3. Once the committee and director agree upon these goals, they should be taken to a full board meeting for a full and frank discussion and approval.
4. Mid-year, the evaluation/compensation committee should meet with the director informally. The director should outline progress toward the agreed-upon goals, and a dialogue should ensue with the committee members.

5. In late spring, the director should write a self-evaluation of progress against goals. Each member of the board should also write a confidential evaluation of the director's performance against those same earlier approved goals. The chair should counsel board members to exclude their own personal agendas and assessment of intangibles such as the director's personal style.
6. The committee should meet again and compare the director's self-evaluation with the board's combined evaluation. A dialogue should follow that provides both praise and affirmation for the success achieved and constructive feedback about areas that still need work.
7. The board chair should write a one-to-two-page summary for the file and report back orally to the entire board on the closure of the process.

The evaluation/compensation committee should then set the director's compensation for the coming year or undertake a formal contract renewal. This should occur at least twelve to eighteen months—no less—before the director's current contract ends. Boards frequently ignore the director's evaluation and compensation until long after all other staff members have been reviewed. The director, whose evaluation and compensation process should come first, is often last or forgotten entirely.

Balance Is the Goal

In conclusion, effective governance in international schools hinges on the ability of boards to maintain a delicate balance between strategic vision and operational management. Successful boards understand that their role is not to micromanage but to provide oversight and direction. Cultivating trust, communication, and mutual respect among board members and between the board and leadership ensures that both long-term goals and immediate needs are met. Boards that invest in ongoing training, encourage open dialogue, and foster healthy partnerships are equipped to navigate leadership transitions and crises with confidence. Ultimately, the most effective boards are those that continually reflect on their practices, adapt to the evolving needs of their communities, and prioritize the well-being of both the school and its students. By doing so, they not only fulfill their governance role but also help steer the institution toward sustainable success, securing a positive legacy for future generations.

Reference

National Association of Independent Schools. (n.d.). Principles of good practice. Retrieved from https://www.nais.org. Accessed 23 July 2024.

Leading the Organizational Culture

Ruth Allen and Patrice Dawkins-Jackson

It usually begins with someone lamenting: "The chats are on fire!" followed by a flurry of "pings" that signal the arrival of multiple screenshots, each taken from online chats involving a variety of stakeholders. These chats can be focused on any number of issues: an alleged bullying incident, a homework assignment, or even the quality of today's pasta lunch. Despite the range of topics, the messages share a common theme: criticism of "The School" and what it is or isn't doing. Although the active participants in the chats are generally in single numbers, the ripple effect is significant, spreading complaints to an audience of hundreds. It is parking-lot gossip on steroids, and while most of these fires can be put out without too much effort, the damage to trust in "The School" often lingers.

This is not, of course, something that is only happening in education. The 2024 Global Risks Report from the World Economic Forum highlights a "deteriorating global outlook, where societal polarization is likely to deepen, and even the concept of "truth" will come under strain." At the same time, the report also emphasizes that hope remains and that there are unique opportunities to rebuild trust, foster optimism, and strengthen resilience in our institutions and societies (Zahidi, 2024). School leaders are critical to this process of strengthening their institutions, influencing both individuals and groups at all levels within their community. Nonetheless, their ability to perform effectively in this role largely depends on the trust they inspire in their colleagues and staff and all stakeholder groups (Burke et al., 2007). If leaders are effective in building trust, they not only strengthen their own resilience but also that of the organization, ensuring that both are more likely to withstand the "slings and arrows" of outrageous talk. If they are effective in building trust, leaders can strengthen the legitimacy of their institutions and subsequently mitigate the impact of any potential crisis.

Although there is extensive research on the importance of trust in schools, much of this has focused on the relationship between individuals as opposed to trust in the institution itself. Unfortunately, experience has shown us that crises can occur even when there is a high level of trust in specific individuals. For example, it's not unusual to hear staff members or parents qualify their complaints with the phrase, "It's not you, I know you are doing the best you can —it's the school," as if the institution itself were some shadowy force, like the Wizard of Oz, hidden behind a curtain, manipulating events with questionable intent. Added to this, there is also a danger that if the focus of trust is exclusively on individuals, when that person moves on, the school's overall stability may be put at risk, and the incoming leader may face a more significant challenge in establishing their place in the community. This highlights the responsibility of school leaders to ensure that trust is embedded in the institution, and not just in individuals. As leaders, we must ensure that we consolidate institutional legitimacy.

So how can we build this trust in the school as an institution? How can we foster a shared understanding (and appreciation) of our strategy and safeguards, our norms and values, and our policies and procedures? How can we, as school leaders, ensure that this foundation of trust enables the institution to withstand the next crisis it is likely to face? In this chapter, we will explore how an analytical framework for institutional legitimacy such as that developed by Bunnell et al. (2017) can act as an enabling structure to support these efforts.

Part 1: Identifying the "Institutional Primary Task"

The ability to set a clear direction aligns with behaviors commonly associated with trust-building leadership styles, such as transformational leadership, and is often perceived as a marker of both individual and institutional competence. Although the direct link between setting direction and trust in leadership has yet to be extensively studied, evidence suggests that providing explicit and engaging guidance positively impacts individual, team, and organizational performance (e.g., Bell, 2007; Ginnett, 2010; Zaccaro, 2001). Leaders who provide a clear and compelling direction are essential to ensuring that all team members view their tasks and goals as meaningful, challenging, and well-defined (Hackman, 2002). By offering this clarity, leaders energize and motivate their team members to pursue shared objectives that are aligned with organizational priorities and that are more likely to be viewed as valuable and reflective of attainable opportunities for personal growth. This ensures that team members remain engaged and assume accountability for progress (Hackman & Wageman, 1986). To set such direction effectively, leaders must not only understand their team's capabilities and the organizational context and culture in which they operate, but they must also provide an enabling structure within which team members can thrive. The analytical framework for institutional legitimacy developed by Bunnell et al. (2017) is one such enabling structure. The first step in implementing this structure is for leaders to identify the school's institutional primary task, that is, the essential, core task that must be fulfilled for the organization (school) to survive.

What Is the Institutional Primary Task?

Many school leaders and their teams spend a significant amount of time developing aspirational mission statements about creating "lifelong learners" or "global citizens," however, fewer articulate their institutional primary task. Unlike mission statements, which are future-focused and aspirational, the institutional primary task is grounded in operational realities and defines "what" we do rather than "why" we do it. The institutional primary task is important to the school's survival, given that if the task is not fulfilled, the school´s very existence is likely to come into question. For example, the basic task of any school is student learning. Any school that does not focus on learning as a task is unlikely to survive as an institution.

Examples of the institutional primary task of a specific school might therefore be as follows:

- To engage students in real-world, project-based learning experiences that enable students to develop the skills of creativity, critical thinking, and collaboration.
- To deliver an internationally recognized curriculum that equips students with the knowledge, skills, and credentials necessary to access higher education opportunities worldwide.
- To provide high-quality instruction that enables students to achieve mastery of common core curriculum standards.

James and Walker (2007) indicate that a focus on the institutional primary task can bring about "a strong feeling of mutual accountability, a high level of trust, and a spirit of collective effort" among teachers (James & Walker, 2007, p. 548), which suggests that establishing clarity in terms of the institution's primary task will enable school leaders to make decisions that strengthen both their personal credibility and the institution's legitimacy, fostering trust at all levels. Bunnell et al. (2016) also emphasize that aligning actions with the school's primary task is critical to creating a sense of legitimacy. For example, they argue that for a school to be legitimately considered international, its primary task must be to deliver an international curriculum. Failure to carry out this task by, for example, implementing a curriculum that is based on purely national standards would undermine its identity as an international school and put at risk the legitimacy of its claim to international status (Bunnell et al., 2017). Similarly, if a school claims to be bilingual, its primary task should include something along the lines of delivering the curriculum through dual language instruction, with operational tasks, such as hiring teachers who are proficient in each of the target languages fulfilled to make the claim legitimate. Conversely, this also means that if a school states that its primary task is to deliver high-quality instruction but then neglects investments in teacher professional development or fails to hire sufficient teachers to implement its programs, credibility is compromised, trust eroded, and the overall sense of legitimacy undermined.

Having clarity in terms of the primary task therefore provides a clear direction that enables leaders to ensure that not only are procedures and practices within the school aligned, but more importantly, that the multiple perspectives and mindsets of individuals are unified in a singular focus that drives all other tasks and activities in the school.

Reflection Opportunity

How would you define your school's Institutional Primary Task?

How does the definition of this task differ from your school's mission statement?

Would all stakeholder groups (parents, teachers, administrative staff, and students) come up with the same definition?

Throughout this chapter, we will provide examples from a fictitious American International School (AIS) to illustrate our ideas and provide a model that could be used to implement the framework. The complete framework for this example school (adapted from Bunnell et al., 2017 and Allen, 2021) can be found at the conclusion of the chapter. To begin, here is the fictional institutional primary task.

> ## American International School: Institutional Primary Task
>
> To deliver a blended (US/Host country) curriculum through student-centered and dual language instruction that promotes bilingualism and provides access to further education in both host country and international contexts.

Part 2: The "Building Blocks" of Institutional Legitimacy

Although identifying the institutional primary task is an important first step, it helps to set a compelling and clear direction. Further support is necessary if leaders are to establish a sustained sense of individual trust and institutional legitimacy. Leaders must understand that their relationship with trust and those with whom they are forging it is emergent and fragile (Marks et al., 2001), and that while trust is built through small, specific actions, it can also, through these same actions, be broken. Once again, providing an enabling structure is vital.

Within their analytical framework for institutional legitimacy, Bunnell and Fertig (2016) indicate that the institutional primary task must be supported by three "pillars of institutionalization" (Scott, 2003, 2014). These pillars, each of which focuses on a different aspect of the organization, are essentially the "building blocks" of legitimacy.

The Regulative Pillar

The regulative pillar includes organizational rules and regulations such as disciplinary codes for students, contractual obligations for parents, and labor regulations for staff, as well as standard operating procedures for various aspects of school operations. It can also include governance structures that set out the roles and responsibilities of leadership in the school, identifying boundaries, for example, between board members and the school administration. For school leaders, the regulative pillar is perhaps the easiest to implement, as it is relatively straightforward and concrete. Rules can be written and published, and systems can be put in place to monitor compliance.

The Normative Pillar

The normative pillar relates to institutional norms, values, standards, and expectations. Unlike the restrictive and prescriptive nature of rules and regulations, norms and values serve as a guiding framework, shaping behavior within the organization while allowing for flexibility and shared understanding. The normative pillar is less concrete than the regulative pillar and, as such, is more complex in terms of implementation. It requires individuals to have a deeper sense of morality than they require to comply with rules and regulations (Scott, 2014). As such, establishing a set of institutional values that communicate organizational culture and consolidate relationships within the school is vital. Without a clear understanding of institutional values, any member of the organization is likely to find themselves on unstable ground, unsure of institutional priorities and related expectations.

Beyond the abstract concept of values, other aspects of the school's operation, such as ensuring that the curriculum is based on a set of recognized and established standards, are also vital within the normative pillar as these standards and expectations relate directly to the institutional primary task of learning, informing instructional practices. Normative practices may also include developing standards for professional staff. Systems of professional evaluation and appraisal are of particular significance, given that a leader who establishes norms, especially when those norms promote adaptability, self-correction, learning, and open communication, boosts organizational performance and strengthens perceptions of their own capability and credibility.

The Cultural-Cognitive Pillar

The cultural-cognitive pillar refers to the shared understandings and processes of sense-making that are necessary for individuals to function as a coherent whole within an organization. It is the most important of the three pillars, as without these shared understandings, elements within the other pillars are likely to fail. However, it is also the most complex to implement as it is abstract and intangible, dealing with the mindsets and beliefs that exist within the organization. Having clarity in terms of the cultural-cognitive pillar is particularly important in international contexts where staff may come from a wide variety of cultural backgrounds and where little can be assumed in terms of shared understandings and perspectives.

By way of an example, in a school setting, the cultural-cognitive pillar might include beliefs about the nature of student assessment and related grading systems, including issues such as: should we be using a standards-based approach or a more traditional grading system that establishes a pass or fail? Do we approach assessment from a growth mindset or a perspective of compliance? Should we factor in "punishments" for late work or give credit for extra effort? All of these questions relate not to the rules, regulations, or even standards of assessments, but to our ingrained beliefs about the purpose of assessment and the way in which it should be used. Another example can be seen in how the cultural-cognitive pillar influences approaches to instruction: Should we take a phonics approach to literacy acquisition, or is balanced literacy the right way to go? Is there a place for direct instruction in the classroom, or should students always be involved in student-centered experiential learning? What is our shared definition of learning? In essence, the cultural-cognitive pillar is driven by our conscious and subconscious beliefs and attitudes toward what we do as educators.

Reflection Opportunity

Where do you spend most of your time as a school leader: Establishing and monitoring rules and regulations, modeling norms and values, or establishing shared understandings and a shared culture?

Should your time be equally divided between all three, or should you focus more on one than another?

Part 3: The Carriers of Institutionalization

According to Scott (2003, 2014), the pillars themselves are evidenced and expressed by a series of carriers: symbolic systems, relational systems, activities, and artifacts. It is through these carriers that the leader exerts influence, and it is within these carriers that their competence as a leader and their ability to establish institutional legitimacy is likely to be measured.

Carrier 1: Symbolic Systems

Symbolic systems represent how rules, regulations, norms, values, and cognitive frameworks embody the identity of an institution. For example, in a British-style school, rules around school uniforms may be deeply connected to cultural expectations and seen as a key component of institutional identity. In contrast, an American-style school might emphasize individual expression, with institutional identity being reflected through norms, rituals, and traditions that promote individuality and school spirit. Having clarity around what is or is not considered an important symbol of identity is a key to institutional coherence and perceptions of legitimacy.

On another level, accreditation agencies frequently stipulate the expected rules and regulations that a school must comply with to be considered legitimate and to acquire the symbolic stamp of approval. A lack of compliance with these rules may result in the loss of accreditation as a symbol of quality and subsequently undermine institutional legitimacy.

In terms of the normative pillar, the key standards and expectations of a school are inevitably symbolized within the curriculum. Schools that do not have a recognized and legitimate set of curriculum standards but instead leave decisions about curriculum entirely to individual teachers are likely to lack credibility. The same is true for student assessment. Without clearly established policies and procedures that represent how student assessment and grading practices should be manifest in the school, the grades that a teacher assigns may be perceived as subjective and lacking in validity. At the same time, many schools now use electronic platforms to house complex grading systems and while these systems may seek to consolidate legitimacy through the supposed objectification of assessment with mathematical algorithms generating results,

Table 7.1 AIS example: Symbolic systems

Regulative Pillar	Normative Pillar	Cultural-Cognitive Pillar
Quality Assurance is represented through accreditation by a US regional/international accreditation organization in addition to that of the host country. Established rules and regulations symbolize school culture and identity (e.g., dress codes, scheduling systems, classroom routines, procedures, etc.). Clearly established policies and procedures for student assessment grading allow for effective monitoring of progress.	Curriculum is based on an internationally recognized set of standards and expectations blended with local requirements. A wide variety of electives and options are offered through which these standards can be attained. Established Institutional values that support inclusion and belonging and are aligned with international-mindedness and global citizenship. All students are expected to reach a level of bilingualism that facilitates access to both host country and international universities.	We believe that… Student agency and choice are a central tenet or fundamental principle of the school program. Both student performance and student behavior should be approached from the perspective of a growth mindset. Bilingualism/multilingualism is important for cognitive flexibility, effective communication, and the capacity to thrive in a globally connected world.

there is a risk that they may conflict with cultural-cognitive expectations of a growth mindset and the use of assessments to promote student agency and learning. For school leaders, it is vital to generate discussions around these issues ensuring coherence in rules, regulations, standards, expectations, and cultural-cognitive beliefs.

Carrier 2: Relational Systems

Relational systems refer to the connections and patterns of interaction between members of an organization that serve as a critical foundation for its functioning. Establishing a clear organizational structure with shared expectations of behavior reduces ambiguity, defines boundaries, and ensures individuals can be held accountable while receiving the support they need to succeed. This accountability can arise through both internal and external mechanisms. External accountability is rooted in situational factors and systems such as performance monitoring or oversight in relation to professional standards and therefore aligns with the normative pillar. Conversely, internal accountability belongs within the cultural-cognitive pillar as it reflects an individual's intrinsic willingness and belief in their responsibility for their actions. Human resources practices such as hiring, compensation, and professional development (Pfeffer & Veiga, 1999) are key here as not only do they impact employee satisfaction, commitment, and performance but they also shape the level of trust employees have in both their leaders and the organization (Gould-Williams, 2003; Whitener, 1997). By fostering a supportive and transparent environment, these practices can reinforce relational systems and further anchor trust within the organization.

Clarity in terms of the cultural-cognitive perception of leadership is also key to relationships within a school. Many schools increasingly expect leadership to be distributed across the organization rather than concentrated in a few individuals. However, without clear norms and established communication channels, this can lead to confusion and even conflict. Developing collaborative norms that can ensure the effective distribution of leadership can enhance perceptions of a leader's benevolence, signaling a commitment to team and follower development. Leaders who enable their teams to leverage diverse resources and work synergistically are perceived as both competent and supportive, reinforcing trust and overall effectiveness.

The broader organizational and cultural context can also have an influence on the relationships within a school. For example, the organizational climate, defined as a relatively stable and enduring environment, is shaped by the perceived values of the organization (Tagiuri & Litwin, 1968) and plays a significant role in fostering or hindering trust. This can prove a challenge, particularly in multicultural contexts that are characterized by diversity. When an individual understands the cultural context within which they are working, they have clarity on how to react and respond to emerging situations, and trust can be consolidated. Without this cultural understanding, the individual may not know how to respond within any given context, resulting in uncertainty, confusion, and hindering trust. Situations like this can generate a sense of frustration and isolate the individual, leading to a perception of incompetence, either in terms of self-image (e.g., "I don't have the skills to be successful here…") or regarding the organization itself (e.g., "This school is a mess–they have no idea how to do things here!").

> **Reflection Opportunity**
>
> Think about the organizational structure of your school. Is there clarity in terms of roles and responsibilities at all levels of the organization? Where might this need to be strengthened?
>
> How would you describe the leadership model of your school? Does it align with institutional norms and values?
>
> Are there aspects of your school and community culture that are unique and may need to be made explicit for someone new to the organization?

Table 7.2 AIS example: Relational systems

Regulative Pillar	Normative Pillar	Cultural-Cognitive Pillar
Governance systems and organizational structures contain clear boundaries and consolidate the right of each level of the school to function without undue interference.	Clear relationships ensure that everyone understands their responsibilities and are able to fulfill their expected roles within established collaborative procedures.	We believe that: Relationships are key to fostering a culture of trust and collaboration. Leadership should be distributed throughout the organization in order to promote a culture of shared responsibility.
Regular communication channels are structured to ensure clarity, consistency, and transparency throughout the organization.	A supportive accountability approach is used to ensure that individuals are held to account for professional standards within a system based on institutional norms and values.	
Procedures and practices related to human resources are followed consistently throughout the organization.		

Carrier 3: Actions

For an organization to be considered legitimate, its actions must align with established rules, regulations, norms, standards, and cultural-cognitive expectations. For instance, if a student behavior policy is clearly outlined in a handbook but not consistently enforced, the institution's legitimacy is compromised. Again, this can be difficult in multicultural contexts where some members of the community may believe a zero-tolerance approach should be taken to student behavior, expecting that leaders will enforce a strict policy for disciplinary incidents with predetermined (often punitive) consequences, while others may believe that a more restorative, flexible approach, focusing on student development and growth should be taken. The same principle applies to professional standards for staff. Policies that allow employees discretion in achieving goals signal organizational trust in their abilities (Guzzo & Noonan, 1994; Iles et al., 1990). However, leaders are often evaluated on enforcing these policies—particularly their fairness or procedural justice—and failing to uphold fairness (e.g., in promotion decisions) can erode trust (MacNeil, 1985). Even when leaders are not involved in creating these policies, their role as enforcers ties their perceived trustworthiness to how these policies are applied. Moreover, the overall supportiveness of the organizational climate—one that values respect, avoids scapegoating, and encourages open dialogue about mistakes (i.e., interactional justice)—further influences trust in leadership. Team leaders are more likely to be respected and viewed as trustworthy in such environments.

Reflection Opportunity

Where would you place yourself on a scale of 1–10 in which 1 = Highly Rigid (adheres to rules and regulations with little adaptation to context) and 10 = Highly Adaptive (Willing to adjust rules and processes based on context and individual needs).

How does your approach impact your actions as a leader and how those actions might be perceived by other stakeholders?

Table 7.3 AIS example: Actions

Regulative Pillar	Normative Pillar	Cultural-Cognitive Pillar
Systems for monitoring compliance with rules and regulations that promote coherence but can be adapted if specific contextual needs are identified. Accreditation visits/inspections carried out by external organizations validate compliance with requirements. Systems for monitoring and evaluating professional performance are established and shared with stakeholders.	Established expectations for a coordinated and coherent pedagogical approach. Standards for professional staff that focus on growth and development are implemented throughout the organization.	We believe that: Students learn best through strategies such as inquiry-based learning and project-based learning. Professional staff have the skills and expertise to operate within clear guidelines and should be trusted with a level of autonomy that empowers them to make meaningful contributions to the schools' goals.

Carrier 4: Artifacts

Artifacts relate to any document or object that helps members of an organization better understand that organization and its role within it. For example, these may include policy manuals, curriculum documents, and published standard operating procedures. Other artifacts such as accreditation certificates or a license to function may be necessary for a school to be considered legitimate and allowed to operate. Similarly, externally certified student results can be considered an artifact that represents school performance. Artifacts can help to communicate the shared beliefs and understandings of the cultural-cognitive pillar; however, they can also represent a risk. For example, if too much weight is placed on student outcomes as represented by student results on standardized tests such as the IB Diploma or Advanced Placement exams it can sometimes lead to behaviors that may be considered unethical such as excluding students from a test in order to boost published results, or implementing a program that drills students in test performance as opposed to focusing on learning (an educational version of the Enron scandal where executives prioritized stock prices over ethical practices due to stakeholder pressure).

Table 7.4 AIS example: Artifacts

Regulative Pillar	Normative Pillar	Cultural-Cognitive Pillar
School accreditation and authorization certificates. Manuals that contain Standard Operating Procedures.	Handbooks that outline and/or define the school's approach to learning. Student outcomes that culminate in a dual US High School and host country diploma.	Our beliefs are shared through: Mission, vision, and values statements posted throughout the school. Regular communications with the school community (newsletters, articles, assemblies, etc.). Visual imagery (photos) of school activities that are in line with the mission, vision, and values.

> **Reflection Opportunity**
>
> What artifacts could you show someone that would help them understand your organization?
> What artifacts exist in your school to demonstrate its legitimacy?

 Bringing It All Together

Leaders can demonstrate their competence and consolidate institutional legitimacy by using an enabling structure such as the analytical framework for institutional legitimacy (Bunnell et al., 2017) that we have explored throughout this chapter. Indeed, leaders must provide such an enabling structure in order to avoid being seen as disorganized, disconnected, or ineffective. An enabling structure can also ensure leaders are able to effectively allocate resources, establish core norms of conduct, and shape team composition (Fleishman et al., 1991; Hackman, 2002) and can help to create a foundation of trust that enables the organization to withstand any specific crisis or the absence of any specific individual. Most importantly, by implementing a structure, leaders can ensure that the school is

Table 7.5 Complete framework for American International School

Institutional Primary Task	To deliver a blended (US/Host country) curriculum through student-centered and dual language instruction that promotes bilingualism and provides access to further education in both host country and international contexts.		
	Regulative Pillar	Normative Pillar	Cultural-Cognitive Pillar
Symbolic systems	Quality Assurance is represented through accreditation by a US regional/international accreditation organization in addition to that of the host country. Established rules and regulations symbolize school culture and identity (e.g., dress codes, scheduling systems, classroom routines and procedures, etc.). Clearly established policies and procedures for student assessment grading allow for effective monitoring of progress.	We have a curriculum based on an internationally recognized set of standards and expectations blended with local requirements. We provide a wide variety of electives and options through which these standards can be attained. We have established Institutional values that support inclusion and belonging and are aligned with international-mindedness and global-citizenship. We expect all students to reach a level of bilingualism that facilitates access to both host country and international universities.	We believe that… Student agency and choice are a central tenet, or fundamental principle of the school program. Both student performance and student behavior should be approached from the perspective of a growth mindset. Bilingualism/multilingualism is important for cognitive flexibility, effective communication and the capacity to thrive in a globally connected world.
Relational Systems	Governance systems and organizational structures contain clear boundaries and consolidate the right of each level of the school to function without undue interference. Regular communication channels are structured to ensure clarity, consistency and transparency throughout the organization. Procedures and practices related to human resources are followed consistently throughout the organization.	Clear relationships ensure that everyone understands their responsibilities and are able to fulfill their expected roles within established collaborative procedures. A supportive accountability approach is used to ensure that individuals are held to account for professional standards within a system based on institutional norms and values.	We believe that… Relationships are key to fostering a culture of trust and collaboration. Leadership should be distributed throughout the organization in order to promote a culture of shared responsibility.

Actions	Systems for monitoring compliance with rules and regulations that promote coherence but can be adapted if specific contextual needs are identified and recorded. Accreditation visits / inspections carried out by external organizations that validate compliance with requirements. Systems for monitoring and evaluating professional performance are established and shared with stakeholders.	Established expectations for a coordinated and coherent pedagogical approach. Standards for professional staff that focus on growth and development are implemented throughout the organization.	We believe that… Students learn best through strategies such as inquiry- based learning and project-based learning. Professional staff have the skills and expertise to operate within clear guidelines and should be trusted with a level of autonomy that empowers them to make meaningful contributions to the schools' goals.
Artifacts	School accreditation and authorization certificates. Manuals that contain standard Operating Procedures.	Handbooks that outline and/or define the school's approach to learning. Student outcomes that culminate in a dual US High School and host country diploma.	Our beliefs are shared through: Mission, vision and values statements posted throughout the school. Regular communications with the school community (newsletters, articles, assemblies etc.). Visual imagery (photos) of school activities that are in line with the mission, vision and values.

Source: Adapted from Bunnell et al. (2017).

not seen as a mysterious magician, working behind the scenes to create a false illusion, but instead, they can pull back the curtains to reveal a team equipped with courage, brains and a heart that is competent, committed and dedicated to effectively supporting students along the road to success.

References

Allen, R. (2021). *Institutional legitimacy in international schools: An exploration of school leaders' perceptions of institutional legitimacy in U.S.-style international schools in Latin America* (Doctoral dissertation).

Bell, A. (2007). Using vision to shape the future. *Leader to Leader, 2007*(45), 17–21. https://doi.org/10.1002/ltl.238

Bunnell, T., Fertig, M., & James, C. (2017). Establishing the legitimacy of a school's claim to be "international": The provision of an international curriculum as the institutional primary task. *Educational Review, 69*(3), 303–317. https://doi.org/10.1080/00131911.2016.1237476

Bunnell, T., & Fertig, M. (2016). International schools as institutions and the issue of legitimacy. *International Schools Journal, 36*(1), 56–64

Burke, C. S., Sims, D. E., Lazzara, E. H., & Salas, E. (2007). Trust in leadership: A multilevel review and integration. *The Leadership Quarterly, 18*(6), 606–632. https://doi.org/10.1016/j.leaqua.2007.09.004

Fleishman, E. A., Mumford, M. D., Zaccaro, S. J., Levin, K. Y., Korotkin, A. L., & Hein, M. B. (1991). Taxonomic efforts in the description of leader behavior: A synthesis and functional interpretation. *The Leadership Quarterly, 2*(4), 245–287. https://doi.org/10.1016/1048-9843(91)90016-U

Ginnett, R. C. (2010). Crews as groups. In *The organizational psychology of teams* (pp. 79–110). https://doi.org/10.1016/b978-0-12-374946-8.10003-2

Gould-Williams, J. (2003). The importance of HR practices and workplace trust in achieving superior performance: A study of public-sector organizations. *The International Journal of Human Resource Management, 14*(1), 28–54. https://doi.org/10.1080/09585190210158501

Guzzo, R. A., & Noonan, K. A. (1994). Human resource practices as communications and the psychological contract. *Human Resource Management, 33*(3), 447–462. https://doi.org/10.1002/hrm.3930330311

Hackman, J. R. (2002). *Leading teams: Setting the stage for great performances*. Harvard Business Press.

Hackman, J. R., & Wageman, R. (1986). Leading groups in organizations. In P. S. Goodman (Ed.), *Designing effective work groups (pp. 134–142)*. Jossey-Bass.

Iles, P. A., Mabey, C., & Robertson, I. T. (1990). HRM practices and employee commitment: Possibilities, pitfalls and paradoxes. *British Journal of Management, 1*(3), 147–157.

James, C., Connolly, M., Dunning, G., & Elliott, T. (2007). Collaborative practice: A model of successful working in schools. *Journal of Educational Administration, 45*(5), 541–555. https://doi.org/10.1108/09578230710778187

MacNeil, I. R. (1985). *Relational contract: What we do and do not know*. University of Wisconsin Law School Digital Repository. https://repository.law.wisc.edu/s/uwlaw/item/27126

Marks, M. A., Mathieu, J. E., & Zaccaro, S. J. (2001). A temporally based framework and taxonomy of team processes. *Academy of Management Review, 26*(3), 356–376. https://doi.org/10.5465/amr.2001.4845785

Pfeffer, J., & Veiga, J. F. (1999). Putting people first for organizational success. *The Academy of Management Executive, 13*(2), 37–48. https://doi.org/10.5465/ame.1999.1899547

Scott, W. R. (2003). Institutional carriers: Reviewing modes of transporting ideas over time and space and considering their consequences. *Industrial and Corporate Change, 12*(4), 879–894. https://doi.org/10.1093/icc/12.4.879

Scott, W. R. (2014). *Institutions and organizations: Ideas, interests, and identities* (4th ed.). Sage.

Tagiuri, R., & Litwin, G. H. (1968). *Organizational climate: Explorations of a concept*. Harvard University Press.

Whitener, E. M. (1997). The impact of human resource management practices on perceptions of organizational performance. *Human Resource Management Review, 7*(4), 389–404. https://doi.org/10.1016/S1053-4822(97)90022-7

Zaccaro, S. J., Rittman, A. L., & Marks, M. A. (2001). Team leadership. *The Leadership Quarterly, 12*(4), 451–483. https://doi.org/10.1016/s1048-9843(01)00093-5

Zahidi, S. (2024). *2024 Global risks report*. World Economic Forum.

Leading Change Begins with Trust

Vicki Denmark, Colin Brown, and Lindsay Prendergast

The Value of Integrity

Managing change as a leader, whether you are experienced or brand new, is a challenge to navigate, and often difficult to recognize the political pitfalls of your decisions. This trap can be minimized by standing firm and knowing who you are as a person and a leader, and what your core values are in the context of education. What are you not willing to forego when faced with resistance or challenges? A solid beginning to your new directorship starts with being loyal to your integrity regardless of the situations or challenges you might encounter.

Leaders new to the position or new to the school are bound to face situations that test their integrity. In fact, this testing is a necessary step to earn the critical trust equity to ensure significant change. Staying true to your values and beliefs and being consistent with your actions, whether they are currently popular or not, will garner long-term trust. Faculty begin to understand that when the new leader says something, it will happen.

Integrity is vital to being a quality and respected leader. Some of the most significant reasons that embracing integrity as a leadership value may positively influence your capacity to have an impact are that it enables you to:

Build trust: When leaders consistently act with integrity, they gain trust from their staff, students, board members, and community members.

Please remember, this is a process, and it takes time to build this trust equity. Sometimes, due to confidentiality, stakeholders will not know you acted with integrity on certain issues for a long period of time.

Set an example: Always remember that leaders are viewed as role models and their words and actions are constantly scrutinized. Their actions and decisions influence the behavior of others. So, when leaders uphold high standards, they are modeling and inspiring others around them to do the same.

Ensure accountability: Leaders with integrity understand that they are accountable for their actions. In leadership, this means that a leader with integrity takes responsibility for their decisions, admits mistakes, and takes thoughtful actions to correct the mistakes.

Foster a positive work culture: Leaders who demonstrate integrity create a school culture and climate where honesty, transparency, and fairness are valued and upheld.

Enhance decision-making: Integrity enables leaders to make decisions based on principles rather than convenience or short-term gain. Compromising your integrity for short-term wins is often enticing, but it significantly damages your reputation as a leader. Ethical decision-making ensures long-term success and sustainability for organizations.

Attract talent and loyalty: Generally, staff want to work for leaders who are trustworthy, take responsibility for their actions, and treat people fairly. Leaders who have integrity earn a great reputation quickly in the education profession, thereby recruiting and retaining staff is usually somewhat less challenging.

For leaders, new and veteran, their integrity can be challenged each day by a myriad of unpredictable circumstances and people. We believe that as a leader, especially when you're new to a school or organization, you take time to deeply reflect on what is important to you as an individual, writing those in a journal, and committing to upholding your integrity regardless of the situation. Yes, some of the board, staff, and community members might not initially like you or your decisions, but, at the end of the day, your integrity stays intact.

Case Study #1

An international, well-qualified, and experienced school leader was hired to replace a principal who chose to retire two years after opening the school. The retiring principal was a generational local hire with family members serving in key positions in the school, administration to facilities, and all positions in between. A teacher informed the new principal of these connections months after assuming the position when a significant disciplinary issue emerged with four 8th-grade students. In short, one of the 8th-grade students brought alcohol in a plastic container to school, indulged, and passed the container to a few other students. The student just happened to be the retired principal's granddaughter. When the chorus teacher, who witnessed this situation happening in her class, brought the students to the principal's office, she reminded the principal of the relationship between the student and the retired principal. She stated, "We should just give these students a few days of sitting in the office as their disciplinary consequence." The chorus teacher was a second cousin to the retired principal, so you're getting the picture here about the predicament that the new principal is in and how her integrity was challenged.

The new principal had a choice: either dismiss the incident or follow the board's policy for students bringing, distributing, and consuming alcohol on school property. What to do? The first option would be to keep "peace" among the many relatives on staff, help the new principal earn short-term acceptance among this group, and stay out of the political dynamics. The second choice, following the board's policies, would uphold the integrity of the new principal's policies but would divide the school and its community.

Let's Reflect

What is the best decision for the collective good of the school and these students?

Is the new principal's integrity damaged if she doesn't follow policy?

Is the new principal's integrity more important than keeping the "peace" at the school?

What Happened Next

The new principal chose to follow the board's policy, which included calling the board president, consulting with the administrative team, and being fully aware of the turmoil that could happen if the students received the disciplinary consequences stated in the board manual. The new principal felt that there should not be preferential treatment for these students, especially considering the severity of the incident.

When you truly lead with integrity, it will likely not be readily or immediately seen by your faculty, staff, and parents. Some of the greatest challenges to your integrity involve decisions you need to make which must be kept somewhat confidential to protect those involved. To the outside observer, without the intricate knowledge of the whole picture, decisions you make with integrity can be construed negatively. In fact, your character is usually questioned or attacked in such scenarios.

Case Study #2

Being relatively new to a school, a Director had to make a challenging decision regarding a veteran teacher who had been at the school for many years and was well loved by the community. She was a favorite amongst the parent community for her sweetness and perceived reputation of being an amazing teacher. However, student learning suffered in her classes. She was uncertified, well past retirement age, and was not able nor wanted to keep abreast of current best teaching and learning practices. While there were numerous attempts to support her in the classroom (including a few action plans), it was clear she did not have the capacity or desire to change. So, the Director, clinging to his integrity and goal of doing what was best for students and student learning, did not renew her contract. The outrage in the community was palpable and many parents questioned the Director's decision-making ability and character. Some parents expressed, "How could he not renew her? This new Director is heartless and is completely wrong. She is really an excellent and sweet teacher."

Leading Change Begins with Trust

 ## Let's Reflect

Imagine the community is highly upset by this situation. What might occur if you try to justify your decision and openly tell parents and other teachers the reasons why it was necessary to non-renew the teacher?

What might the outcome be if you continue to support the teacher, positively and publicly recognize her previous service to the school, and endure the negative sentiments from some of the community?

 ## What Happened Next

The Director chose to act with integrity and not openly share his reasoning because of the negative impact it would have on the teacher and the students. When confronted, he shared,

> The division is moving in a new direction next year, but we are very grateful for the outstanding service this teacher has provided over the years. She is a kind and compassionate educator, and we wish her the very best.

It would have been very easy for the Director to show data and give his reasoning to get a reprieve from the onslaught of attacks (short term win), but it would have hurt the teacher and students involved. While navigating this period was very uncomfortable, once the new academic year started with a new dynamite teacher, parents could then appreciate the decision made and some trust equity was earned. It also demonstrated to the community that the Director always maintained integrity even when it was challenging to do so. This resolution can be inspiring for change.

 ## Knowing Your Staff

Often, a new leader is hired to change the school, such as improve student achievement, implement a new program, or rebuild the school's culture. When the board members express there are specific facets of the school they want to be changed, that could generally translate to meaning that they wish the identified change to happen fast. The challenge you will encounter is balancing the push to implement change while also managing effective and sustainable change. Establishing trust and support during this balancing act is a skill set that leaders in similar situations must immediately demonstrate. Knowing that schools are complex, people-centric, and dynamic organizations adds a dimension to change management that non-education organizations can pay less attention to. Why? In schools, the change management process relies heavily on the willingness and acceptance of your staff, students, board members, and community to adjust their mindsets and perspectives.

New leaders faced with implementing change immediately can easily (albeit inadvertently) disrupt the culture, make uninformed decisions, and be viewed as an autocratic leader if a change management process is not understood and followed. For example, knowing the climate and daily routines of the school, its current status, and the relationships among the staff members can be a catalyst for change. As a new school head, it could take a few months to begin to understand the school's current reality, which includes having a pulse on the culture and climate, traditions, norms, and implicit practices.

Identifying Faculty's Acceptance of Potential Change

Shifting from the status quo takes effort, usually involves displacing the current mindset, and may be, subsequently, somewhat uncomfortable. Compounding this unpleasant feeling is the thought that the change being made may only be temporary or could be detrimental. No wonder the word change conjures up an initial sense of uneasiness or resistance.

Regardless, in progressive schools that embody continuous improvement, change is not only inevitable but necessary to avoid stagnation. As the leader of change, it is imperative you have a good understanding of your faculty and where they are in the transition process. Identifying the mindsets and attitudes of your staff can present an early opportunity to begin strategizing where you may accelerate engagement or where you may need to provide additional support or strategic communication.

Consider these example categories that describe common ways individuals respond in the face of change:

Early Supporters: Every school head needs to identify this group early in the change process. No need to worry; this group generally makes themselves known to the school head in advance of any change. The early supporters (ES) are immediately aligned with the change you are proposing, and they support you. It is important to recognize and show appreciation for their support and look for ways they can be actively involved in the change. Additionally, identifying and empowering ESs who have "political clout" (for example, individuals who are highly trusted by most of the community) will enable the change to gain momentum.

Group Thinkers: Although it is tempting to want a large portion of your staff to conform to your views to maintain cohesion or harmony, group thinkers can be detrimental to the change process. Staff members in this category need to focus less on suppressing their dissent and focus more attention on the best outcome for the school. They can be complacent and unaware of their conformity over being an independent thinker. As a school head, you want to include a portion of this group in meetings or committees with faculty who are critical thinkers skilled at asking questions that promote expressing an opinion based on knowledge, experiences, and facts. The smaller the group to include group thinkers, the better because there is more accountability or exposure for them to engage and express their perspectives on the proposed change.

Middle of the Roaders: These faculty members are not sure about you or the vision. They will test or question you and are unsure about investing in you and change (remember, change takes effort). It is crucial you recognize this group, not write them off, and, in fact, spend the greatest amount of time and effort helping them get to know you and your vision. Once they believe in you and your vision, they will become ardent supporters. Additionally, they can become your critical advocates because they will ask the difficult questions that could be your blind spots. They can also become your most authentic and passionate leaders.

Opposing Mindsets: Most times, there is nothing you can do to change these people. They actively resist change and refuse to believe in you and the vision. They may try to sabotage every effort you make and try to rally support from the Middle of the Roaders. Many times, they will spread misinformation or make false assertions to tarnish you, cast doubts, and disrupt the change. They are also likely to chastise or try to discredit and/or ridicule the ESs. These individuals will significantly challenge your integrity, are highly toxic, and need to be removed to enhance the school climate and culture.

Silent Faculty Members: For school heads, this group of faculty members, regardless of size, might be the most difficult to work with during the change process. They will be easy to identify because they generally avoid discussions, show passive resistance to the change, and demonstrate a lack of enthusiasm for the school's new direction or head. Sometimes, school heads mistakenly regard the silent faculty member group as not lending support or considering sabotaging the change effort. It is unwise for school heads to have these thoughts about the silent faculty members. Consider instead that this group or individuals within this category take longer to determine if the change is good for them or the school and need time to listen to all viewpoints. For this group, continue to reach out and invite them to disclose their views or concerns, and demonstrate active listening techniques even when you might disagree with their opinions. Remember not to shut down communication; instead, we should provide them opportunities to contribute and open their minds. Finding ways to engage the silent faculty members will show a school head's commitment to understanding various perspectives and people's hesitations to embrace change. Silence doesn't always indicate this group's lack of support.

Remember that the categories are not rigid. The point is to move faculty members into supporters but learn from everyone about what are their perspectives on change, the vision, the culture, student learning, etc. The categories provide an opportunity to prioritize where support is most needed.

Change Management

While you are in the stage of learning your staff and understanding them through the lens of how they most likely will react to change, we suggest that you also become a student of change management itself. There are a plethora of change theories in the research literature and not all can be adaptable in their truest textbook form when you are in the midst of initiating and implementing change, while also managing and leading the daily operations of the school. One change theory that we propose to consider adapting as your process is the ADKAR model, developed by Jeffrey Hiatt in 2006. The ADKAR model (Awareness, Desire, Knowledge, Ability, and Reinforcement) for change management is based on the principle that organizational change can only happen when individuals change and adapt or embrace the change process and its eventual outcomes. Each phase of the ADKAR model is operationalized below in the context of change management in schools.

Awareness Phase

The Awareness Phase generally occurs during the first few months of the school head's tenure or anytime change or reform is on the horizon. The purpose of this phase is to focus on and convey to stakeholders the reasons why change is needed. Think of this first phase of change management as exploring the school's landscape. This means that the school head engages in self-reflection and has clarity about the change before communicating the details to stakeholders. A simple way to ensure there is clarity is to consider these self-reflection questions that require data gathering, stakeholder conversations, and synthesizing the information:

- What do I know about the school and its history with change or reform?
- What were the past successes and challenges associated with change or reform?
- To what degree were the staff members involved in the change management process?
- How much training do the staff members have in change management?
- How do I know now is the best time to implement change?

Of course, there are other questions you might consider before communicating the desired change to stakeholders. Still, the questions above are an excellent beginning to the ongoing self-reflection process school heads should continuously engage in during the change process. The awareness phase is binary: stay aware of self and become aware of others' status or feelings about change.

Before communicating the change to your staff, develop a communication plan to engage them in discussions about the change. The primary goal should be communicating the need for change to all stakeholders by providing rationale backed with data and the risks of not moving forward. By convening a small group of willing staff at the onset of the change, your team is empowered to collaboratively develop a communication plan to execute and design the strategy to ensure that its format meets the needs of each stakeholder group. Effective strategies for communicating to the broader community might include open forums, recorded videos that concisely describe the change, surveys, structured meetings, or digitized newsletters. Try to convey the same message in each format and allow time or implement a simple process for stakeholders to provide input. A mistake many leaders make once they allow stakeholders to "weigh in" is not employing a "feedback loop" – communicating the feedback received and what was revised or altered due to the input. This step is critical to effectively implementing the communication plan. You will gain respect and credibility when you are transparent with the feedback results and any revisions to the change proposed based on the feedback.

While immersed in the Awareness Phase or when entering the Desire Phase, taking an inventory of how your stakeholders react to the communication about the change presents another opportunity to collect feedback. Although people tend to move in and out of the categories described below, developing an awareness of what these categories mean to the change process can assist you with customizing communication or thinking about different strategies to use to increase staff members who support the change process.

Desire Phase

Just because you communicated well and did your best to ensure awareness about the change during the Awareness Phase, this does not mean that you should conflate these outcomes to indicate stakeholders want or desire the change. Moving along the change management process to the Desire Phase could suggest it is time to continue explaining the need for the change. Or, in an ideal state, this phase might indicate that the stakeholders choose or want to support and engage in the proposed change. For school heads, the desire phase could be the most challenging of the five phases. Why? The reason goes back to what we know about motivating and influencing people to believe, embrace, and be active in the change or reform proposed. Change disrupts what is known and comfortable, which means that the school head needs to demonstrate patience and continue communicating and listening to stakeholders who express hesitation or criticism about the proposed change. Keep in mind that your stakeholders might be aware of the change but not want the change to happen. Therein lies the complexity of this phase. We have a few strategies that a school head can use to build a desire for change.

Strategies to Support Stakeholders in the Desire Phase

- Find influential staff members and give them leadership roles to assist with assuring their peers of the needed change.
- Proactively identify and address any internal and external barriers to overcome concerns.
- Invite the naysayers or silent members to engage in two-way dialogues and actively listen to their concerns.
- Refrain from being judgmental or expressing frustration. Stay positive.
- Consider revising or revisiting the communication methods. Discern if the messaging was clear, positive, and presented without emotionally charged words.

Knowledge Phase

This phase of the ADKAR change management model is significant because it indicates that you have solid information from stakeholders on the acceptance and support for the change or reform. Transitioning your school and faculty into the Knowledge Phase will take time and patience, along with intentional data collection. Be sure to revisit the information and data gathered from the implementation of the communication plan (see Awareness Phase), and use the results to determine which, if not all, of the faculty members need training on how to adapt to the change. Your staff might say that they are knowledgeable about change, but as the school head, it is best to reestablish purpose with everyone so that there is no misunderstanding about responsibilities, skills, resources, and processes that will be impacted. You've likely been in organizations long enough to know that learning how to embrace and be a positive contributor to the change process does not always come easily. Therefore, in this phase, take the opportunity to stand side by side with your staff to learn and grow together. As Robert Boyce, a renowned historian states, "Knowledge is power. Knowledge shared is power multiplied."

Strategies to Support Stakeholders in the Knowledge Phase

- Share the data results from the communication plan with your staff. Be transparent about what worked well and what needs improvement.
- Talk to your staff. Listen for their excitement and concerns. Keep an open mind and ask questions to be sure you understand their perspectives as well as their depth of knowledge.
- Involve stakeholders when making the decision about the training sessions. Focus on the needs of the collective group and find ways to address individual or outlying needs.
- Be ready to slow the change process if you find there is concern or if the training did not meet your staff's needs. Sustainable change takes time and having knowledge about what to expect will serve everyone well in the future.
- Continue to communicate in a variety of ways (and model too) the expectations for adapting to change.

Ability Phase

Remember the professional development sessions you have attended? Did you leave the sessions full of content knowledge but have challenges when it became time to apply the new learning? In this phase, you might experience or realize the same feeling with your staff.

The Ability Phase is about moving beyond gaining knowledge about change to enabling your staff to perform, use the skills learned, and demonstrate their competencies. It's the phase where knowledge turns into action, and it involves providing the most appropriate resources and support to ensure staff members are as confident as possible to engage in change. As the school head, without effectively leading this phase, even a highly motivated and informed staff might struggle to make the change sustainable, which can jeopardize the success of the overall change initiative.

Just as students benefit from differentiated instruction, your staff members might also indicate that their competency and confidence level need a boost before applying the new skills and behaviors that are required for the change to occur. If you hear from your staff that there are gaps in their knowledge or their skills need refinement, then again, slow down and meet their needs instead of taking the leap to implement the change initiative. Essential questions to employ in this phase might be, "Do staff members have the necessary skills and knowledge to implement and support the change initiative?" You will want to informally assess each staff member's ability to support and engage in the change initiative by providing opportunities for their voices to be heard, either through quick questionnaires or listening sessions.

Strategies to Support Stakeholders in the Ability Phase

- Address skill gaps: Identify skill gaps and offer additional training or resources to close these gaps. Your staff may need more time or practice to develop the ability to apply the knowledge they've learned.
- Remove barriers: Identify and address any obstacles preventing staff members from successfully making the change. This could be a lack of time, outdated processes, or conflicting responsibilities. Removing these barriers enables your team to focus on learning and applying new behaviors.
- Provide ongoing feedback: Monitor your staff's progress and provide constructive feedback to help them refine their abilities and ensure they move in the right direction.
- Offer mentorship and coaching: Assign mentors or coaches who can provide personalized guidance as employees work to implement the change. These mentors can offer tips, answer questions, and give confidence to struggling people.

Reinforce Phase

This change management process's final phase is about keeping the momentum, engagement, and desire in place. Although this phase appears at the end of the five-phase process, reinforcement strategies merit application throughout the change journey. For example, when your staff is immersed in the act of change, this is a time to carefully monitor, collect data, and determine where the successes and gaps exist (Fullan, 2001). In change management, reinforcement means striving to sustain the change so that staff members do not revert to old behaviors or opposing perspectives. Sometimes the strategies are as simple as communicating appreciation to individuals, celebrating successes along the way, modeling a positive change management perspective, and staying completely engaged in the change process.

However, reinforcing the change's importance can require staff members to receive additional training sessions, extended timelines, or new resources. Hiatt (2006) emphasizes the importance of reinforcement: "Without reinforcement, a person or group may perceive that the effort expended during the transition was not valued. They may seek ways to avoid the change, and their desire to change will diminish."

The school's culture can also be negatively impacted if your staff members lose interest in the change process. A small group of staff might drift into becoming "opposing voices," as they begin to question the viability and purpose of the change, which can easily expand to a larger group, thus causing a fracture in the school's culture (Goleman, 2000). If this happens or if you have a hint that the fracture could occur, then immediately act and reinforce the good that the change initiative is doing for the school. Remember that reinforcements are most effective when they occur throughout the change process instead of waiting near the end of the initiative.

Strategies to Support Stakeholders in the Reinforce Phase

- The recognition or reward is personalized to the individual, meaning the verbal or written communication is not generic.
- Either the director/school head or a staff member who is in a leadership position provides recognition or rewards.
- The recognition is received in a timely manner.
- Any additional training or information is based on your staff members' feedback and your observations of their behaviors and attitudes.

Sustaining meaningful change in a school environment requires continuous engagement, adaptability, and reinforcement of the change process.

As school heads navigate the complexities of leading change, the ADKAR model offers a structured approach that prioritizes awareness, builds desire, fosters knowledge, develops ability, and reinforces long-term commitment. Successful change management is not a one-time effort but an ongoing process that relies on clear communication, active listening, and intentional support for stakeholders at every stage (Maxwell, 2007). By recognizing the challenges inherent in change, addressing concerns proactively, and celebrating progress along the way, school leaders can create a culture where change is embraced rather than resisted. Ultimately, effective change management fosters a dynamic, resilient school environment where both educators and students thrive in a culture of continuous growth and improvement.

Bridging the Gap Between Theory and Practice

Understanding integrity and change management in isolation is insufficient; true leadership emerges when these concepts are synthesized and applied to daily practice. As an educational leader, your role is not only to embrace these principles yourself but also to create an environment where they become embedded in the culture of your school. The challenge lies in moving from theoretical understanding to practical application in a way that is meaningful, sustainable, and impactful (Brown, 2018).

Establishing a Leadership Framework

To effectively apply the learning from integrity and change management, it is helpful to develop a structured leadership framework that guides decision-making, communication, and action.

Consider the following components:

1. Vision and Core Values:

    - Clearly define and articulate the core values that will guide leadership decisions.
    - Align the vision of the school with the principles of integrity and strategic change.
    - Communicate this vision consistently to all stakeholders.

2. Building Trust and Credibility:
   - Model integrity in everyday interactions, ensuring transparency and consistency.
   - Establish trust by being honest about challenges and engaging stakeholders in solution building.
   - Create feedback loops where concerns are acknowledged and addressed (Edmondson, 1999).
3. Strategic Change Management:
   - Utilize the ADKAR model to assess where individuals and groups are in the change process.
   - Develop tailored strategies for addressing resistance and increasing buy in.
   - Ensure professional development opportunities that support capacity building in change implementation.
4. Decision-Making and Ethical Leadership:
   - Use a values-based decision-making process to navigate complex situations.
   - Balance the needs of various stakeholders while remaining committed to long term goals.
   - Be prepared to make difficult decisions that align with the integrity driven vision.

Action Steps for Implementation

Applying integrity and change management in educational leadership requires intentional action. Here are specific steps to guide the process:

1. Conduct a Leadership Self-Assessment:
   Take time to reflect on your leadership strengths and areas for growth, particularly in relation to integrity and change management. Consider how your values align with your actions and how effectively you navigate organizational change while maintaining trust and transparency. Engage in self-assessment by examining past decisions, challenges, and successes to identify patterns in your leadership approach. Additionally, seek feedback from peers, mentors, and staff

to gain a well-rounded perspective on your impact. Encourage honest and constructive input by creating a culture where feedback is valued, and use these insights to refine your strategies, enhance communication, and build stronger relationships within your school community.

2. Engage Your Team in the Change Process:

    Identify key influencers among faculty and staff who can serve as change champions, as their credibility and leadership can help build momentum and encourage broader engagement. These individuals can model a positive attitude toward change, address concerns among their peers, and serve as liaisons between leadership and staff. Foster open dialogue about the need for change by creating structured opportunities for discussion, such as focus groups, town halls, or one-on-one meetings, where stakeholders can express their thoughts, ask questions, and offer ideas. Actively listen to concerns, validate emotions, and provide clear, data driven reasons for the change to build trust and transparency. By involving stakeholders in shaping the process – whether through advisory committees, collaborative planning sessions, or pilot programs – you cultivate a sense of ownership and shared responsibility. This inclusive approach not only increases buyin but also leverages the collective expertise of your team, leading to a smoother and more sustainable transition.

3. Develop a Sustainable Change Strategy:

    Implementing phased changes rather than abrupt shifts provide individuals and organizations with the necessary time to adapt, reducing resistance and increasing the likelihood of long-term success. This approach allows for gradual adjustments, enabling stakeholders to familiarize themselves with new processes, systems, or expectations without feeling overwhelmed. Additionally, continuously assessing progress through data analysis and stakeholder feedback ensures that strategies remain effective and responsive to emerging challenges. By regularly evaluating outcomes and making data driven adjustments, organizations can refine their approach, address potential obstacles proactively, and sustain momentum toward their goals.

4. Embed Integrity in Organizational Culture:

    Recognizing and rewarding behaviors that align with ethical leadership and integrity reinforces a culture where honesty, transparency, and responsibility are valued and consistently demonstrated. Publicly acknowledging individuals who uphold these principles not only motivates them to continue their ethical conduct but also inspires others to follow their example. Establishing clear policies and practices that promote accountability and fairness further strengthens this commitment by providing a structured framework that ensures ethical behavior is not only encouraged but also expected and consistently upheld. These policies should include transparent decision-making processes, mechanisms for reporting ethical concerns, and fair consequences for misconduct, creating an environment of trust and reliability. Additionally, implementing mentorship programs plays a crucial role in developing future leaders with a strong ethical foundation. By pairing experienced leaders with emerging professionals, organizations can provide guidance, role models, and real-world scenarios that help instill ethical decision-making skills. Through regular dialogue and practical experiences, mentees gain a deeper understanding of how to navigate complex ethical challenges while maintaining integrity. Together, these strategies create a sustainable culture where ethical leadership becomes ingrained in an organization's identity, ensuring long term trust, credibility, and success.

Measuring Success and Adapting for Growth

Applying these principles effectively requires ongoing evaluation. Consider the following indicators of success:

Stakeholder engagement: Are faculty, staff, students, and families actively involved in decision-making processes?

Trust and morale: Has there been an increase in trust, collaboration, and overall morale within the school?

Change adoption: Are new initiatives being implemented with sustained commitment and effectiveness?

Ethical decision-making: Are difficult decisions being made with integrity, even in challenging circumstances?

As a leader, your ability to synthesize integrity and change management will define the culture and effectiveness of your school. By remaining reflective, adaptable, and committed to ethical leadership, you can foster an environment where both students and educators thrive. The journey toward effective leadership is continuous, but with a clear framework and purposeful action, the impact of your leadership will be lasting and transformative.

References

Brown, B. (2018). *Dare to lead: Brave work. Tough conversations. Whole hearts*. Random House.

Edmondson, A. (1999). Psychological safety and learning behavior in work teams. *Administrative Science Quarterly, 44*(2), 350–383. https://doi.org/10.2307/2666999

Fullan, M. (2001). *Leading in a culture of change*. Jossey-Bass.

Goleman, D. (2000). *Emotional intelligence: Why it can matter more than IQ*. Bantam Books.

Hiatt, J. (2006). *ADKAR: A model for change in business, government, and our community*. Prosci.

Maxwell, J. C. (2007). *The 21 indispensable qualities of a leader: Becoming the person others will want to follow*. Thomas Nelson.

Merriam-Webster. (2024). Resilience. In Merriam-Webster.com dictionary. Retrieved February 28, 2025, from https://www.merriam-webster.com/dictionary/resilience

Neff, K. D. (2011). *Self-compassion: The proven power of being kind to yourself*. William Morrow.

Guiding Teachers through Change

Myron Dueck and Colin Brown

Educational communities are incredibly dynamic systems, and the role of the leader is to guide their teams through layers of complexity in service of the ultimate goal–student learning. Taking on the challenge of leadership comes with numerous 'givens,' and though there are far too many for a book, let alone a single chapter, let's acknowledge three unavoidable realities. First, there's the reality of constraints. We have yet to meet a school leader who is not challenged by a lack of time, resources or people. For this reason, we will spend some time exploring theory, but far more on practical tools and strategies that the reader can use right away. Second, leadership involves navigating change. Whether it's being hired to lead a new school, developing and adopting policy, adjusting to political shifts, or the emergence of generative AI, a school leader must be prepared to lead through times of innovation and revision. This chapter will provide tools and strategies for transitioning to what is waiting *just around the corner*. Third, our school communities consist of three very different, but interrelated groups: students, teachers, and parents. While there are general approaches to leadership that apply to all our community members, there are also specific challenges and needs inherent in leading instructors. For this reason, helping teachers embrace change is the focus of this chapter.

Resoundingly, education is all about student learning, and leadership *should* play a critical role. Unfortunately, our use of 'should' reflects the ideal, not necessarily the reality. Many school leaders may not recognize that improving student learning *is* their primary obligation. In their very timely book, *Leadership for Deeper Learning* (2021),

Richardson, Bathon, and McLoed argue that leading through educational reform takes courage to push the status quo, always believing that things can be *better*.

Stepping into a new school, leaders are immediately faced with challenging the status quo. Many leaders have been asked, 'Why are we making this change? We have always done it this way and it works well enough.' There are a lot of things that we've *done before*. Having students write lines on the board is one of many archaic approaches we used to employ to change inappropriate behavior, but obviously we've recognized the need to adopt more effective approaches.

Leadership is becoming inseparable from change. Richardson et al. (2021) further cite compelling research that 'leadership is a critical factor in establishing the conditions necessary for successful student learning' (p. 3). Perhaps most importantly, they lay down a challenge to all school leaders that, 'it is the adaptability to context and willingness to lead change that distinguish leaders from mere administrators' (p. 3).

Readers drawn to this book are likely interested in expanding their role from mere administrators to that of a dynamic leader. Considering the complexity of our schools and the need for leaders to be courageous and daring, this chapter will seek to answer three questions:

What are a few guiding principles to support teachers through change?

What are some specific approaches to meet the diverse needs of today's teachers?

What are some strategies, tools, and ideas surrounding change that are both practical and transferable, and that school leaders can use right away?

Three Guiding Principles

In this section, we will share three ideas that exist at the 30,000-foot view of change. Bump into anyone who has taken a keen interest in sharing leadership strategies, and they'll have a few 'go-to' rules. Suffice it to say, there are thousands of adages, concepts, and guidelines out there on the topic of leadership. Here are three.

The Four Stages of a Paradigm Shift

The term 'paradigm shift' was popularized in 1962 by the American physicist and philosopher Thomas Kuhn. To give it a contemporary definition, we asked Microsoft Co-Pilot's artificial to describe a paradigm shift, and here was the first result:

> Essentially, a paradigm shift occurs when the prevailing framework or model used for understanding a phenomenon becomes incompatible with new evidence or phenomena, leading to the adoption of a new theory or perspective. It's like a transformative leap that reshapes how we think and approach problems.
>
> (OpenAI, 2024)

Whether it's a shift in teacher assessment practices, introducing a new proficiency scale to parents, or guiding students to think critically and problem-solve, sometimes we need to literally change our thinking and the thinking of our community members. The bad news: it's hard. The good news: it's predictable.

The next time you are using Microsoft Word; you have its author to thank – Richard Brodie.

Besides designing the most prolific word processing program ever (and being an accomplished poker player), Brodie wrote two books, one entitled, *Virus of the Mind*. In this intriguing read, Brodie uses examples from the scientific world, such as Darwin's 1859 theory of natural selection, to illustrate that new ideas tend to 'rub people the wrong way at first and produce predictable reactions' (Brodie, 1995, p. 3). Brodie argues that just about any fundamental shift in thinking typically involves these four stages:

1. **Complacency/Marginalization** – At first a new idea is ignored or dismissed as it does not pose a serious threat to the status quo.
2. **Ridicule** – If the new idea persists, detractors resort to mockery or laughter. They make fun of the notion hoping that it will be put to rest.
3. **Criticism** – If the new idea gains a foothold in their community or society, the resistors dig in for the fight. Here we see an

attack – verbally, emotionally, and even physically on the new idea and those who've adopted it. Imagine the challenges faced by the school leader facing the criticism stage described in the example below:

> A new Director had just begun his tenure at a school where the introduction of standards-based grading and reporting (SBGR) had been led by three of the school's teachers who, with limited understanding of it, had struggled so much to implement the change schoolwide that the whole school community vehemently opposed it. In fact, some families were pulling out of the school because of it. In numerous initial parent meetings, he was confronted with,
>
> 'You don't like that SBGR stuff, right?'
>
> He responded, 'Well, yes, I do, because it is incredibly effective for student learning. But on the other hand, I do not necessarily support the way it is currently being implemented.'
>
> Uniting students, teachers, and parents to change their fixed mindset about SBGR would require a transformative leap, but it was expected. Ironically, once this shift occurred, he was confident many of the passionate 'non-believers' become the strongest advocates.

4. **Acceptance** – Once a critical mass of people embraces the new paradigm, it achieves psychological and intellectual acceptance – you have made it!

    When you are next attempting to usher in a fundamental change to your school, and it's meeting significant resistance, it can be helpful to identify the stage you're in, understand what is coming next, and know that you are not alone. A leader proposing change will require courage – the road to acceptance is tough. While each of the first three stages are challenging, Stage 3 is the steepest hill to climb. That is not to say there is no value inherent in the challenge. The 'criticism' stage is a good time to genuinely listen, reflect on arguments made, and seek greater clarity as to why there is resistance. Consider this example of a school leader navigating the challenges presented in Stage 3.

A Head of School mistakenly bypassed this stage early in his career. After listening to the English Language Arts (ELA) faculty and various specialists, the team decided that a change be adopted to a new reading program and tracking system throughout the elementary school. Upon hearing the resources could also be translated into Spanish, the Head of School proposed that the Spanish Language Arts (SLA) teachers also adopt this new program. After a month, the ELA teachers had adopted the program with fidelity and improvement was apparent.

The successes in ELA however, were not being experienced by the SLA teachers – they were barely making any progress. Frustrated, and armed with data to show this resistant group the positive impact on learning (in English), Colin gathered the SLA teachers for a discussion.

First, let's acknowledge an undeniable fact. If you approach a potentially contentious meeting with an open mind and genuinely listen, even if you have your own specific agenda, most times you will learn something valuable. In this case, the resistors were provided a forum to share their reasons for discontent. They liked the idea of the program and even the approach taken, but they were hesitant to adopt it for concrete reasons. It turned out the Spanish translation was 'choppy' and many of the translated words were not culturally appropriate nor relevant. 'No wonder there was resistance!,' he reflected. Fortunately, the group was able to brainstorm a solution that benefitted student learning. In retrospect, this should have been done in the first place! Nonetheless, readers are reminded that Brodie's Stage 3 can be a great opportunity to revisit and deeply reflect on the paradigm shift being proposed.

Leading Change Is a 'Desirable Difficulty'

Speaking of changes being tough, Bjork and Bjork (2011), cognitive psychologists at UCLA, wrote a chapter in the *Psychology of Everyday Life* entitled, *Making Things Hard on Yourself, but in a Good Way: Desirable Difficulties to Enhance Learning*. They argue that long-term understanding and memory are built on the foundation of struggle. They write, '…optimizing learning and instruction often requires going against one's intuition, deviating from standard instructional practices, and managing one's own learning activities in new ways' (p. 57). This notion is related to what Wilson et al. (2019) call the *'Eighty Percent Rule.'* They suggest that there is a 'sweet spot' of difficulty – a 'Goldilocks zone' (p. 2) where the learner seeks challenges at the edge of their competency. The challenge is not so difficult that they give up, but not so easy that it's a breeze.

If according to Brodie, 75% of a paradigm shift involves increasing resistance, and Bjork and Bjork (2011) contend that deeper learning is embedded through difficulty, you could argue that the growth of a change leader requires resistance. In fact, we should seek it! It's how we learn, develop resilience, and leverage experience to tackle the next hurdle. Just as the criticism stage rests on the brink of acceptance, know that you are growing your capacity as a leader through the inescapable challenge of the role.

The Unavoidable Need for Dialogue, Relationships, and 'Trust Equity'

We have seen it many times. A leader wants to make a change, 'move the needle,' and transform the school into a better place. Perhaps through noble intentions, impatience, or pressure, they skip much of the dialogue stage and just push through with a policy. They 'draw the line' as a firm message that their expectations will be upheld! This type of leadership, relying on the power base of position or title, is incredibly tempting. It's efficient and quick. To be clear, in times of crisis or emergency, decisions often need to be made without much consultation. But that is the exception more than the norm for contemporary educational leadership.

One of the most effective leaders Myron ever worked with often said, 'Policies just avoid difficult conversations,' and it is so very true. This leader often reminded his faculty that while it may appear that an edict will solve the problem, if key members of the community do not see the purpose or reasons for the change, compliance on the surface too often masks the rumblings that move underground. Besides losing the conversation, a leader may also find that people can comply with a policy and still achieve their original intention in another way. Consider this example of how firm policies can hinder a desired change:

> Jason is a new Head of School in a school that has several traditionally minded teachers who assign grades for effort, participation, and punctuality. One Upper School teacher, Mr. Smith, locks the classroom door at the beginning of class, and while tardy students are eventually let in, the process allows Mr. Smith to note the infraction, and three late arrivals contribute to a 5-point deduction to the student's term grade. Jason's goal is to shift the entire school to a standards-based grading model. An obvious first step is to eliminate egregious grading practices such as locking the door and reducing the grade for each student admitted thereafter. It's clear to Jason that a student's Physics grade should not be lowered at term-end because their parents dropped them off late for school one too many times. At the first staff meeting of the year, Jason announces that a school-wide grading document will be developed. But in the meantime, he announces an initial policy to the entire staff: No more deductions to students grades for arriving late to class!
>
> Confident that the problem has been solved by the policy, it's not until much later in the year when he realizes the problem still exists, but it's taken another form. A parent seeks him out after a Board meeting,
>
> 'Hey Jason, what do you think of Mr. Smith's bell quizzes?'
>
> Jason is caught off guard and asks the parent to elaborate.

'Well, my son has received three zeros this term for missed quizzes. These one-minute quizzes count for grades, and Mr. Smith starts them immediately after the bell. Any student late to class misses the quiz, and there is no opportunity for them to make up the assessment.'

The next morning a frustrated Jason, now lacking sleep, visits the teacher and a confrontation ensues. Jason believes the teacher's 'bell quizzes' are a policy infraction, while the teacher contends that he's adhering to Jason's policy. In the teacher's opinion, he is not reducing scores for late arrival, these are missed quizzes.

Jason could continue to introduce policies:

No More Bell Quizzes. No More Locked Doors. Students Must Have an Opportunity to Reassess

What Jason may soon realize is that, sure enough, policies just avoid difficult conversations. After forming a staff grading committee that includes the aforementioned teacher, many staff conversations, and a year-long pilot, Jason recognizes that a shift in thinking serves the school much better than a list of policies. A year later Jason's school has an agreement supported by staff and parents:

> At [insert school name here] grades are assigned to communicate a student's academic achievement according to the established learning standards for any given subject. A separate 'Habits of Scholarship' indicator reflects behaviors related to punctuality, class preparation, and integrity.

All Aboard! Strategies for Change!

When a leader is introducing a change, and some of the staff members are not embracing it, it can be incredibly useful to identify which category teachers are in (as outlined in Chapter 7). We will focus on the 'Early

Supporters' (ES) and 'Middle of the Roaders' (MR) as these people are critical for embedded change to occur.

Imagine you want to introduce changes to your school's grading policy, specifically eliminating the grading of homework because it is not necessarily an accurate reflection of student learning and progress. You passionately present the idea at your staff meeting. Your short presentation cites a few authors, some research and failure rate data, and you promise to revisit the conversation at the next meeting.

An Early Supporter (ES) may follow up with you and share something like: 'I am totally on board, and I am getting rid of grading homework today. I will just tell students I am not grading their homework anymore. In fact, I'm going to get rid of homework altogether.' This ES is exhibiting attributes of 'keen, but inexperienced.'

Another ES might share, 'Initially I was struggling with your homework grading proposal, but after sleeping on it I'm starting to like it. My partner also teaches here and after chatting about it we agree that students are likely just copying from each other. But one of the challenges I see is that homework is important, and some students will not do it if I don't assign a grade. Again, this is an example of 'keen, but inexperienced.'

A MR might confront you the next day with, 'This seems to be another one of those "in theory" types of changes. In theory, it makes sense, but interacting with these students every day, I just cannot see how it will work. Students will not do their homework, and this will negatively affect their learning.' This example of an MR highlights the 'hesitant but intrigued.'

As you can see in these examples, they are all open to the principle or concept of the change, but they lack the experience, tools, and strategies to implement it. Stated another way, they *lean into* the conversation, the process, the change. The leader's primary role in this situation is to provide support, guidance, and opportunity. This is a critical point to make: if you are leading change and have people supporting the idea, or not vehemently opposing the change, you must be actively involved and provide the necessary time and support systems to actualize the change.

Consider the following examples of change processes in action. What do you notice about the teachers' reactions?

Scenario 1: During the middle of a school year, a principal wanted to implement and mandate a peer observation approach for all teachers. The principal shared the idea at a faculty meeting and was looking for early volunteers to learn the process and try it out. Teachers volunteered (around ten Early Supporters) and were keen on the idea. The principal sent a quick email to them outlining the process, took them all through an instructional round protocol, and then guided the debrief of the observation. He then followed up with an email telling these teachers to organize a time to do follow-up instructional rounds by themselves. Over a two-month period, only one or two independent instructional rounds were conducted. Although the principal reminded/told them to do more, he was surprised people were not conducting them. By the end of the year, no additional instructional rounds occurred.

Scenario 2: The leadership team was looking to enhance teaching through implementing a weekly backward design curriculum development approach. The idea was to clearly highlight and focus on the standards/learning targets taught and assessed throughout the week. The idea was initially presented at a whole school faculty meeting during orientation week before the school year started. Teachers had time to work in groups to review, develop questions, and discuss this new approach. Throughout the week, teachers were provided designated time to better understand the process with colleagues and administration. The leadership team modeled examples for all faculty and was actively involved with the various faculty groups as they began trying to produce this new approach. Teachers were expected to try one and submit it at the end of the second week of school for leadership to review.

Throughout this process, leadership was proactively ready to collaborate with faculty and work through the stages with them. This was certainly a considerable time commitment for leadership, but it proved valuable. Once the initial plans came in, they were immediately reviewed, and feedback was given within two days.

> Close approximations to the goal and meeting the expectations were praised and detailed improvement suggestions were outlined. This process was ongoing. Additionally, if some faculty members were clearly struggling, leadership set up one-to-one meetings and worked collaboratively with the teacher to build an exemplar. Teachers felt very supported and comforted by the fact leadership actively walked with them through the process. Three critical elements of this process included professional development time, focused faculty meetings, and collaborative planning opportunities. The results were immediate. Faculty demonstrated additional understanding, they displayed an increased willingness to discuss challenges and were observed sharing new learnings and exemplars while celebrating successes. Further, designated PD time was given to create new plans. This process continued throughout the year and leadership was ever present and actively involved in the process. By the end of the year, 90% of the faculty were successful with the innovative format.

Reflection Opportunity

Looking at these two scenarios, what do you believe were the significant differences that led to different outcomes?

Responding to Unique Mindsets

While it is important to spend time and effort with the ESs and MRs, it is equally important to not overly invest in devout 'Naysayers.'

Returning to the original scenario about not grading homework, there might be teachers who will completely oppose the direction. They are adamant about not making changes and may confront you with, 'This change you are proposing to our homework grading policy is a really bad idea. We have a long-standing tradition at this school where we expect responsibility, academic rigor, and preparing students for university. These new 'trendy' policies erode the moral fabric of our community.'

This faculty member could be in the category MR, but most likely falls into the category of 'Naysayers.' They are 'able but unwilling.' They probably have the experience and skills to adopt the change, but they resist it because they lack the motivation, willingness, or mindset to try it. Earlier we equated willingness to a faculty member who leans in, but in this case, with arms crossed, the naysayer leans out of the conversation. You suspect that their 'moral fabric' argument is likely disguising their reluctance to spend the time exploring alternative approaches. The role of the leader is to provide research and real-world examples, to support the 'why.' Leaders are reminded that too many conversations in this category will result in draining time, energy, and motivation. Inevitably, these 'Naysayers' will need to either get on board or look for a new environment that best aligns with their mindset.

Try, Then Change: Shifting Minds through Experiences

Some traditional approaches to instruction, assessment, grading, and reporting are exceptionally hard to change. In a perfect world, all a school leader would need is a great set of presentation slides, an impassioned plea, and a wee magic wand, and kazoo, teachers are no longer lecture-based with multiple-choice tests in hand.

The fact of the matter is that long-standing behaviors and thinking are hard to change. We have all heard and read of 'confirmation bias;' our human tendency to seek out and prefer information that supports our preexisting beliefs (Nikolopoulou, 2022). It turns out a major culprit is 'cognitive entrenchment' and we as leaders need to be aware of it. Phan and Ngu (2021, p. 1) cite several features of 'cognitive entrenchment':

- The longer we practice something the more it forms a basis for our personal and emotional needs
- Perceived 'expertise' may stifle one's willingness and motivation to be innovative, flexible, and 'creative to ongoing changes'
- Resistance to change can satisfy three fundamental needs: (1) reduction of cognitive load, (2) the need for efficiency, and (3) our desire for comfort and stability

Considering this list, it's a wonder we change at all! In his recent book, *Engaging Parents and Families in Grading Reforms* (2023), Dr. Thomas Guskey offers a refreshingly new twist concerning shifting teachers' mindsets and practices. He argues that experiences have a much greater capacity to shift our thinking than arguments, data, and impassioned speeches. Rather, Guskey argues that a paradigm shift occurs when educators try something, and then possibly have a surprisingly good outcome. It's this positive emotional experience that can dramatically shift one's thinking. It's similar to the hypercorrection effect referenced by Wiliam in *Embedded Formative Assessment* (2018). The more entrenched we are in an incorrect assertion, the deeper the learning experience once we are corrected. If you've ever said something like, 'Seriously? I've been wrong about that all this time?' you've probably experienced the hyper-correction effect.

You might be thinking that getting teachers to try something is not any easier than convincing them of a new idea. The good news is that it can be. Here are a few ideas:

Contentious Issue Conversation Starters

Early in his career, Myron was teaching at a school where the administration sought to challenge teachers who were 'cognitively entrenched' in traditional grading and assessment practices – and he was certainly one of them. Specifically, he was one of the main critics of re-assessments. As he writes in *Grading Smarter Not Harder* (Dueck, 2014),

> ...whenever the topic of retesting arose, I was one of the first to shoot it down...The tests I administered were not just assessing my students learning, but also measuring and helping to entrench such valuable attributes as a good work ethic the ability to concentrate strong study skills to rule thevalue of tests by allowing students to retake them seem to mean nothing short of absurd.
>
> (pp. 90–91)

A relatively simple template helped encourage Myron, and a few of his equally resistant colleagues to try an ongoing assessment system even though most staff were far from believing in it philosophically. Figure 9.1 is a version that Myron has since used with many school groups. For the next few examples, we will focus on resistance to ongoing assessment, but the reader could use it for any variety of topics. These are great informal conversation starters as they provide support to the willing and voice to the 'Middle of the Roaders.' This useful tool keeps the conversation transparent and public, not behind closed doors, and may just provide the nudge that some people need to try something new.

Offer ongoing assessment opportunities to encourage learning.

"Retesting allows both teachers and learners to make learning the fixed standard and time the variable." (Dueck, M. 2014. *Grading Smarter Not Harder: Assessment Strategies That Motivate Kids and Help Them Learn.*)

Benefits/Pros *"What will work for me…?"*	**Challenges/hurdles** *"I may have a problem with…"*

Questions?
"I am wondering about…"

Ideas/Next Steps
"Hey, I just thought about something!"
"My next step on this is…"

Figure 9.1 Assessment focus #2

Source: Contentious Conversation Starter, ©Myron Dueck, 2021.

Agreements over Policy: Disagree and Commit, and Pilot It

While we emphasize reassessment as the subject of change throughout this chapter, we want to highlight that the processes and tools in this chapter can be adapted to help with many other topics, issues, or challenges. In our work supporting school leaders through the change process around assessment and grading, we have seen examples where the beliefs around assessment were certainly cognitively entrenched. Resistance to ongoing assessment was reflected in statements such as, 'We have a tradition of rigorous education – retests erode that tradition,' 'Kids won't study if they know they have a redo,' or, 'The real world is not a place of second chances!.'

In these instances, it is quite clear that staff will not be easily convinced by diving into the merits or potential benefits of retests. There is merit in going back to earlier in the change process a little, change the narrative, and give people the confidence to try. Three simple leadership tools have proven paramount:

1. **Agreements over Policy**

    Beliefs form the basis of our decision-making. They act like a metaphorical ship's rudder when we are figuring out how to navigate a challenging situation. Keeping in mind that we've discussed that beliefs are very hard to change, perhaps it might be more effective to add beliefs or remind people of ones they already hold. This can help push people to 'try.'

    The faculty in the example above may be inclined to first spend time discussing mistakes, and not ones related to schooling. We would visit blunders we have made in life with them. Myron, for example, often shares one of his long-standing errors – walking away from the oven when broiling French fries – and how a smoke-filled kitchen contributed to his memory and learning. The staff is invited to engage in a discussion involving sports, music, and even their teaching, and how over time we adjust our learning based on mistakes and missteps.

    We have also discussed the obligation we have to recognize when a shift in understanding has occurred. Like when an athlete has significantly

Table 9.1 Ongoing assessment: 'Agreements' over 'policy'

Ongoing Assessment: 'Agreements' Over 'Policy'
1. Learning takes time ... and *more* time can result in *more learning*.
2. We learn from our mistakes ... and *more* mistakes can result in *more* learning.
3. Our goal is for all students to strive for mastery ... and for us to acknowledge it.

improved her 100m dash time, we don't average her year-long results. It was not the time for 'policy,' but rather to encourage dialogue, exploration, and innovation. In the end, we came up with the following agreements (Table 9.1). We wanted the idea of reassessment to take hold, ferment, and percolate. We were one step closer to the 'try' stage.

This might be a good time for the reader to stop and consider how 'agreements over policy' might assist a staff conversation. The more contentious the topic, the greater the effectiveness in exploring broader agreements. For instance, it might be easier to first establish parameters for how we treat other human beings, than it would be for staff to buy in on a specific grading policy.

2. **Disagree and Commit**

An effective strategy used by many school leaders to reach a decision is called 'Disagree and Commit.' According to Guskey (2023):

> Credit for developing this strategy is usually given to Scott McNealy of Sun Microsystems, but it's also attributed to Andrew Grove of Intel and Jeff Bezos of Amazon (Origbo, 2017). The origins of disagree and commit, however, can be traced to the strategies used by military leaders to plan battle campaigns.
>
> (p. 28)

Guskey is certainly correct. In the lead up to the 1944 D-Day Allied landings in France, the United States Navy, Army, and Airforce generals were far from united on how the invasion should be conducted. According to Anthony Beevor's (2009) book, *D-Day – The Battle for Normandy,* internal rivalries were one of the main stressors for Eisenhower, contributing to his incredibly unhealthy coping mechanism of 'smoking up to four packs of Camel cigarettes a day' (p. 2).

The struggles the Generals experienced in planning the invasion serve as a poignant example of 'disagree and commit.' Despite enormous gaps between the generals as to how the invasion should be conducted, once everyone had their say, Eisenhower made the final decision and everyone committed to it.

In *Engaging Parents and Families in Grading Reforms* (2023), Guskey argues that the 'disagree and commit' strategy serves two key purposes:

1. It communicates that all perspectives have value. Everyone involved in the decision-making process has the chance to voice their point of view and have it considered.
2. It helps foster a sense of belonging among individuals in the organization who come to see the essential nature of working together. With a sense of belonging comes loyalty and a willingness to take the risks involved in innovation (Rowland & Pivcevic, 2022) (pp. 28–29).

Let's return to our example surrounding resistance to ongoing assessment. With a staff divided on the merits of giving students more than one opportunity to demonstrate learning but wanting to encourage a climate of innovation and risk-taking, we knew that consensus would be nearly impossible. Perhaps giving people the license to try a new approach, without a sense of permanence, might be the best move. It's time for a 'pilot.'

3. **Pilot the Change**

    Do you want to chew on gravel?
    No.
    Don't worry, we're just piloting it.
    Ok, give me a handful…

While proposing a pilot is not as crazy as asking someone to chew gravel. It's just a spin-off of the adage shared earlier: 'Policy just avoids difficult conversations.' A good pilot program welcomes dialogue before policy is adopted. According to Ashkenas and Matta (2021) with the

Guiding Teachers through Change

Harvard Business Review, the purpose of a pilot is to 'reduce the risk of failure across the entire organization by testing the idea in a small, controlled setting so that you can further refine your solution before you roll it out' (para 1). Further, they underscore that once a pilot is successful, the change needs to be malleable and personalized for different levels and subject areas to foster collaboration and innovation. They encourage leaders to 'create the conditions that allow individuals and teams to adapt the solution to their unique circumstances and make it their own.'

In 2023, while working with many British Columbia schools, Myron helped teachers and administrators tackle a brand-new Ministry proficiency scale. He created the following document to assist departments in defining the proficiency levels (Figure 9.2). Many educators were finding it incredibly challenging to shift away from the use of letter

How would you describe: ☐ evidence of learning ☐ a student that is...	
PROFICIENT	**EXTENDING (SOPHISTICATED)**
DEVELOPING	**EMERGING (BEGINNING)**

	EMERGING	DEVELOPING	PROFICIENT	EXTENDING
The Provincial Proficiency Scale	The student demonstrates an initial understanding of the concepts and competencies relevant to the expected learning.	The student demonstrates a partial understanding of the concepts and competencies relevant to the expected learning.	The student demonstrates a complete understanding of the concepts and competencies relevant to the expected learning.	The student demonstrates a sophisticated understanding of the concepts and competencies relevant to the expected learning.

Figure 9.2 Example template for teachers to describe what levels look like in their context

grades and percentages, finding that the headings for the scale were too vague and unfamiliar. Questions such as these abounded:

> What does extending look like?
> What's the difference between 'Developing' and 'Proficient'?

To answer these questions, each grade level or department was given the task of describing what a certain level might look like specific to their context.

Here's an example of an upper school social studies department that sought to first establish student characteristics specific to the levels of 'Emerging' and 'Extending':

How would you describe: ☐ evidence of learning ☑ a student that is...	
PROFICIENT	**EXTENDING (SOPHISTICATED)** Articulates understanding through a variety of mediums and ways Applies learning to new contexts or situations Takes risks Perceptively connects separate ideas
DEVELOPING	**EMERGING (BEGINNING)** With support, begins to take a position May know a concept but needs assistance in applying it

	EMERGING	DEVELOPING	PROFICIENT	EXTENDING
The Provincial Proficiency Scale	The student demonstrates an initial understanding of the concepts and competencies relevant to the expected learning.	The student demonstrates a partial understanding of the concepts and competencies relevant to the expected learning.	The student demonstrates a complete understanding of the concepts and competencies relevant to the expected learning.	The student demonstrates a sophisticated understanding of the concepts and competencies relevant to the expected learning.

Figure 9.3 Example completed template by a social studies teacher

Guiding Teachers through Change

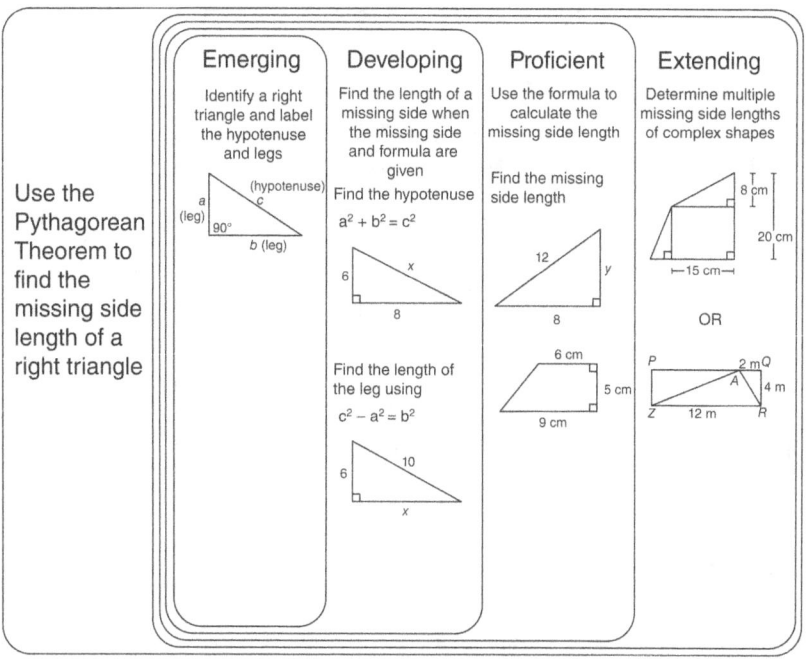

Figure 9.4 Example completed template by a math teacher (examples courtesy of Rebecca Brisson and Myron Dueck, adapted from Chris Hunter and Marc Garneau of the British Columbia Association of Math Teachers)

Recall that Ashkenas and Matta contend that an effective leader allows different teams within the organization to adapt a pilot to meet their specific needs and context. Consider this example of a middle school math teacher developing a 'progression' for students to understand what the proficiency scale means at the grade 8 level when tackling the Pythagorean Theorem.

The Pen-Toss: Feeling the Need for Change

As mentioned earlier, all the words in the world may not compel a teacher to change. They sometimes need to feel it.

A few years ago, Myron came across an interesting document. Designed by Lisa O'Reilly, based on Anderson and Krathwohl's (2001) Revised Bloom's Taxonomy, it was a table with knowledge dimensions on the vertical or Y axis, and cognitive dimensions on the horizontal or X

Standard(s)/Objective(s): _____

My audit: ☐ unit/summative test ☐ unit plan ☐ other: _____

Bloom's Revised Taxonomy Worksheet	Cognitive Process Dimension					
	1 Remember Recognizing or recalling knowledge, facts or concepts. **Verbs:** define, describe, identify, know, label, list, match, name, outline, recall, recognize, reproduce, select, state, locate	**2 Understand** Constructing meaning from instructional messages. **Verbs:** illustrate, defend, compare, distinguish, estimate, explain, classify, generalize, interpret, paraphrase, predict, rewrite, summarize, translate	**3 Apply** Using ideas and concepts to solve problems. **Verbs:** implement, organize, dramatize, solve, construct, demonstrate, discover, manipulate, modify, operate, predict, prepare, produce, relate, show, solve, choose	**4 Analyze** Breaking something down into components, seeing relationships and an overall structure. **Verbs:** analyze, break down, compare, select, contrast, deconstruct, discriminate, distinguishes, identify, outline, investigate	**5 Evaluate** Making judgments based on criteria and standards. **Verbs:** rank, assess, monitor, check, test, judge	**6 Create** Reorganize diverse elements to form a new pattern or structure. **Verbs:** generate, plan, develop, create, invent, organize, construct, produce, compile, design, devise
Factual Knowledge Basic elements used to communicate, understand, organize a subject: terminology, scientific terms, labels, vocabulary, jargon, symbols or representations, and specific details such as knowledge of events, people, dates, sources of information.						
Conceptual Knowledge Knowledge of classifications and categories, principles, theories, models or structures of a subject.						
Procedural Knowledge Knowing how to do something: performing skills, algorithms, techniques or methods.						
Metacognitive Knowledge The process or strategy of learning and thinking, an awareness of one's own cognition, and the ability to control, monitor and regulate one's own cognitive process.						

(The Knowledge Dimension)

Developed by Lisa O'Reilly, MA. Based on Anderson, L.W., & Krathwohl (Eds.). (2001). A Taxonomy for learning, teaching, and assessing: A revision of Bloom's Taxonomy of Educational Objectives. New York: Longman.

Figure 9.5 Example completed table of knowledge dimensions

axis. He immediately saw the potential for this table to serve as a type of audit for teachers to conduct on a unit plan, test, or series of topics. He took Lisa's table and made the minor adjustment of adding a few lines and checkboxes at the top of the document (see Figure 9.5).

In a professional development event Myron was leading 20 teachers were going to be looking at their assessment practices and the depth of learning they were intending to assess. He asked each teacher to bring along one of their favorite end-of-unit tests. Once teachers were seated, he asked them to individually go through their assessment, question-by-question, and determine where on the table each question best fit. Take the following question as a possible example of what teachers reviewed:

1. Define the term 'antagonist.'

    Virtually every learning standard, and most test or project prompts, are really an intersection of a verb and a noun, the cognitive dimension and the knowledge dimension. To determine the cell representing this intersection, the teacher would first identify the verb or action. 'Define' is found in the '1. Remember' column. Next, they identify the knowledge dimension. 'Antagonist' represents terminology and therefore belongs in the 'Factual Knowledge' row. Therefore, the teacher would put a little 'I,' 'x,' or checkmark in the first cell, the intersection of 'Remember' and 'Factual,' and move on to the next question.

    Consider the next question example:

2. Identify the character in your novel study that most represents the 'antagonist.'

    The verb in this question is 'identify' and it's found in both '1. Remember' and '4. Analyze.' If this was, say, a science question asking the student to, 'identify the liver on this diagram' then 'identify' would be in the '1. Remember' column.

Back to our ELA example. The teacher considers the nature of the question and determines they are asking the student to analyze the character and therefore uses the cognitive dimension column '4. Analyze.' Next is the knowledge dimension. If the student will simply be compiling a list of attributes they know pertain to an antagonist, and relating them to a character, it's likely in the 'Factual' row and again we place a 'tick' or 'I' in the corresponding cell.

Thus far, the teacher's audit table would look like this (Figure 9.6).

About 10 to 15 minutes into the exercise, a teacher muttered something that won't be quoted and proceeded to toss her pen into the corner of the room. Nobody was injured. After freeing herself of her writing device, the high school English Language Arts teacher then shoved her test to the far edge of the table and declared, 'I'm done with this activity!.' She had noted on the table about 20 questions of her assessment. Can you speculate what part of the table was most populated with ticks?

You likely guessed it...the upper left portion. Her students were doing a lot of remembering facts.

Bloom's Revised Taxonomy Worksheet	Cognitive Process Dimension					
	1 Remember — Recognizing or recalling knowledge, facts or concepts. **Verbs:** define, describe, identify, know, label, list, match, name, outline, recall, recognize, reproduce, select, state, locate	2 Understand — Constructing meaning from instructional messages. **Verbs:** illustrate, defend, compare, distinguish, estimate, explain, classify, generalize, interpret, paraphrase, predict, rewrite, summarize, translate	3 Apply — Using ideas and concepts to solve problems. **Verbs:** implement, organize, dramatize, solve, construct, demonstrate, discover, manipulate, modify, operate, predict, prepare, produce, relate, show, solve, choose	4 Analyze — Breaking something down into components, seeing relationships and an overall structure. **Verbs:** analyze, break down, compare, select, contrast, deconstruct, discriminate, distinguishes, identify, outline, investigate	5 Evaluate — Making judgments based on criteria and standards. **Verbs:** rank, assess, monitor, check, test, judge	6 Create — Reorganize diverse elements to form a new pattern or structure. **Verbs:** generate, plan, compose, develop, create, invent, organize, construct, produce, compile, design, devise
Factual Knowledge — Basic elements used to communicate, understand, organize a subject: terminology, scientific terms, labels, vocabulary, jargon, symbols or representations, and specific details such as knowledge of events, people, dates, sources of information.						
Conceptual Knowledge — Knowledge of classifications and categories, principles, theories, models or structures of a subject.						
Procedural Knowledge — Knowing how to do something: performing skills, algorithms, techniques or methods.						
Metacognitive Knowledge — The process or strategy of learning and thinking, an awareness of one's own cognition, and the ability to control, monitor and regulate one's own cognitive process.						

Standard(s)/Objective(s): _____

My audit: ☑ unit/summative test ☐ unit plan ☐ other: _____

The Knowledge Dimension

Developed by Lisa O'Reilly, MA. Based on Anderson, L.W., & Krathwohl (Eds.). (2001). A Taxonomy for learning, teaching, and assessing: A revision of Bloom's Taxonomy of Educational Objectives. New York: Longman.

Figure 9.6 Example audit table completed by a teacher

'This is not me! This is not the nature of my classroom! I don't teach like an encyclopedia!,' declared the fourth-year teacher.

Myron assured her that his first audit experience wasn't much different.

'Isn't it nice to find that out early in your career?' he asked. 'I only discovered this 15 years in.'

Two weeks later the ELA teacher had revamped her assessment questions to reflect the depth of verbiage in the learning standard. Once she saw and felt the state of assessment in her classroom, she was motivated to change it. To be clear, there's nothing wrong with assessing whether students remember and understand. What many teachers find after performing a self-audit is that their student prompts are overly weighted to those types of questions, and they are not predominantly assessing the types of verbs found in the learning outcome such as analyze, evaluate, and design.

Leading Change: Prepare for the Challenge

There is an inherent juxtaposition for any school leader. On one hand, we typically find ourselves in schools that have traditions, established policies and many other entrenched practices. Often these things contribute to the strengths and legacy of the school and may form the very reason many families invest their time and money to enroll their children. In many cases our schools have brand recognition; parents are proud to have their child wear the shirt with our school logo. On the other hand, as leaders, we inherit the mantle of responsibility to improve the school, shift thinking and practices, and always strive to be better. Compounding this challenge is that as time marches on, the ground will always move under our feet. Changes in educational theory, political shifts, technology, staff changes – the unknowns waiting just around the corner are endless.

During his opening keynote for the 2024 EARCOS Educators Conference, entitled, *Ch-Ch-Ch-Changes 2024,* Myron challenged participants to embrace the difficulties surrounding change. A recurring theme in that keynote was embodied in this slide:

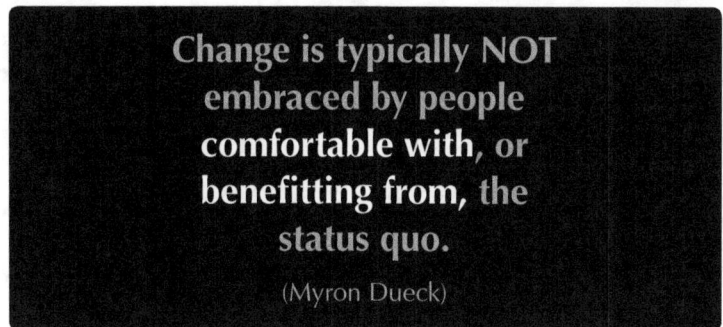

Figure 9.7 EARCOS Keynote

Source: Ch-ch-ch-Changes (2024).

If you're looking for comfort and benefit in the status quo, we might suggest a path different from educational leadership. Leading through change is not easy, but it is incredibly rewarding. So, if you're up for the challenge of shifting mindsets, first for the teachers in your school, and then to observe the impact on student learning, we trust that the ideas and tools shared in this chapter assist you in that journey.

References

Anderson, L. W., & Krathwohl, D. R. (2001). *A taxonomy for learning, teaching, and assessing: A revision of Bloom's taxonomy of educational objectives*. Longman.

Ashkenas, R., & Matta, N. (2021). How to scale a successful pilot project. *Harvard Business Review*. https://hbr.org/2021/01/how-to-scale-a-successful-pilot-project

Beevor, A. (2009). *D-Day: The battle for Normandy*. Penguin.

Bjork, R. A., & Bjork, E. L. (2011). Making things hard on yourself, but in a good way: Creating desirable difficulties to enhance learning. In M. A. Gernsbacher, & J. R. Pomerantz (Eds.), *Psychology and the real world* (2nd ed.). Worth Publishers.

Brodie, R. (1995). *Virus of the mind: The new science of the meme*. Integral Press.

Dueck, M. (2014). *Grading smarter not harder: Assessment strategies that motivate kids and help them learn*. ASCD.

Dueck, M. (2021). *Giving students a say: Smarter assessment practices to empower and engage*. Association for Supervision & Curriculum Development (ASCD).

Dueck, M. (2024, March 21–23). Ch-Ch-Ch-Changes 2024. *Opening keynote presented at the 2024 EARCOS Educators Conference*, Shangri-La Hotel, Bangkok.

Guskey, T. (2023). *Engaging parents and families in grading reforms*. Corwin.

Kuhn, T. S. (1962). *The structure of scientific revolutions*. University of Chicago Press.

Microsoft Copilot. (2024, July 16). What is meant by a paradigm shift [AI-generated response]. OpenAI. https://copilot.microsoft.com/

Nikolopoulou, K. (2022). *What is confirmation bias?* Scribbr. https://www.scribbr.com/research-bias/confirmation-bias/

O'Reilly, L. (n.d.). *Revised Bloom's taxonomy table for auditing assessment practices.* [Unpublished document].

Origbo, T. (2017). The origins of "disagree and commit" in leadership strategies. *Harvard Business Review.*

Phan, H. P., & Ngu, B. H. (2021). A case for cognitive entrenchment: To achieve optimal best, taking into account the importance of perceived optimal efficiency and cognitive load imposition. *Frontiers in Psychology, 12,* 662898. https://doi.org/10.3389/fpsyg.2021.662898] (https://doi.org/10.3389/fpsyg.2021.662898

Richardson, J. W., Bathon, J., & McLeod, S. (2021). *Leadership for deeper learning: Facilitating school innovation and transformation* (1st ed.). Routledge.

Rowland, D., & Pivcevic, P. (2022). *The leadership book: A guide to effective decision-making and change management.* Pearson.

Wiliam, D. (2018). *Embedded formative assessment* (2nd ed.). Solution Tree.

Wilson, R. C., Shenhav, A., & Straccia, M., et al. (2019). The eighty-five percent rule for optimal learning. *Nature Communications, 10,* 4646. https://doi.org/10.1038/s41467-019-12552-4

10 Leading for a Flourishing Society

Kam Chohan and Michael Johnston

Understanding the Bigger Context: A World of Complexity

Multiple generations have had the sinking feeling that humanity is at its worst. How do you suppose students were feeling in 1945 as they witnessed two atomic bombs being dropped devastating hundreds of thousands of lives? As authors we can personally remember living in fear as a middle school student thinking a bomb was going to be dropped in Canada as we practiced duck and cover in the 1970s. When "We Are the World" came out in the 1980s, people felt paralyzed to help the millions of kids their age who didn't even have access to basic needs. We remember thinking how can this be so? Our outlook on the state of the world has a tremendous amount to do with how we view our own ability to make positive change whether it be at a micro or macro level.

Throughout history, every generation has felt that the challenges of their time are uniquely overwhelming. From the devastation of World War II to the fear of nuclear attacks during the Cold War, to the widespread hunger and inequality highlighted in the 1980s, these feelings of despair are not new. What has changed is how we interact with and perceive the world's complexity. Today, instant access to global news via technology gives us a heightened awareness of crises, yet it also offers unprecedented opportunities to engage, connect, and create change.

The world has always been complex; it comes down to how we interact, view, absorb, and embrace that complexity that really matters. Human behavior stays the same throughout world history, it is the technology that changes. Humans repeat the mistakes of the past over and over but our access to this information has changed drastically over time due to technology. In North America in the 1980s, you would not have heard about a missing child in another state, province, or country. There were no 24-hour news channels, never mind access to any news story at the tip of our fingers on a mini-computer that is always connected. People could not access a network of millions of people around the world to institute large-scale change. Now we do, as witnessed by the Arab Spring in 2010. The perception that things are more complex and beyond our reach is a matter of how we approach interconnectivity and ideally embrace complexity to understand this ever-connected world of systems embedded in systems embedded in systems. Education can play a major role in preparing generations of students who not only embrace complexity but also have the desire and skills to contribute to their community and beyond. What role does a school leader play in making sure this can be an outcome?

Shouldn't school be the place students learn how to go from caring about creating change to being able to do so in impactful ways? Students learn about these critical issues throughout the school day but often are not allocated the time, tools, and support needed to tackle them in meaningful ways. Whether it is a club, a class, or a personal passion project, students have the capacity and desire to create a better future; all we need to do in schools is create the time, teach the tools, mentor, and step out of the way. As leaders, we play an integral role in making sure this is a reality.

As educators, we must acknowledge this complexity and embrace it, rather than be overwhelmed by it. The rapid evolution of technology has created an interconnected world where information is readily available, but it has also made it easier to feel powerless in the face of global challenges. Yet, education can empower students to navigate and shape this world. Schools should not just teach about problems; they should equip students with the tools, mindset, and confidence to take meaningful action. Leaders in education play a pivotal role in ensuring that students transition from simply caring about issues to being able to address them in impactful ways.

The Myth of Choosing between Academics and Authentic Learning

There is a perception in schools that we must choose between strong academic outcomes or authentic learning experiences that matter. This is not true. Academic outcomes improve when we foster deep thinking and action-oriented learning. The question most widely asked is about sacrificing academic results by learning in a different way. The two-year *Knowledge in Action Efficacy Study* (Rosefsky, 2021) aimed to find out if using a Project Based Learning (PBL) approach could both give a deeper conceptual understanding and produce good results on external assessments for Advanced Placement (AP). Their findings showed equal and, in most cases, better results on the AP exams for students engaged in this approach. In some cases, students performed significantly better, especially those with more diverse learning needs. At least 80% of the students in the study stated the greatest value was the ability to apply what they have learned to their lives outside the classroom.

Guiding Staff through a Mindset Shift

Often what is in our control when planning learning engagements is more than we perceive. From the macro choices we make in structuring the schedule to the micro choices of the teachers' daily lesson plans, there is so much more in our control than we think. Why don't more schools foster an approach to learning that allows students to embrace complexity and take authentic action on issues they are passionate about? Many of the barriers come down to the perception that academic rigor will be sacrificed if we allow students to dig into the messy, complex issues that matter to them. Rigor itself is a loaded word that is often misinterpreted and misused. Rigor comes from the word rigid which implies inflexibility and hardship. In this ever-changing and adaptive world that we live in, is this really the goal? Could we not be aiming for human flourishing instead, with vigorous and healthy growth? It does not have to be a choice between content or process, it's concept and action through authentic process and reflection that we can aim for.

Having students dig into complexity and act on an issue is not more work, it's just different work. It is different work that needs to be championed by leaders from the school vision to the professional development required to support teachers to operationalize the plan. A school leader's responsibility is to guide communities through a process to ensure "the why" of the school is aspirational and meaningful. Imagine a world where every school was working towards serving others and the planet. The collective impact would be tremendous.

An example is from St. Joseph's Institute International in Singapore where the vision simply reads: *Learn, Inspire, Serve*. Schools around the world review their mission and vision on a regular cycle. Is yours aspirational, clear, and purpose-driven? Once a vision is clearly articulated, a leader's job is to help the community shape a strategy that communicates the importance of this work. A school can go from providing authentic opportunities in some places because those passionate teachers know what and how to guide students to a culture of service where it just becomes what we do, day in and day out.

Changing ingrained beliefs about academic rigor requires a strategic, multi-layered approach. School leaders must act as facilitators, creating conditions for teachers to see, experience, and believe in the value of authentic learning. Below are practical strategies to help shift staff mindsets:

Redefining Rigor and Academic Excellence

Many educators equate rigor with traditional methods such as rote memorization, heavy workloads, and standardized assessments. However, rigor should instead reflect deep, meaningful engagement with content, critical thinking, and the ability to apply knowledge in real-world contexts (Blackburn, 2018).

Practical Application

Using examples from research (e.g., Wagner, 2008) to show that rigor is about depth of learning rather than difficulty of tasks, encourage teachers to reflect on the most meaningful learning experiences in their own lives—chances are, they were authentic and relevant.

Analyze current practices: Have teachers audit their lesson plans to identify tasks that promote surface level knowledge versus those that encourage deep understanding and application.

Develop a shared definition of rigor: Facilitate a collaborative session where staff define what rigor means in the context of their school. Encourage them to focus on cognitive engagement, problem-solving, and student agency rather than traditional difficulty measures.

Modeling Authentic Learning through Professional Development

School leaders must give teachers firsthand experiences with authentic learning to shift their perceptions. Experiencing project-based learning (PBL), design thinking, and real-world problem-solving can help educators understand the benefits.

Practical Application

Engage teachers in project-based learning: Run a PBL experience during professional development, where teachers tackle a real-world issue at the school (e.g., redesigning learning spaces, improving student engagement). Through this, they can see the complexity, relevance, and academic rigor of the approach.

Use lesson study protocols: Implement cycles where teachers design, observe, and reflect on lessons that integrate authentic learning elements (Lewis et al., 2006).

Visit model schools: Arrange school visits or virtual meetings with institutions that have successfully integrated authentic learning without sacrificing academic excellence.

Demonstrating the Impact with Research and Data

Teachers are more likely to embrace change when they see evidence that it benefits students. Providing research-based data on the impact of authentic learning can help alleviate concerns.

Practical Application

Present research findings: Share studies such as the Knowledge in Action study (Rosefsky, 2021), which found that students in Pleased AP courses performed as well or better on standardized tests while demonstrating deeper conceptual understanding.

Showcase student work: Create a portfolio of student projects that align with academic standards, highlighting both process and outcomes.

Use student and teacher testimonials: Gather reflections from educators and students who have participated in authentic learning, emphasizing the impact on engagement, comprehension, and retention.

Aligning Assessment Practices with Authentic Learning

One of the biggest concerns educators have is how to assess learning in nontraditional ways. School leaders must help teachers explore and implement alternative assessment strategies that maintain rigor while supporting authentic learning.

Practical Application

Introduce performance based assessments: Support teachers in developing rubrics for presentations, portfolios, and interdisciplinary projects that align with learning objectives (Wiggins, 1998).

Use competency-based grading: Shift from traditional grading to mastery based assessment, where students demonstrate understanding through real-world applications (Guskey, 2019).

Host public exhibitions of learning: Encourage students to present their projects to authentic audiences, such as industry professionals or community members. Seeing students confidently articulate their learning can help shift teacher mindsets.

Providing Structural Support for Authentic Learning

Mindset shifts require systemic changes to sustain new approaches. Leaders must ensure that school structures—such as scheduling, collaboration time, and policies—support the integration of authentic learning.

Practical Application

Reconfigure schedules to allow for interdisciplinary work: Implement flexible scheduling to create longer blocks for deep inquiry and project-based work (Kallick & Zmuda, 2017).

Build professional learning communities (PLCs): Establish PLCs where teachers collaboratively design, implement, and reflect on authentic learning experiences (DuFour & Eaker, 1998).

Encourage community partnerships: Facilitate connections between teachers and local businesses, organizations, and experts to create realworld learning opportunities for students.

Bringing It All Together

Shifting from a content driven, standardized assessment culture to one that embraces authentic learning requires leadership, intentionality, and support. By redefining rigor, providing professional development, using research to build confidence, aligning assessments, and structuring schools to support real-world learning, school leaders can create an environment where deep learning and academic excellence coexist. The future of education depends on preparing students to think critically, solve real-world problems, and apply knowledge in meaningful ways—without sacrificing the academic skills they need to succeed.

The Power of Connection and Belonging in Learning

A student's ability to flourish is deeply connected to their sense of belonging. Until students feel valued and included their ability to learn and grow remains limited. Schools play a crucial role in creating environments where students not only gain knowledge but also discover their identity and place in the world. We can't underestimate the power of simple acts like encouraging students to see things from someone else's perspective or to lend a helping hand. Exercises like these teach empathy in a way that textbooks can't. And when students learn to walk in someone else's shoes, they not only grow as individuals but also make their communities stronger. Until we feel a sense of belonging can we really learn and flourish? It's about more than just building knowledge; it's about creating a sense of connection—not only with their peers but also with the wider community and, ultimately, with themselves. Team projects, community service, and respectful dialoguing within the school can make a huge difference. When students feel valued and included, they begin to see themselves as part of something bigger, which can be life changing.

> ## Reflections on Human Flourishing: The Core of Education
> *Kam Chohan, Executive Director, ECIS*
>
> Human flourishing is something I have often thought about and attended many seminars, lectures, and discussions on. For me, it is a state of optimal functioning in all aspects of a person's life. It's more than just being happy—it involves developing a sense of purpose, life satisfaction, and good mental, physical, and social health. Flourishing is also a life of service and defines a life well lived.
>
> When I first decided to become an educator, I knew it was my purpose. As a child, I often played at being a teacher, but due to a lack of representation in my own school life—I never had a teacher of color during my education—I never believed it was an option for me. Now, after many years in education, a large part of my human flourishing has been dedicating my life to teaching and learning.

Education is a transformative tool that cultivates essential skills, values, and mindsets necessary for individuals to lead fulfilling, meaningful lives. Education focuses on holistic development, emphasizing well-being, character, relational skills, and ecological responsibility over traditional academic metrics. That's the kind of education that really sticks with people, long after they've left the classroom. Schools such as the Ibiza Project focus on well-being and flourishing, recognizing that education should be about more than preparing students for jobs or exams. Human flourishing is about more than preparing them for jobs or exams; it's about giving students the tools to navigate the ups and downs of life with confidence, compassion, and resilience.

Service as a Way of Being

Well-being is on every school's strategic plan and to achieve this we really need to ensure we provide opportunities for all stakeholders to engage in serving others and our planet. The impact on our well-being is profound when we do good for others. These kinds of experiences keep us well, increase happiness, and give us greater purpose in this complex world. Research shows that engaging in acts of service increases happiness, reduces stress, and fosters a sense of purpose (Lyubomirsky et al., 2005). Neuroscientific studies, such as those conducted by Serve Cerebral, highlight how serving others activates reward centers in the brain, leading to longterm benefits in emotional resilience and mental health. Leaders can make this part of the core of work rather than a peripheral action. Serving others and the planet does not have to be something extra or a hobby; it can fundamentally become a driving force in our lives for wellbeing far past our formal schooling experience. School leaders need to ensure that the adults in the organization are motivated and professionally prepared to support these kinds of opportunities for all ages of students.

Integrating Service into School Culture

To embed service as a core value, schools must make structural and cultural shifts that encourage and sustain engagement. Service learning, mentorship programs, and real-world projects help students connect their education to a larger purpose. When students see the tangible impact of their learning, they develop a sense of agency and responsibility. For example, initiatives where students provide aid to marginalized communities or run business projects that lead to employment opportunities show that learning can extend beyond the classroom and create real change. Research indicates that students involved in service learning develop stronger leadership skills, increased empathy, and a greater sense of civic responsibility (Eyler & Giles, 1999).

As school leaders, we have experienced the transformation these approaches can have on all stakeholders. Senior leaders can impact the outcomes systematically for student learning, school operations, teacher development, parent engagement, local connections, and global impact. School leaders can foster the same skills and approaches in teachers and students to tackle local and global issues. It is a daunting but exciting charge we have as leaders, but the outcomes for learning and for our planet are worth the time invested. Consider these opportunities for deepening the value of service across a school.

Embedding Service Learning into the Curriculum

Embedding service learning into the curriculum transforms it from an occasional extracurricular activity into a meaningful and sustained part of students' academic experiences. When service learning is seamlessly integrated into daily instruction, it enhances both academic engagement and personal growth by providing students with authentic opportunities to apply their knowledge in ways that address real-world challenges.

The key to effective integration is aligning service projects with specific academic objectives, ensuring that students see clear connections between their classroom learning and their contributions to the community. This alignment allows students to deepen their understanding of subject matter while developing critical thinking, problem-solving, and collaboration skills. For example, a science class studying environmental sustainability might partner with a local organization to analyze water quality in nearby streams, while a history class exploring social movements might create an oral history project that amplifies the voices of underrepresented community members.

Beyond reinforcing academic concepts, embedding service learning fosters a sense of purpose, civic responsibility, and empathy in students. When they witness firsthand how their learning can make a tangible impact, they become more engaged and motivated learners. Additionally, integrating service learning into the curriculum encourages interdisciplinary collaboration among teachers, strengthens school-community partnerships, and supports the development of well-rounded, socially conscious individuals.

By making service learning a natural and intentional part of the educational experience, schools empower students not only to master academic content but also to become active, informed, and compassionate contributors to society.

Reflections on Service Learning

Kam Chohan, Executive Director, ECIS

I've seen firsthand how service learning can ignite something incredible in students. There's a moment when students step out of the classroom and realize that what they've been learning has real-world value—that it can make a tangible difference. During my time as a teacher, I ran several modules that were project based. One group of my students ran an event for a business module, and one of the students gained a summer job from one of the organizations they worked with. At Educational Collaborative of International Schools (ECIS) we provided a university scholarship for a student who had set up an initiative in Athens, where twice a week, students and staff provided conversation, food, blankets, and other essentials to the unhoused population. Though that student left the school five years ago, the initiative continues. These experiences give students a sense of responsibility and a connection people who may not be in their schools and their daily environments. We hope they start to see themselves as agents of change, with a sense of agency. But it doesn't stop there. These kinds of activities also help students build skills that will serve them for life. Teamwork, problem-solving, empathy—these are things you can't learn from a textbook alone. Working on real-world projects teaches students how to communicate, collaborate, and think creatively. They begin to understand the value of listening to different perspectives and working toward a common goal. And perhaps most importantly, they learn that their actions, no matter how small, can have a ripple effect on the world around them.

Strengthening Community Partnerships

Sustained, impactful service projects thrive on strong, reciprocal relationships between schools and community organizations. By establishing partnerships with local nonprofits, businesses, and governmental agencies, schools can create opportunities for students to engage in meaningful, real-world work that extends beyond the classroom. These collaborations not only enrich student learning but also provide tangible benefits to the community, fostering a culture of shared responsibility and mutual growth.

Effective community partnerships are built on clear communication, shared goals, and a commitment to long-term engagement. Schools should take the time to understand the needs and priorities of local organizations, ensuring that service projects align with real challenges while also supporting students' academic and personal development. For example, a partnership with a local food bank could integrate lessons on nutrition, economics, and social justice, while collaboration with a city planning department might involve students in sustainability initiatives or urban development projects.

Engaging with professionals and community leaders exposes students to different career paths and real-world problem-solving experiences. These partnerships can also lead to mentorship opportunities, internships, and pathways for students to remain involved in civic engagement beyond their school years. Additionally, involving students in community-based projects nurtures essential skills such as collaboration, adaptability, and cultural awareness—qualities that prepare them to be responsible, engaged citizens.

By investing in strong community relationships, schools ensure that service learning is not just an isolated experience but an ongoing, embedded practice that fosters deep connections between students and the world around them. When schools and community organizations work together as true partners, both benefit from the shared expertise, resources, and commitment to creating positive change.

The Lifelong Impact of Service

Ultimately, fostering this sense of connection and purpose doesn't just benefit the students; it enriches the entire community. When students feel valued and supported, they bring that positivity back into their relationships present and future. They become role models for others, showing what's possible when we work together for a common good. And as educators, seeing this transformation happen is one of the most fulfilling parts of the work we do. It always reminds us why we started this journey in the first place and fills us with hope for the future.

As educators, we have the privilege of shaping not just the minds but the hearts of our students. It's a big responsibility, but it's also an incredible opportunity. By focusing on human flourishing—on helping students develop purpose, resilience, and a sense of connection—we can guide them toward lives that are not just successful, but meaningful. Education is about so much more than academics. It's about preparing students to face the world with courage and compassion, to build relationships, and to leave the planet a little better than they found it.

Leading for Flourishing and Systemic Impact

There appears to be a will on the part of many K–12 educators to facilitate the kind of learning that gives greater purpose and growth of skills and character. What is needed is to find the way. Traditional content-driven curriculum and assessing students on memory recall in standardized ways is not what today's learner needs. A more connected, student-driven, and emergent curriculum will create generations of deep thinkers and systemic practitioners with strong values and character.

For education to truly support flourishing, it needs to happen in environments where everyone feels safe, included, and valued. A space that respects diversity and actively works toward equity can make a world of difference for students. At ECIS, this is something woven into every part of training because we know how powerful it can be. Schools can create these kinds of spaces by implementing policies that actively combat bullying, promoting cultural understanding, and making sure students have access to mental and emotional support when they need it. Inclusive education isn't just beneficial for some students—it's something that enriches everyone. It helps broaden perspectives and creates a deeper understanding of the world we live in.

When schools commit to inclusivity fully and truly, they give students the chance to develop empathy and recognize that the world is filled with all kinds of people, each with their own stories and perspectives. For students in international communities, this might feel like second nature because they're often surrounded by people from different cultural and linguistic backgrounds. But for many others, this kind of exposure isn't a given. That's why it's so important to intentionally create opportunities for students to learn about and connect with people who are different from them. Helping students understand other cultures doesn't just prepare them for the world; it helps them be better, more compassionate contributors to it.

Creating inclusive spaces in schools can promote collaboration and mutual respect. These spaces give students a sense of belonging, which is so essential to their growth. When students feel like they're part of a supportive and welcoming community, they're more likely to take risks, engage in learning, and thrive in ways that go beyond academics. Inclusive school cultures don't just make learning environments better—they prepare students to succeed in an interconnected world. By valuing diversity and fostering respect, schools can give students the tools they need to flourish, no matter where life takes them.

Education is one of the most powerful tools we have for helping students flourish. It equips them with the skills and perspectives they need to engage meaningfully with the world and to care deeply about both society and the environment. Harvard Human Flourishing Program (n.d.) states that reimagining education as a space where flourishing isn't just a side goal—it's the focus, and to do that, it takes teamwork. Educators, students, parents, and communities all need to come together to create environments where flourishing is at the heart of everything we do.

As educators, we have a chance to take this even further. Our role isn't just to teach but to inspire students to dive deeper into what excites them. Whether it's encouraging students to start an after-school group, participate in a club, or even launch a community project, these activities give students ownership of their learning and help them discover their strengths. Imagine schools hosting events where students and teachers come together to brainstorm new initiatives. It's a simple way to foster leadership and remind students that their ideas matter.

Student Voices Lead the Way

One way to nurture this is by encouraging students to find their voices and work on the things they're passionate about. The world we live in today offers so many unique opportunities that didn't exist even a decade ago. For example, I've seen how activities like Esports can bring students together in ways that go beyond the traditional classroom. These leagues allow students to connect with peers from different places, breaking down barriers and creating new opportunities for collaboration and growth. It's amazing to see how something like gaming can help students build friendships, share their interests, and even involve the wider school community, including parents. These kinds of ventures not only spark joy but also give students a sense of purpose and belonging. We even had an Esports demonstration at our most recent Leadership Conference, in which students from ACS International School in partnership with DAIGON Esports played a game of Rocket League, which was engaging and educational for all 450 delegates. Afterwards, they hosted a panel where students who played in the match were able to talk about the personal benefits and flourishing that Esports has allowed them to have in within their school communities.

A Call to Action: Education as a Force for Good

By leading with kindness and support, educators can help students see the bigger picture: that flourishing is about much more than individual success. It's about making a positive impact on the people and places around us. When we help students thrive—not just academically, but as compassionate and well-rounded individuals—we're not just shaping their future. We're shaping a better world.

As we reflect on the journey of exploring human flourishing through education, we are reminded of the incredible power schools must shape not just individuals but entire communities. Education is so much more than a means to academic success—it's a way to nurture purpose, resilience, and connection in our students. By embracing a holistic approach to teaching, one that prioritizes well-being, empathy, and inclusion, we create the foundation for lives that are both meaningful and impactful (VanderWeele, 2017). By shifting our focus from rigid structures to meaningful, purpose-driven learning, we can transform education into a powerful tool for societal progress. Students deserve an education that prepares them not just for exams but for life. And as educators, we have both the opportunity and the responsibility to make this vision a reality.

As educators, our responsibility is to model the values we hope to instill curiosity, kindness, and a commitment to the well-being of others.

It's about showing students that they are part of something bigger, that their voices matter, and that their actions can make a difference. When we lead with this mindset, we aren't just teaching lessons; we're helping students build lives of purpose and joy. Ultimately, the goal of education is not just to prepare students for the future but to inspire them to shape it. Together, we can create a world where flourishing isn't just an ideal—it's a reality for all. And that, for me, is the greatest purpose of this journey as an educator.

Our children need it. They deserve it. Our future depends on it.

References

Blackburn, B. (2018). *Rigor is not a four-letter word*. Routledge.

DuFour, R., & Eaker, R. (1998). *Professional learning communities at work: Best Practices for enhancing student achievement*. Solution Tree.

Eyler, J., & Giles, D. E. (1999). *Where's the learning in service-learning?* Jossey-bass.

Guskey, T. R. (2019). *On your mark: Challenging the conventions of grading and reporting*. Solution Tree Press.

Harvard Human Flourishing Program (n.d.). *Flourishing Network*. Harvard University. https://hfh.fas.harvard.edu/flourishing-network-HFH

Kallick, B., & Zmuda, A. (2017). *Students at the center: Personalized learning with habits of mind*. ASCD.

Lewis, C., Perry, R., & Murata, A. (2006). How should research contribute to instructional improvement? *The Teachers College Record, 108*(12), 2407–2422.

Lyubomirsky, S., Sheldon, K. M., & Schkade, D. (2005). Pursuing happiness: The architecture of sustainable change. *Review of General Psychology, 9*(2), 111–131.

Rosefsky, F. (2021). *Knowledge in action efficacy study: Evaluating project-based learning in AP courses*. National Center for Learning and Evaluation.

VanderWeele, T. J. (2017). On the promotion of human flourishing. *Proceedings of the National Academy of Sciences of the United States of America, 114*(31), 8148–8156. https://doi.org/10.1073/pnas.1702996114

Wagner, T. (2008). *The global achievement gap: Why even our best schools don't teach the new survival skills our children need—And what we can do about it*. Basic Books.

Wiggins, G. (1998). *Educative assessment: Designing assessments to inform and improve student performance*. Jossey-Bass.

11
Leading with Resilience

Bloodine Barthelus and Shauna Hobbs-Beckley

Leadership development in education predominantly occurs on the job. While many leaders complete leadership training and earn additional certifications, they often find a lack of ongoing training tailored to the unique challenges and demands of their profession. When such training is available, it typically focuses on the mechanics and logistics of leadership—what is required for student success—rather than addressing the personal, emotional, and relational aspects of the role.

Yet, the reality is that educational leadership demands resilience and a high degree of emotional intelligence to navigate the profession's complexities. Leaders must consistently demonstrate social and emotional competence to meet the demands of a VUCA (volatile, uncertain, complex, ambiguous) environment, requiring nothing less than resilient leadership.

In this chapter, we define resilience as "the ability to recover from or adjust easily to misfortune or change" (Merriam-Webster, 2024). We explore the essential components necessary to cultivate resilience, beginning with the importance of leaders embracing their humanity through authenticity and honoring the humanity of others by demonstrating empathy. By fostering genuine connections, leaders can enhance their insight and effectiveness.

We also aim to humanize leadership by redefining success, emphasizing the value of learning from missteps, and treating failures as opportunities to model humility. This approach encourages leaders to adopt a learner's mindset, engaging with their work and life through curiosity and wonder.

Finally, we conclude the chapter with practical strategies to help leaders sustain and model resilience over the long term in ways that support both their personal and professional well-being.

DOI: 10.4324/9781003581451-11

Resilient Leadership: Embodying Emotional Intelligence and Authenticity

Resilience in leadership is rooted in authenticity and emotional intelligence—a skill set that goes beyond understanding and managing your own emotions to include recognizing and responding to the emotions of others. Emotional intelligence serves as the bridge between your authentic self and your leadership presence, enabling you to lead with integrity and genuine connection. Leading authentically means embracing and integrating your identity, values, and lived experiences into every aspect of your role. It's about showing up fully, with the vulnerability to be real and the courage to connect meaningfully with your team.

Leaders with high emotional intelligence are better equipped to make balanced, informed decisions, even under pressure. Their ability to stay composed helps them focus on long-term goals while managing immediate challenges. More importantly, this emotional grounding enables them to empathize with team members, consider diverse perspectives, and make inclusive decisions that reflect the collective needs of the team. Emotional intelligence, when rooted in an authentic connection to one's identity, becomes a powerful tool for fostering trust and building resilient organizations.

Daniel Goleman, a leading expert on emotional intelligence, identifies five key components: self-awareness, self-regulation, motivation, empathy, and social skills (Goleman, 2000). Among these, self-awareness serves as the cornerstone of resilient leadership. For leaders, self-awareness isn't just about understanding emotions in isolation; it's about recognizing how your identity—your experiences, beliefs, and values—shapes your actions and decisions. Leaders who embrace their identity and bring their whole selves to their roles are better positioned to connect with others authentically. This self-knowledge enables leaders to leverage their strengths, address areas for growth, and model transparency and trust.

By weaving self-awareness into their leadership practice, leaders can embrace their biases and limitations, creating space for collaboration and feedback that fosters humility and openness. This approach strengthens team dynamics and nurtures a culture of inclusivity. When leaders openly share how their identity informs their perspective, they model a level of authenticity that inspires others to do the same. This creates an environment where team members feel valued and empowered, contributing to a shared sense of purpose. Ultimately, this collective authenticity and trust lay the foundation for resilience—not just for the leader, but for the entire organization.

Motivation is another critical pillar of emotional intelligence, closely tied to identity and authenticity. Leaders driven by a clear sense of purpose—one that aligns with their values and personal mission—demonstrate resilience even in the face of adversity. When leaders are grounded in their identity, their motivation is not just about achieving external goals but also about fulfilling an internal commitment to their values and beliefs. This intrinsic drive inspires determination and optimism, even during challenging times.

Authenticity amplifies this motivation. When leaders lead from a place of genuine self-expression, their passion and commitment become visible and contagious. Team members are inspired to match that energy, knowing they are part of a shared mission that feels both meaningful and attainable. This alignment between a leader's identity and their leadership style creates a ripple effect, elevating morale and fostering collective resilience.

Bringing Your Whole Self: The Catalyst for Resilient Leadership

Bringing your whole self to work is not just a feel-good concept; it is a powerful tool for resilience. Authentic leadership requires that you embrace your identity, values, and vulnerabilities without reservation. When you bring your whole self to work, you establish a foundation of honesty and openness that builds trust and creates meaningful connections. This authenticity strengthens relationships and fuels motivation, enabling leaders to navigate complexity and adversity with increased perseverance.

A Case Study: Shauna Hobbs-Beckley's Leadership Journey

I have often found that when leaders are not fully authentic, they spend significant energy maintaining facades. This energy could be better used to solve problems, innovate, or connect with their teams. Authenticity provides clarity, which is crucial during difficult moments. It enables you to focus on what truly matters and make decisions aligned with your values, even when faced with external pressures.

My own journey toward authenticity as a leader was fraught with challenges. During my first year as a principal in a conservative southern state, I found myself hiding a significant part of my identity—my same-sex relationship. I was in a committed partnership with someone in a prominent profession, and together, we decided to start a family. While I was thrilled about this upcoming chapter, I felt unable to share my joy openly with my colleagues or the community. The societal stigma surrounding same-sex relationships in that environment fueled my fear of judgment and discrimination, keeping me silent. This secrecy took a toll on my energy and confidence, forcing me to compartmentalize my personal and professional lives in a way that was both exhausting and unsustainable.

The turning point came when I announced my pregnancy during an end-year evaluation. Despite being praised as one of the district's most effective principals just 24 hours earlier, I was called into the superintendent's office. I was told I should resign or take a leave of absence. The community's response was swift and harsh, with petitions circulating for my removal—often led by people who had never met me. In that moment, I realized that hiding who I was had not protected me; it isolated me. I decided to lead from a place of authenticity, embracing my whole self, regardless of the consequences.

When I finally allowed myself to be fully seen, something unexpected happened: my faculty rallied around me. Their support reinforced that authenticity builds trust, even in challenging environments. By embracing my full identity in leadership, I created deeper connections with my team, fostering an environment of mutual respect and resilience. This authenticity motivated me to persevere through a trying time and ultimately made me a more effective leader.

That period tested every ounce of resilience I had. Ultimately, I made a choice: I would not hide anymore. I decided that my identity and personal life were not liabilities but integral parts of who I was as a leader. I stood firm, and to my surprise, my faculty stood with me. Their support helped me remain in my position and taught me an invaluable lesson about authenticity. By shielding others from my personal truths, I shielded myself from genuine connection. From that point forward, I promised to show up as my full self in my leadership role, not the curated version I thought others wanted to see.

This decision transformed my leadership. I became more present, empathetic, and transparent. I found that authentic leadership fostered deeper trust and collaboration within my teams. Resilient leadership starts with bringing your whole self to the table—and it's a commitment that liberates not just the leader but everyone they work with.

How Authenticity Fuels Motivation and Resilience

When leaders bring their whole selves to their roles, they create a deeper connection to their work. This connection strengthens their motivation, which is essential for navigating complexity and adversity. Motivation derived from authenticity has a ripple effect: it inspires teams to engage more fully, invest in their work, and persevere through challenges.

Consider this: when you lead authentically, your team sees someone who owns their story or admits vulnerabilities. This honesty fosters a sense of psychological safety, where team members feel empowered to bring their authentic selves to the table as well. In this environment, creativity thrives, and people are more willing to take risks and innovate, knowing their contributions are valued.

Authenticity also equips leaders with resilience to face challenges head-on. When your leadership is grounded in your identity and values, you have a clear compass guiding your decisions. This clarity becomes particularly valuable in moments of crisis or uncertainty, enabling you to respond decisively while staying true to your principles. Moreover, leading with authenticity eliminates the mental strain of maintaining a facade, freeing up cognitive and emotional resources to focus on problem-solving and strategic thinking.

Practical Strategies for Cultivating Authentic Leadership

Authentic leadership is not a destination; it is a journey that requires intentionality, reflection, and practice. It is about aligning who you are with how you lead—integrating your values, experiences, and beliefs into your actions and decisions. Authentic leaders inspire trust, foster meaningful connections, and create environments where their teams feel empowered to thrive.

The following strategies provide actionable steps to help you cultivate authenticity in your leadership. From self-reflection to fostering psychological safety, each strategy is designed to strengthen your ability to lead with integrity, empathy, and purpose. By embracing these practices, you not only enhance your own effectiveness as a leader but also contribute to a culture of trust, resilience, and inclusivity within your organization. Leadership rooted in authenticity isn't just about what you do—it's about who you are and the impact you have on those around you.

Embrace self-reflection: Authentic leadership starts with knowing yourself. Take time to reflect on your values, beliefs, strengths, and areas for growth. Use tools like journaling, personality assessments (e.g., Myers-Briggs or StrengthsFinder), or feedback from trusted colleagues to deepen your self-awareness. Ask yourself: Am I leading in alignment with my values? And how can I better integrate who I am into how I lead?

Align actions with values: Leadership decisions should reflect your core values. When facing complex situations, take a moment to evaluate whether your actions align with what you believe is right and just. This alignment not only reinforces your confidence and clarity as a leader but also serves as a moral compass during uncertainty. By leading in alignment with your values, you cultivate a sense of authenticity that strengthens your ability to make consistent, principled decisions. This, in turn, builds trust with your team, as they can clearly see your integrity and commitment to doing what is right.

Be transparent: Authentic leaders are open about their decisions, challenges, and thought processes. Share not only what you are doing but why you are doing it. Whether it's a challenging budget decision or a strategic shift, letting your team understand the rationale fosters trust and collaboration.

Share your story: Sharing parts of your personal journey can humanize your leadership and strengthen your connections. Be intentional about what you share, ensuring it is appropriate for your audience and relevant to the moment. For instance, sharing a time you overcame a professional setback can inspire resilience in your team.

Admit mistakes and model learning: Authentic leaders don't strive for perfection; they embrace growth. When you make a mistake, acknowledge it openly and share what you've learned. This strengthens your credibility and models a growth mindset for your team.

Seek feedback regularly: Authentic leaders are not afraid to ask, How am I doing? Create structured opportunities for your team to provide feedback—whether through one-on-one conversations, surveys, or anonymous suggestion boxes. Demonstrate that you value their feedback by acting on it whenever possible. When it's not feasible to act on the feedback provided, simply letting staff know what will be done instead and why fosters understanding and transparency. This approach reassures your team that their voices are heard and encourages a willingness to continue providing feedback in the future.

Practice empathy and active listening: Listening deeply and seeking to understand others' perspectives are hallmarks of authentic leadership. During conversations, focus entirely on the speaker—ask clarifying questions and validate their experiences. This fosters trust and shows that you care about their thoughts and feelings.

Set boundaries and model balance: Authentic leadership includes demonstrating that well-being matters. Be clear about your boundaries—whether it's family, self-care, or professional limits—and respect others' boundaries as well. Modeling this balance reinforces the idea that leaders are people first.

Cultivate psychological safety: Create an environment where your team feels safe to share ideas, take risks, and voice concerns without fear of judgment or retribution. Regularly check in with team members, encourage diverse viewpoints, and celebrate learning from mistakes.

Champion inclusiveness and equity: Authentic leaders recognize and value their team members' diverse identities, experiences, and perspectives. Actively work to amplify underrepresented voices, ensure equitable opportunities, and challenge biases—including your own. This demonstrates your commitment to fairness and strengthens trust.

Live your authenticity consistently: Being an authentic leader isn't a one-time choice; it's a daily practice. Show up as your true self in every meeting, decision, and interaction. Consistency builds trust and allows your team to understand and rely on your leadership style.

Engage in ongoing learning: Leadership evolves, and so should you. Commit to continuous personal and professional growth through books, podcasts, training, or peer mentoring. Authentic leaders demonstrate that learning never stops, inspiring their teams to do the same.

 ## Why These Strategies Matter

By implementing these strategies, you demonstrate to your team that leadership isn't about perfection; it's about showing up with integrity, vulnerability, and a commitment to growth. Authentic leadership inspires trust, deepens engagement, and ultimately builds a culture where individuals feel empowered to bring their whole selves to work. When leaders lead authentically, they create a ripple effect that fosters authenticity and resilience throughout their teams.

 ## Social and Emotional Intelligence: Leading with Empathy and Insight

In today's educational landscape, resilient leadership requires more than strong organizational skills or a strategic vision. It calls for a deep, nuanced understanding of social and emotional intelligence (SEI) as a foundation for empathetic, insightful leadership that can withstand the challenges of a VUCA environment—characterized by volatility, uncertainty, complexity, and ambiguity. Education leaders, perhaps more than ever, must cultivate a reflective and emotionally aware approach to their roles, honoring both their humanity and the humanity of those they lead.

One of the fundamental truths of leadership is navigating not only life's inevitable ups and downs but also understanding how these shifts impact both the leader and those they serve. Leaders often fall into the trap of believing that their position of authority requires them to always have answers at the ready, inspire others in the face of adversity, while maintaining an image of joy, optimism, and unshakable dedication, no matter the circumstances.

This idealized version of leadership is reinforced by the way we celebrate leaders—focusing on their moments of triumph, their "mountaintop" achievements, and their ability to overcome monumental challenges. While these stories are inspiring, they often leave current leaders questioning their own adequacy when they don't measure up to these polished portrayals. What's missing from these narratives is the full journey—the struggles, missteps, and learning moments that paved the way to greatness.

For every celebrated leader hailed as a role model, there's an untold story that doesn't fit into a brief, polished introduction. These sound bites, though inspiring, often obscure the deeper journey—the full climb of the mountain. Real leadership embraces the truth that mountains are rarely smooth, linear ascents. Instead, they are marked by landings and valleys that form the foundation necessary to support the peaks we aspire to reach.

It is in these valleys—these pauses and challenges—that social and emotional intelligence is forged. Through intentional personal development and learning, leaders have the opportunity to build character, confront their limitations, and choose time and again, whether to grow or remain stagnant. A decision to grow requires a focus on the development of social and emotional intelligence which allows leaders to navigate their role with insight and resilience.

Social and Emotional Intelligence for the Educational Leader

The Collaborative for Academic, Social, and Emotional Learning (CASEL) (n.d.) states that social and emotional learning is an integral part of human development and defines it as,

> ...the process through which all young people and adults acquire and apply the knowledge, skills, and attitudes to develop healthy identities, manage emotions and achieve personal and collective goals, feel and show empathy for others, establish and maintain supportive relationships, and make responsible and caring decisions (CASEL, n.d.).

The ability to perceive, understand, and manage emotions—both in oneself and in others—creates a stable foundation from which leaders can address the challenges and stresses that arise daily in their work. Leaders with high SEI can navigate complex interpersonal dynamics, make better decisions under pressure, and create environments where both students and staff feel understood and supported. Importantly, SEI helps leaders recognize their own limitations and stress signals, equipping them to take proactive steps to maintain their mental and emotional well-being. Michael Fullan, in *Leading in a Culture of Change*, stressed the importance of social and emotional intelligence well when he stated, "It should come as no surprise then that the most effective leaders are not the smartest in an IQ sense but are those who combine intellectual brilliance with emotional intelligence" (Fullan, 2001, p. 71).

Honoring One's Humanity to Lead with Clarity and Empathy

One of the most powerful aspects of SEI is the opportunity it gives leaders to honor their humanity. When educational leaders understand and manage their own emotions, they are better positioned to lead with clarity and empathy, offering a stabilizing presence to their school communities. Honoring one's humanity begins with self-awareness—a clear understanding of one's emotional triggers, motivators, strengths, and areas for growth. It is also an understanding of one's identity that supports a love and appreciation of self, and a willingness to continue to peel back one's layers with curiosity and wonder rather than judgment; to applaud when appropriate and adjust when required without defensiveness. It requires leaders to acknowledge their vulnerability, recognizing that emotions like anxiety, frustration, and even loneliness are a natural part of the leadership journey. By identifying and accepting these emotions, leaders can approach their roles from a place of compassion rather than from emotional reactivity leading to clearer thinking and a more supportive environment for everyone in the school community.

The leader who appreciates that leadership does not negate their humanity but augments it will be able to leverage authenticity to show up in a way that is liberating for themselves and for those they serve. It will allow them to serve with empathy as they are attuned to their own emotions and can more easily understand the emotions of others, offering support that is sensitive to their staff and students' unique challenges. In a world where reactivity is prevalent, an empathetic leader can sit with others in their pain and discomfort, fostering a culture of psychological safety, where team members feel valued, heard, and empowered to bring their full selves to work. This safety is essential for resilience, as it allows educators and leaders alike to adapt, innovate, and recover from setbacks together.

Leadership Growth through Personal Development and Self-Reflection

So, how does a leader faced with the ongoing challenges of leading in the global educational space ensure that they approach their role and their lives from a place of resilience? It begins with intention and one that is focused on ongoing growth. Leaders committed to their personal and professional development can better navigate complex challenges and sustain a positive impact over time. There is strength in accepting that even as a leader, there is always more to be learned and that no one, even the one tasked with steering the ship, knows everything about anything. This acceptance creates space for growth, fosters a willingness to challenge one's own assumptions and behaviors, honors one's humanity, and allows others to extend a level of grace and accountability that builds a community of learning and connection.

It is quite probable for leaders to engage in a myriad of personal and professional development opportunities and never shift in their approach and way of being. The critical element of change is self-reflection as it supports leaders to pause, assess, and learn from their experiences. Regular reflective practice allows leaders to examine both successes and failures, fostering greater insight into their decisions, actions, and relationships.

An excellent example of this came during a professional development session for school leaders focused on self-awareness. The facilitator used a metaphor to illustrate how others' perceptions of us might differ from how we see ourselves. One leader shared a story: each morning, he made a point to greet his staff as they arrived. However, as the day progressed and he became immersed in managing the school, he no longer saw a need to greet staff in the halls. Over time, he received feedback that staff found it rude when he walked past them without acknowledgement.

In that moment, the leader realized that while he was focused on the tasks at hand, maintaining a sense of humanity in his interactions throughout the day was critical for those under his leadership. This "aha" moment came as a direct result of his willingness to reflect on the feedback and apply the insights shared during the professional development session.

The leaders in that session grappled with the gap between their intentions and the unintended impact often communicated by their staff, families, or students. The discussion highlighted that growth through reflection lies in the space between intention and impact. For leaders striving to embody social and emotional intelligence, the key is to confront the discomfort of misunderstanding and actively explore the challenges and opportunities within that space. This willingness to reflect and unpack the misalignment is crucial for fostering growth and building stronger connections with those they serve.

Embracing Feedback as an Essential Tool for Insight and Growth

Feedback can be one of the most valuable resources for leaders seeking personal growth. By embracing constructive feedback, leaders gain a clearer understanding of how others perceive their actions and communication, allowing them to make adjustments that enhance their effectiveness. While receiving feedback can sometimes be uncomfortable, it is crucial for building resilience. Leaders who view feedback as an opportunity for growth are more likely to build stronger relationships with their teams and create a culture of continuous improvement within their schools.

To harness the full power of feedback, leaders can actively seek it out, soliciting input from trusted colleagues, mentors, and even staff members. This openness to feedback signals humility and a willingness to grow—qualities that reinforce a resilient mindset and promote a learning culture within the school.

Actionable Strategies for Cultivating Reflective Practice and Seeking Feedback

Feedback is a powerful tool for insight and growth. Leaders who seek and embrace feedback demonstrate humility and a commitment to improvement. Though it can be uncomfortable, feedback strengthens relationships and fosters a culture of learning.

Below are a few strategies that can maximize the benefits of feedback:

- **Establish a reflective routine**: Dedicate time to journal or record thoughts. Ask key questions like: *What went well? What way of being supported this success? What could improve? How did I handle challenges? Am I showing up as the type of leader that I choose to emulate?*
- **Engage in peer coaching**: Partner with another leader to share honest reflections and offer mutual support founded on empathy, accountability, and support.
- **Create a culture of feedback and responsiveness**: Use a variety of feedback tools such as anonymous surveys and 360-degree evaluations paired with a clear and transparent reflection process that highlights an appreciation and a responsiveness to feedback.
- **Build a support network**: Rely on mentors, colleagues, or coaches for honest, unbiased feedback and encouragement that is supportive of ongoing growth.

By embedding social and emotional intelligence, reflective practice, and a commitment to feedback into their leadership approach, educational leaders can build the resilience they need to lead with empathy, insight, and sustainability. In doing so, they not only achieve professional success but also find fulfillment and balance in their personal lives, sustaining their passion and well-being throughout their careers.

Redefining Success: Embracing Failure as a Learning and Innovation Tool

Psychological Safety: The Foundation of Resilient Teams

Resilient leadership is not just about the leader's ability to adapt and persevere; it's about cultivating those same qualities in others. This requires creating an environment where team members feel psychologically safe—a culture where they can take risks, voice concerns, and even fail without fear of humiliation or retribution. Without psychological safety, team members may feel hesitant to share ideas or feedback, leading to lack of innovation and creativity. Leaders can establish psychological safety by actively encouraging open communication and demonstrating empathy towards team members. This involves listening attentively, acknowledging diverse perspectives, and providing constructive feedback. Additionally, setting clear expectations and recognizing contributions can help build trust and confidence within the team. A leading scholar on the subject, reveals that teams with high levels of psychological safety are more innovative, adaptive, and effective (Edmondson, 1999). When people feel safe, they share ideas, experiment, and learn from failures. Conversely, in environments lacking psychological safety, individuals often hold back, stifling creativity and collaboration.

A Case Study: Shauna Hobbs-Beckley's Leadership Journey, *Continued*

Early in my tenure as a school leader, I noticed a troubling pattern among my staff. They were hesitant to propose bold ideas or admit that a strategy wasn't working. It wasn't that they lacked creativity or initiative; they feared failure—and the potential repercussions of admitting it. To address this, I focused on fostering a more open and supportive environment. I started by holding regular meetings where everyone was encouraged to share their thoughts and ideas without judgment. I also made a point to publicly acknowledge and celebrate efforts, even when they didn't lead to immediate success, reinforcing the message that learning from failure is a valuable part of growth. To break this cycle, I normalized failure as part of learning.

One of the ways I did this was by sharing my own professional missteps. During team meetings, I recounted times when my strategies fell flat, or I misjudged a situation. I didn't stop at the failure itself; I explained what I learned from it and how it shaped my approach moving forward. By sharing my own vulnerabilities, I demonstrated that even leaders are not infallible, fostering a culture where team members felt more comfortable to do the same. This transparency not only humanized my leadership but also strengthened the trust within the team. Embracing vulnerability as a leader helps to create an environment where everyone feels valued and empowered to contribute their best ideas. This transparency sent a clear message: mistakes are not just acceptable—they are essential for growth.

One memorable example that shaped my understanding of leadership involved my early tenure leading an international program where I lacked cultural experience. Initially, I presented my vision for what the program needed, unintentionally overlooking the unique needs and values of the school community. Stakeholders were hesitant to voice concerns or share ideas, reflecting a broader absence of psychological safety—a crucial element I had failed to cultivate.

As I reflected on this experience, I realized that my approach leaned heavily on generalized best practices rather than taking the time to understand the cultural context and priorities of those impacted. I learned that good leadership is not about having all the answers but about creating an environment where others feel safe to express their perspectives, knowing their voices will be valued.

While my proposed approach might have ultimately aligned with the community's needs, my failure to engage them in the process created unnecessary setbacks. Recognizing this misstep, I regrouped with the team, stepping back to let them lead the discussions and address the issues from their unique perspective. This shift not only resolved immediate challenges but also taught me the critical importance of honoring and incorporating cultural context into decision-making. By adapting my approach, the program flourished, serving as a powerful reminder that successful leadership requires listening, collaboration, and a willingness to evolve based on the needs of those you serve. This shift not only strengthened the program's impact but also deepened trust and engagement within the community. It highlighted the importance of leaders being attuned to the unique cultural context and priorities of their communities, ensuring that decisions align with shared values and aspirations.

The community later shared that this experience gave them the confidence to take risks in the future, knowing their voices would be valued regardless of the outcome. That's the power of psychological safety: creating an environment where individuals feel secure in expressing ideas, taking chances, and sharing concerns without fear of judgment or retribution. This trust fosters innovation, collaboration, and a stronger, more cohesive community.

Transparency in Leadership: A Case Study

Transparency, often considered a cornerstone of trust by leadership experts and practitioners alike, requires more than openness—it demands intentionality and inclusivity. It means providing clear communication about decisions, including the rationale behind them, and actively engaging stakeholders in the process. Yet, the urgency of leadership can sometimes cloud its execution.

A Case Study: Shauna Hobbs-Beckley's Leadership Journey, *Continued*

Early in my tenure at an international school, I faced the challenge of filling a critical leadership position quickly. While the process was thorough and ultimately brought forward a highly capable candidate, the speed of the decision left many feeling excluded from the process. This exclusion underscored the importance of balancing efficiency with the need to engage others meaningfully. Transparency in such moments isn't just about explaining what was done; it's about ensuring that people feel heard and valued, even when timelines are tight. Reflecting on this experience, I recognized that fostering trust through transparency requires proactive communication and intentional efforts to include the community, regardless of the constraints.

When the time came to hire for another leadership role, I knew the approach had to change. I acknowledged the previous process's lack of transparency and committed to a more inclusive, visible process. We partnered with an outside organization, International Schools Services (ISS), to manage the hiring process, ensuring impartiality. Department chairs conducted initial interviews, narrowing the pool to the top candidates, while board representatives handled the narrowing to the final selection of two.

Acknowledging past mistakes opened the door to meaningful dialogue. I said, "The process wasn't as inclusive as it could have been, and I want to ensure this one is better." That moment shifted the energy in the room. What could have been a contentious discussion became an opportunity for collaboration and improvement.

Resilient leaders are resilient not because they avoid mistakes but because they learn from them. Failure isn't the opposite of success; it's a prerequisite. Research on failing forward emphasizes that leaders who openly address their missteps foster a culture of learning and innovation (Maxwell, 2007). By modeling this, leaders demonstrate that setbacks are not dead ends but rather detours on the road to growth.

Practical Strategies for Fostering Psychological Safety

Model vulnerability: Share your own failures and what you learned from them. This signals to your team that mistakes are part of the process, not something to fear.

Create structured opportunities for risk-taking: Encourage staff to propose and test creative ideas but provide a framework for accountability. For example, after every brainstorming session, assign roles and establish timelines for follow-up.

Celebrate lessons learned: When a project doesn't proceed as planned, focus on what was gained rather than what was lost. Dedicate time during team meetings to reflecting on lessons learned from setbacks.

Provide clear expectations: Be clear about goals, roles, and expectations while allowing room for creativity, because as Brené Brown (2018) says, "Clear is kind." Clear guidance fosters trust and empowers teams to take risks and grow within a supportive framework.

Solicit feedback regularly: Create multiple channels for staff to share their thoughts and concerns, whether through anonymous surveys, one-to-one check-ins, or open forums.

By integrating these strategies into your leadership practice, you can build a resilient team capable of facing challenges head-on.

Sustaining Resilience over the Long Term

Education is not for the faint of heart. As leaders, you help shepherd the realm of possibility for the next generation. You pave the way for teachers, staff, families, and students to stand in community with one another despite differing perspectives, viewpoints, and ideologies. You are tasked with maintaining balance and a semblance of normalcy in a VUCA (volatile, uncertain, complex, ambiguous) environment. While this responsibility often comes with the expectation of perfection, let us take a moment to acknowledge that perfection does not exist. What belongs in this space of expected excellence is the willingness to embrace your humanity and lead from a space of authenticity.

Leadership resilience recognizes that challenges are ever-present, shaping not only the educational space you are called to lead but also impacting your personal life. It acknowledges that some days may feel so overwhelming that showing up strong in your professional role seems impossible—and vice versa. Resilience means accessing a sustaining depth within yourself, drawing from a reservoir of resources, support, and strategies that nurture your humanity. However, this reservoir must be intentionally built and consistently maintained over time.

The demands of educational leadership are significant, requiring a delicate balance between competing priorities and the constant pressures of guiding school communities. Sustaining resilience over the long term is essential for thriving in your role without sacrificing your well-being. This section explores practical strategies for maintaining resilience, practicing self-compassion, and leveraging community and collaboration.

Practical Strategies for Maintaining Resilience in a High-Pressure Environment

Resilience is not a fixed trait but a skill that can be cultivated and strengthened over time. For leaders in high-stress environments, developing habits and routines that promote mental and emotional well-being is crucial. Here are some effective strategies:

Delegate and set boundaries: Establishing and respecting personal boundaries is essential. This might include setting designated "off hours" for pausing work communication, dedicating time to personal commitments, or learning to say no to tasks that would overwhelm your capacity. Boundaries help prevent burnout and preserve energy for both personal and professional responsibilities.

Prioritize self-care: Leaders often experience guilt when considering activities solely for their well-being. Thoughts such as, "How can I think about myself when others are struggling?" or "I'll prioritize self-care once school is out," are common. However, neglecting self-care limits your ability to lead effectively. Your best day becomes better when you are well-rested, nourished, and supported. Taking care of yourself also sends a clear message to your community about the importance of self-care. Regular exercise, healthy meals, meditation, reading, and hobbies can help leaders recharge. Even brief moments of rest can prevent chronic stress and provide resilience against daily challenges.

Develop a reflective practice: Reflection helps leaders gain perspective and make intentional choices in response to stress. Journaling, mindfulness, nature walks, or brief "pause" moments during the day can foster a reflective mindset, enhancing clarity and strengthening resilience.

Use micro-recovery techniques: Small opportunities for recovery throughout the day can make a significant difference. Simple practices like breathing exercises, short walks, or moments of silence allow leaders to reset and approach tasks with renewed focus.

Practice self-compassion: Dr. Kristin Neff (2011), a leading researcher on self-compassion, describes self-compassion as "turning compassion inward." She identifies three essential elements:

1. Mindful Awareness: Recognize and accept the pain or challenge you are facing without exaggeration or dismissal.
2. Self-Kindness: Approach yourself with grace and care during moments of failure, suffering, or inadequacy—offering the same kindness you would extend to a loved one.
3. Common Humanity: Understand that your experiences are part of the shared human condition. Recognizing this connection helps foster resilience by reminding you that you are not alone in facing challenges (Neff, 2011).

Leaders often feel immense pressure to perform perfectly, but resilience grows when you allow yourself grace. By leaning into self-compassion, you create space to prioritize your needs, fostering inner strength and reducing the risk of burnout.

Leveraging Community and Collaboration to Sustain Resilience

Isolation is a common challenge for leaders, especially when facing difficult decisions or high-stakes responsibilities. Resilience, however, is often strengthened through community and collaboration. Surrounding yourself with a supportive network provides strength, insight, and encouragement through the highs and lows of leadership.

Build a support network: Identify trusted colleagues, mentors, and peers who understand the demands of leadership. Engaging with this network can provide fresh perspectives, emotional support, and practical advice. Peer support reinforces resilience by reminding leaders that they are not alone.

Collaborate for collective growth: Sharing knowledge and responsibilities with your team can reduce stress and create a more balanced workload. Collaboration fosters a culture where all members feel valued and empowered, strengthening the entire community and creating an environment where resilience thrives.

Engage in professional development communities: Resilient leaders are lifelong learners. Participating in professional development networks or attending workshops provides tools for managing stress while connecting with others who face similar challenges. These communities offer valuable spaces for shared learning and encouragement, enhancing resilience across the educational landscape.

By embracing these strategies, educational leaders can sustain resilience throughout their careers. The pursuit of resilience is not just about surviving challenging times but about thriving—fostering fulfillment and remaining steadfast in your purpose as an educator and leader.

Looking Ahead: Leading with Resilience for a Global Impact

As global education becomes the reality of our interconnected world, leaders must embrace their role not only as educators but as architects of inclusive, empathetic, and transformative communities. The demands of global education call for leaders who can navigate diverse cultural landscapes, adapt to complex challenges, and inspire collective growth.

Resilient leadership, grounded in emotional intelligence and authenticity, is essential for meeting these demands and shaping the future of education.

The vision for global education leadership extends beyond managing systems or implementing policies—it requires fostering environments where students, educators, and families feel seen, valued, and empowered. Leaders who embrace resilience and authenticity bring clarity and compassion to their decision-making, creating a ripple effect of trust and collaboration that strengthens communities. Emotional intelligence, the ability to connect deeply with oneself and others, equips leaders to handle the complexities of global education with empathy and insight. By actively listening, showing vulnerability, and cultivating psychological safety, resilient leaders model behaviors that build inclusive and supportive school cultures.

To sustain this level of leadership, prioritizing social and emotional well-being is as vital as professional development. Leaders must recognize that their capacity to inspire and guide others depends on nurturing their own resilience. Reflective practices, seeking support networks, and setting clear boundaries allow leaders to recharge and focus on their mission. In doing so, they demonstrate that self-care is not a luxury but a necessity—one that reinforces their ability to lead with purpose and authenticity.

Honoring one's humanity is at the heart of transformative leadership. It requires embracing not only one's strengths but also vulnerabilities, fostering a culture where everyone feels valued and empowered to bring their authentic selves to the table. By leading with courage and integrity, resilient leaders set the stage for progress, innovation, and unity within their communities. This approach redefines leadership in global education, positioning it as a force for inclusivity, empathy, and enduring impact.

Resilient leaders who embody emotional intelligence and authenticity inspire change far beyond their immediate circles. They transform challenges into opportunities for growth, encourage collaboration across diverse perspectives, and foster environments where all voices matter. By prioritizing connection and inclusivity, these leaders leave a legacy that shapes not only the present but the future of education, ensuring that the global education landscape thrives for generations to come.

In leading with resilience, authenticity, and emotional intelligence, we not only adapt to the demands of global education but transform them into opportunities for meaningful growth, deep connection, and lasting impact.

References

Brown, B. (2018). *Dare to lead: Brave work. Tough conversations. Whole hearts*. Random House.

Collaborative for Academic, Social, and Emotional Learning (CASEL) (n.d.). What is SEL? Retrieved from https://casel.org/what-is-sel/

Edmondson, A. (1999). Psychological safety and learning behavior in work teams. *Administrative Science Quarterly, 44*(2), 350–383. https://doi.org/10.2307/2666999

Fullan, M. (2001). *Leading in a culture of change*. Jossey-Bass.

Goleman, D. (2000). *Emotional intelligence: Why it can matter more than IQ*. Bantam Books.

Maxwell, J. C. (2007). *The 21 indispensable qualities of a leader: Becoming the person others will want to follow*. Thomas Nelson.

Merriam-Webster. (2024). Resilience. In Merriam-Webster.com dictionary. Retrieved February 28, 2025, from https://www.merriam-webster.com/dictionary/resilience

Neff, K. D. (2011). *Self-compassion: The proven power of being kind to yourself*. William Morrow.

Driving Leadership
A School Leader's Journey

*Shannon Hobbs-Beckley,
Laura McBain, Ariel Raz,
and Richard Boerner*

The role of a school leader is a dynamic journey, much like navigating a complex road trip. From merging onto the freeway to finding the flow of the open road and finally exiting gracefully, each phase requires distinct strategies, skills, and mindsets. This chapter explores these stages, drawing on personal experiences and research insights to illuminate the path of education leadership.

Phase 1: Getting on the Freeway

Starting as a school leader often feels like navigating a congested on-ramp of a busy highway. You're trying to find your place amidst a fast-moving system, unsure of the right speed or lane. This stage is about establishing presence, building trust, and learning the nuances of a new environment—all while grappling with the steep learning curve that comes with the role. The key is to enter with clarity and intention rather than speeding ahead without a roadmap.

Entering with Empathy: Listening to Your School Community

Before making any major decisions, effective leaders take the time to listen. Much like a driver checking their mirrors before merging, leaders need awareness of their surroundings. This means engaging with teachers, students, parents, and staff to understand the culture, strengths, and concerns that shape the school community. Active listening can be achieved through structured listening sessions, empathy interviews, or simply being present in school hallways, classrooms, and community events. Building authentic relationships early ensures that leadership decisions are informed by the people they will affect most.

Transitioning into a new leadership role requires humility and an openness to learning. Much like merging onto a busy freeway, leaders must find the right moment to enter the flow without disrupting it. This involves listening deeply to the people within the organization—teachers, students, parents, and community members—to understand their perspectives, challenges, and aspirations. The goal is to build relationships and trust, which are foundational to any successful leadership journey. Leaders who take the time to listen are better equipped to identify opportunities and avoid missteps.

Establishing Credibility as a New Leader

Leadership credibility is not assumed—it is earned through consistent action, transparency, and responsiveness. Whether you are an internal hire or new to the institution, demonstrating a willingness to learn, acknowledging past successes, and leading by example builds confidence in your leadership (Kouzes & Posner, 2017). Early on, it is critical to listen more than you speak, showing that you value the expertise and institutional knowledge of those around you. Research suggests that leaders who actively engage in open communication and foster a culture of trust create stronger, more effective teams (Garmston & Wellman, 2016).

Being visible and engaged—attending school events, visiting classrooms, and holding open office hours—helps establish trust (Grissom et al., 2013). School leaders who prioritize relationship-building and take time to understand the culture and values of the school community are more likely to gain stakeholder buy-in and ensure long-term success (Fullan, 2020). Additionally, following through on commitments, communicating openly about decisions, and admitting when adjustments are needed solidify your reputation as a leader who is thoughtful, principled, and dedicated to the community's success (Bryk & Schneider, 2003).

The Power of Presence

One of the most important behaviors a leader can adopt early and often is being visible and engaged within the school community. Research has shown that principals who are frequently seen in hallways and classrooms are more likely to create thriving school cultures (Grissom et al., 2013). In practical terms, this means showing up where the work happens—not just in offices or meetings but in the daily lives of students, teachers, and staff. For instance, a study revealed that school leaders who consistently spend time outside their offices build stronger connections and foster a culture of trust and collaboration.

This kind of presence signals more than just attentiveness; it demonstrates commitment and builds trust. An experienced school leader once emphasized the importance of never rushing decisions, suggesting that thoughtful observation and engagement are critical during the early stages of leadership.

Lessons from Missteps

One leader's experience highlights the importance of building trust before implementing major changes. Tasked with developing a strategic plan within a tight timeframe, they worked tirelessly to craft a vision they believed would set the school on a transformative path. While the governing board embraced the vision enthusiastically, the leadership team's response was far more skeptical. The ambitious plan, introduced without sufficient collaboration or buy-in, felt overwhelming to the team.

Recognizing the misstep, the leader pivoted. They redesigned the planning process to involve the leadership team more deeply, transforming it into a collaborative effort. This not only improved the quality of the plan but also strengthened relationships within the team, laying the groundwork for future successes. The experience underscored the importance of pacing and relationship-building in the early stages of leadership.

Design Thinking for Leaders

Applying design thinking principles can help leaders take an iterative, human-centered approach to problem-solving. The process—empathize, define, ideate, prototype, and test—ensures that changes are developed with real input from those affected (Brown, 2009). By centering decision-making on stakeholder experiences, leaders foster innovation that is both meaningful and sustainable (Liedtka, 2018).

Empathize: Effective leadership starts with understanding the needs, challenges, and aspirations of students, teachers, and parents. This phase involves active listening, conducting interviews, and gathering qualitative and quantitative data to uncover key insights (IDEO, 2015).

Define: Once leaders gather insights, they must synthesize the information to clearly define the problem. A well-defined problem statement ensures that solutions are addressing root causes rather than symptoms, increasing the likelihood of successful implementation (Buchanan, 1992).

Ideate: In this stage, leaders encourage brainstorming sessions that promote diverse perspectives and innovative solutions. Schools can foster creativity by bringing together interdisciplinary teams, using structured techniques such as mind mapping or rapid idea generation (Martin, 2009).

Prototype: Rather than implementing large-scale changes all at once, leaders can develop low-risk, small-scale prototypes that allow for real-world testing. This might involve piloting new instructional strategies, modifying scheduling approaches, or testing new communication methods with parents (Brown, 2009).

Test: Feedback is essential. Leaders should analyze the effectiveness of prototypes, gather feedback, and refine solutions based on real-world use. This iterative approach helps reduce resistance to change and ensures that innovations are well-aligned with stakeholder needs (Liedtka, 2015).

Design thinking not only enhances problem-solving but also promotes a culture of collaboration, adaptability, and innovation in schools. By embedding design thinking into leadership practices, school leaders can create environments where continuous improvement is the norm, rather than the exception.

Merging into Leadership with Intention

As a leader navigates the on-ramp of a busy highway it requires patience, awareness, and strategic decision-making. Leaders who take the time to listen, build trust, and establish credibility set themselves up for long-term success. Rushing into change without understanding the landscape can create unnecessary friction, while a deliberate and empathetic approach ensures smoother transitions and stronger stakeholder engagement.

By embedding design thinking principles and fostering a culture of collaboration, leaders can align their vision with the needs of their school community and drive meaningful, sustainable change. The early stages of leadership are critical, not just for personal credibility but for establishing the foundations upon which future success will be built.

With a thoughtful and human-centered approach, school leaders can merge seamlessly into their roles, gaining the trust and confidence of their teams while setting the stage for long-term innovation and progress. Just as a driver must remain alert and adaptable, leaders must continuously assess their environment, respond to feedback, and refine their strategies—ensuring that their journey leads to a thriving and dynamic school community.

Phase 2: Getting into the Flow

As school leaders work to accelerate their vision and drive innovation, it's essential to recognize that this journey is not a race—it's about knowing how to manage traffic. Transformational leadership demands not only internal reflection but also a willingness to experiment and adapt. One of the most critical skills for any leader is navigating the pace of trust—new initiatives can only gain traction when a significant portion of your community is ready to move with you. The common mistake new leaders make is launching change without first assessing the leadership skills and cultural dynamics at play within their unique school context.

Assessing Your Own Acceleration Skills

Every leader brings their own unique set of skills shaped by their identity, experience, and leadership style. As new leaders, we must build self-awareness about how we lead. Do we lean toward a democratic approach, where collaboration is key? Or do we prefer a servant leadership style, putting the needs of others at the forefront? Whether you lead with an autocratic or laissez-faire style, the most effective leaders know that the "right" way to lead depends on the current needs of the school community.

Self-awareness is the foundation of great leadership. To be truly effective, leaders must understand their strengths and areas for growth within each leadership style. This knowledge allows them to build a strong team—one that complements their skills and fills the gaps where they may be less experienced. Effective leadership is not about doing everything yourself; it's about building the right support systems and resources around you. This includes human resources—placing the right people in the right roles—and ensuring that operational resources, such as finances and materials, are aligned to support your school's vision.

After assessing yourself, it's crucial to expand your view and see the broader landscape around you—this means understanding the school community from multiple perspectives. Perhaps most importantly, is the student experience. As leaders, our primary responsibility is to enhance the learning experiences of students within our institutions. To do this effectively, we need more than just data on student performance; we must also gain a deeper understanding of the lived experiences of the students we serve. One powerful way to achieve this is by "shadowing" students for a day. This firsthand experience provides valuable insights into how students engage with the pedagogies, content, and structures that the school has in place.

Another powerful tool for school leaders is "shadowing" different parts of the system. This involves moving beyond observing students, but also immersing yourself in the experiences of teachers, operations staff, and parents. By shadowing these key stakeholders, leaders can uncover both the strengths and the pain points within the system and gain a clearer understanding of where resources and attention need to be directed.

> ## Questions to Guide a Shadowing Experience
>
> What does the daily experience of teachers really look like?
> How do their days start and end, and what's shaping their experience of the school environment? Which aspects of the school's organization are hindering their ability to teach effectively—and which elements are empowering them?
> How do parents perceive and experience communication from teachers, leadership, and the administration? Which parents are actively speaking up, and which voices are missing or need more attention?
>
> These questions aren't just about gathering data—they are about uncovering the areas within your school community that are ripe for improvement and experimentation toward the strategic vision you have in mind for your community

Creating Conditions for All Stakeholders to Accelerate

The human brain seeks routine, pattern and predictability. As the work accelerates and the landscape changes, it is natural that some members of the school community will ask questions, express reluctance, or even resist continuing along the journey. These are the kinds of defining moments mentioned above: how will you respond and ensure that you have not rocketed ahead?

Change leadership is as much about creating stability as it is about driving innovation. The human brain is wired for routine, pattern recognition, and predictability (Rock, 2008). As a leader, you will inevitably encounter resistance, reluctance, or uncertainty from members of the school community when accelerating new initiatives. This is a natural response to disruption, as individuals seek to understand how changes impact them and their roles (Heifetz et al., 2009). How you navigate this resistance—whether through proactive communication, adaptive leadership, or stakeholder engagement—will determine whether your school community continues moving forward together or stalls due to uncertainty and confusion (Kotter, 2012).

Providing Clear Signals

In times of change, school leaders must signal stability and direction to stakeholders. Research shows that organizations that fail to provide clear communication during transitions risk increased anxiety, misinformation, and resistance (Bridges, 2009). One of your most valuable leadership tools is your ability to consistently reinforce core values and the long term vision, ensuring that stakeholders remain aligned with the school's purpose.

To extend the driving metaphor, leaders must:

> **"Honk your horn"** by continuously articulating the established vision and shared destination. Reiterate the "why" behind the work, reinforcing the school's overarching mission and keeping the focus on long term educational goals.
>
> (Fullan, 2020)

> **"Shine your headlights"** to illuminate core values and grounding principles. By making these foundational commitments visible in meetings, policies, and daily interactions, leaders create a sense of psychological safety for stakeholders.
>
> (Schein, 2017)

> **"Use your turn signals"** to prepare people for upcoming shifts. Leaders who communicate proactively about changes—outlining the rationale, timeline, and expected outcomes—help stakeholders feel more prepared and engaged in the transition.
>
> (Bolman & Deal, 2017)

When the road ahead feels ambiguous or unstable, these signals act as markers, guiding your school community back to the fundamental purpose of the work. Leaders who effectively communicate both stability and direction foster trust, motivation, and shared commitment among educators, students, and families (Bryk & Schneider, 2003).

Responding with Agility

Even with a well-structured plan and clear signals, unexpected disruptions are inevitable. Effective leaders understand that agility—the ability to assess, respond, and adapt quickly—is essential for maintaining momentum in schoolwide transformation (Pfeffer & Sutton, 2006). Research highlights that organizations with adaptive leadership structures are better positioned to navigate uncertainty and leverage challenges as opportunities for growth (Heifetz et al., 2009).

Agility in leadership requires both active listening and structured feedback mechanisms. Leaders must create opportunities to read the "gauges" and signals of their school community, ensuring that they are attuned to emerging needs and concerns (Tschannen-Moran, 2014). This can be achieved through:

Listening Sessions and Focus Groups—Providing structured spaces for teachers, students, and parents to voice their experiences ensures that leaders gather qualitative insights about how changes are affecting stakeholders (Kraft & Dougherty, 2013).

Surveys and Data Analysis—Regular feedback through surveys allows leaders to quantify stakeholder sentiment, identifying patterns and adjusting strategies accordingly (Bryson, 2018).

Cross Departmental Collaboration—Strong connections between operational and academic departments ensure that logistical challenges (e.g., scheduling, technology, staffing) do not become roadblocks to innovation (Senge, 2006).

The trust built during the onramp phase of leadership provides the foundation for making timely and effective adjustments during implementation. Leaders who demonstrate responsiveness and flexibility—rather than rigidly adhering to initial plans—are more likely to sustain change efforts and keep their communities engaged in the process (Kotter, 2012).

Grow from a Fleet to a Convoy

Renowned adult communications expert Jennifer Abrams (2009) speaks and writes about the phenomenon of educator training programs where educators are trained to plan, teach, assess, and interact with students. All are central to the work of being an educator in the classroom. It is much less common, however, for educators to be trained how to work deeply and effectively with adult colleagues. In fact, it is these relationships and job expectations that frequently present some of the greatest challenges.

Herein lies the potential, the challenge, and the risk as a leader in this part of the journey. A highly trained and tuned fleet of individuals and departments can be both an asset and an obstacle to achieving innovation. As a small group, they may individually collaborate, innovate, grow and develop, but it comes at the risk of doing so in isolation and decelerating the schoolwide change you are looking for. Guiding these teams and departments to come together into a cohesive convoy characterized by shared destination, seamless communication, agile approaches, and emergency procedures is essential for your leadership work at this stage.

Removing the Barriers for Acceleration

You may find that your ability to respond with agility is hampered by barriers and that the only course of action is to begin moving or dismantling them. These barriers are often in the form of operational challenges. To truly accelerate change, leaders must address these operational gaps first, ensuring that the foundational infrastructure—whether human, financial, or material—is in place to support the vision. In the metaphor of navigating the freeway, sometimes leaders must "clear the wrecks" before they can move forward. This may involve fixing operational inefficiencies, establishing strong support teams, and making sure that resources are in place to allow everyone in the school community to move forward together. While this may feel like a slower start, the payoff comes when the foundational work is done, allowing the school to move more quickly and effectively toward its larger goals.

Fixing Bureaucratic Inefficiencies

Many schools operate under complex bureaucratic structures that create unnecessary hurdles. Streamlining decision-making processes by clarifying roles, empowering teams, and reducing approval bottlenecks can help ensure that teachers and staff can act efficiently (Bolman & Deal, 2017).

For instance, teachers may have great ideas for the classroom, but without the proper resources or staffing, their ability to implement those ideas is hindered. In another example, if a teacher has an innovative idea for a new interdisciplinary course but must navigate weeks of approvals through multiple layers of administration that initiative loses momentum. A leader who recognizes this can develop a faster, more transparent proposal system, allowing educators to pilot small-scale versions of their ideas before full implementation (Ashkenas & Matta, 2021).

Strengthening Support Systems

Leaders must ensure that support structures are robust enough to sustain change. This includes:

- Building cross-functional teams that bridge gaps between instructional, operational, and administrative staff (Hargreaves & Fullan, 2012).
- Providing adequate staffing to prevent teacher burnout and ensure that new initiatives do not feel like an added burden (Kraft & Papay, 2014).
- Establishing mentorship programs where experienced teachers support those adopting new practices (Lave & Wenger, 1991).

Schools that invest in ongoing coaching and professional development create a culture of continuous learning, reducing resistance to change and increasing the likelihood of successful implementation (Guskey, 2002).

Fueling Progress: Aligning Resources with Vision

A leader's vision for school improvement is only as effective as the resources that support it. To accelerate change, leaders must align financial, human, and material resources with strategic priorities (Bryson, 2018).

Prioritizing Financial Investments: Budget constraints often limit educational innovation, but strategic leaders know how to reallocate resources effectively. This may include:

- Reallocating discretionary funds toward teacher training, technology integration, or curriculum redesign (Odden & Picus, 2020).
- Pursuing grants and external funding sources to supplement school budgets (Grubb & Allen, 2011).
- Partnering with community organizations to provide additional resources, such as industry mentors or supplemental learning opportunities (Warren et al., 2009).

By investing wisely in high-impact areas, leaders ensure that change initiatives are sustainable and scalable rather than short-lived pilot programs.

Ensuring Equitable Access to Resources: True acceleration requires ensuring that all students and educators have equitable access to resources that enable success (Darling-Hammond, 2010). This includes:

- Ensuring that classrooms across the school have the same level of technological access and instructional materials.
- Providing targeted support for under-resourced student populations, such as additional learning interventions or after-school programs (Dweck, 2006).
- Addressing staffing shortages by creating teacher leadership pathways that allow experienced educators to take on mentoring roles without leaving the classroom (Ingersoll & Strong, 2011).

Without equity-driven leadership, acceleration efforts risk leaving some members of the school community behind.

The Payoff of Clearing the Road Ahead

Removing barriers to acceleration is not a one-time fix. It is an ongoing process of identifying constraints, dismantling inefficiencies, and ensuring that operational structures align with the school's long-term goals. While taking the time to fix broken systems, strengthen support structures, and align resources may feel like a slower start, the payoff is immense. By creating a solid foundation, leaders enable smoother implementation, greater teacher buy-in, and more sustainable innovation. Schools that invest in clearing the roadblocks before pushing forward can accelerate more effectively allowing educators, students, and the entire school community to move forward together with confidence.

Phase 3: Exiting

If merging onto the freeway is about finding your safe position amongst the traffic flow and maintaining speed is about hitting your stride, exiting is a delicate art of slowing down with intention. Transitioning leadership is not just about leaving—it's about ensuring that what has been built endures and that the successor is set up for success. This phase is as much about legacy as it is about letting go.

Capturing Institutional Wisdom

One of the greatest gifts an outgoing leader can give is the knowledge, insights, and institutional memory accumulated during their tenure. Leadership transitions risk a loss of organizational knowledge if structured systems for knowledge transfer are not in place (Fullan, 2020). Capturing institutional wisdom—the practices, values, and lessons that define a school's culture and operations—is critical for continuity. Without deliberate efforts to preserve this wisdom, the organization can experience unnecessary disruptions, inefficiencies, or a loss of strategic momentum.

To address this, some schools use tools to map out the strengths and gaps within the organization. For instance, a school may develop an exercise to align the skills of the incoming leader with the needs of the leadership team. By identifying areas where the new leader could bring fresh perspectives or strengthen existing initiatives, the organization is able to navigate the transition more smoothly. Such tools may include:

1. **Creating a Leadership Transition Document:**
    A comprehensive transition document should include key priorities, ongoing projects, essential relationships, strategic goals, a nd reflections on past challenges and successes (Kotter, 2012). This provides the incoming leader with a roadmap for understanding the current state of the school and its priorities.

2. **Mapping Organizational Strengths and Gaps:**
   Some schools conduct leadership audits that align the skills of the incoming leader with the needs of the organization. By identifying where the new leader can bring fresh perspectives or strengthen existing initiatives, the transition is more strategic and intentional (Bryk et al., 2010).
3. **Developing a Leadership Pipeline:**
   Long-term capacity building includes succession planning—creating internal pathways for future leadership. Schools that invest in leadership development ensure that when a transition occurs, there are capable internal candidates ready to step into leadership roles (Leithwood et al., 2020).

Creating Systems for Long-term Impact

Building long term capacity means creating frameworks that will endure beyond an individual leader's tenure. This includes documentation, leadership pipelines, and adaptable structures for continuous reflection and adjustment.

The Role of a Leader Emeritus

Another innovative approach is the concept of a "leader emeritus." This idea reframes the role of the outgoing leader as a bridge between the past and the future. Rather than stepping away entirely, the emeritus leader serves as a silent mentor, offering guidance and support when needed without overshadowing the new leadership (Tschannen-Moran, 2014).

In practice, an emeritus leader might help the incoming leader navigate sensitive issues or provide historical context for longstanding policies. This continuity can be invaluable, especially in the early stages of a transition. For instance, a "leader emeritus" may:

- Provide historical context on longstanding policies and decisions.
- Act as a confidential advisor for the new leader during the initial months of transition.
- Help with community relations, ensuring a smooth transition for staff, students, and parents.

However, this role must be carefully defined. The outgoing leader should not overstep or interfere with the decision-making authority of the new leader. Clear boundaries must be established to support wise decision-making without undermining the successor's autonomy (Bolman & Deal, 2017).

Preparing the Organization

A smooth transition also requires organizational readiness. Practical steps, such as organizing resources like shared drives and documentation, can make a significant difference for the incoming leader. Ensuring that these resources are accessible and well-structured helps set a positive tone for the transition. Institutional resources must be structured to ensure continuity. Key documents, policies, and institutional knowledge should be stored in an accessible and organized format. Additionally, conducting an audit of ongoing projects and responsibilities helps the incoming leader prioritize key initiatives effectively.

Additionally, outgoing leaders can play a crucial role in shaping the narrative of the transition. By framing the change as an opportunity for growth rather than a loss, they can help the community embrace the new leader with optimism and support. This involves communicating clearly and frequently with all stakeholders about the reasons for the transition and the qualities of the incoming leader. Outgoing leaders play a vital role in this process by publicly expressing confidence in their successor, reinforcing trust among stakeholders (Tschannen-Moran, 2014). Furthermore, clearly defining continuity plans helps the school community understand how the transition will be managed and what to expect.

Finally, engaging stakeholders throughout the transition fosters transparency and stability. Hosting listening sessions or town halls provides a platform for addressing concerns and ensuring open communication. Additionally, offering mentorship opportunities for key staff members supports continuity and helps maintain institutional knowledge. By focusing on these three key areas—organizing resources, communicating the transition narrative, and engaging stakeholders—the transition process can be managed effectively, ensuring a smooth and stable leadership shift.

Balancing Legacy and Letting Go

Perhaps the most challenging aspect of exiting is balancing the desire to leave a legacy with the need to let go. Leaders often develop deep emotional connections to their schools, making it difficult to step away. However, the most effective transitions occur when outgoing leaders empower their successors to make their own mark. The goal is not to preserve every detail of past leadership but to ensure that the school's guiding principles remain intact (Fullan, 2020). Leaders must recognize that schools evolve, and with new leadership come fresh perspectives and innovations that contribute to growth. One leader reflected on this balance, noting the importance of preserving the school's core values while giving the new leader the freedom to innovate. Striking this balance ensures continuity while fostering growth and evolution within the organization.

Equally important is trusting the successor's vision. Just as teachers eventually step back to let students apply their learning, outgoing leaders must allow the new leader to take the reins without interference (Leithwood et al., 2020). Offering encouragement and support is valuable, but micromanaging or second-guessing decisions can hinder progress. Trust in the new leadership fosters confidence and stability within the school community.

Finally, transitioning out of leadership involves redefining one's professional identity. Many outgoing leaders experience a sense of loss or displacement after stepping away from a role they have deeply invested in (Bridges, 2009). Developing a new focus—whether through mentoring, consulting, or other educational leadership opportunities—can help navigate this transition successfully. By embracing change, supporting the successor, and finding a meaningful post-leadership role, outgoing leaders can ensure a legacy of lasting impact.

Exiting with Purpose and Confidence

A school leader's departure is not the end of their impact—it is a strategic transition that ensures long-term institutional success. The most effective leadership exits are marked by thoughtful planning, knowledge transfer, and a commitment to organizational continuity.

By capturing institutional wisdom, creating systems that endure, preparing the school community, and letting go with grace, leaders ensure that their legacy is not just about what they built—but about how well they prepared others to continue the journey.

Conclusion: Leading with Intention, Agility, and Legacy

Leadership is rarely a straight road. It's a winding journey that demands adaptability, courage, and a deep sense of purpose. By embracing the challenges of each phase—entering the freeway, maintaining speed, and transitioning out—school leaders can navigate their journey with confidence and leave a lasting impact on their schools.

In the early stages, successful leaders take the time to listen, build trust, and establish credibility. They recognize that leadership is not about asserting control but about understanding the culture and needs of the school community. By entering with humility and presence, they lay the foundation for meaningful relationships and informed decision-making.

As momentum builds, leaders must strike a balance between driving innovation and maintaining stability. True transformation happens when leaders assess their acceleration skills, align their vision with the school's needs, and create conditions where all stakeholders can move forward together. This requires not only clear communication and strategic planning but also the agility to respond to challenges and resistance along the way. Ensuring that bureaucratic inefficiencies are addressed, and operational structures are strengthened allows for sustainable progress rather than short-lived change.

Finally, exiting leadership is not just about stepping away—it is about ensuring continuity and empowering the next generation of leadership. A thoughtful transition safeguards institutional knowledge, maintains community trust, and sets up future leaders for success. The most effective school leaders understand that their legacy is not just in what they build but in how well they prepare others to carry the work forward.

Leadership is not a solitary endeavor. It is a shared journey shaped by the people, values, and aspirations of a school community. By leading with intention, adapting with agility, and embracing the responsibility of legacy, school leaders create a lasting impact—one that extends beyond their tenure and ensures a thriving, dynamic learning environment for years to come.

References

Abrams, J. B. (2009). *Having hard conversations*. Corwin Press.

Ashkenas, R., & Matta, N. (2021). How to scale a successful pilot project. *Harvard Business Review*. https://hbr.org/2021/01/how-to-scale-a-successful-pilot-project

Bolman, L. G., & Deal, T. E. (2017). *Reframing organizations: Artistry, choice, and leadership* (6th ed.). Jossey-Bass.

Bridges, W. (2009). *Managing transitions: Making the most of change* (3rd ed.). Da Capo Lifelong Books.

Brown, T. (2009). *Change by design: How design thinking creates new alternatives for business and society*. Harper Business.

Bryk, A. S., & Schneider, B. (2003). *Trust in schools: A core resource for improvement*. Russell Sage Foundation.

Bryk, A. S., & Schneider, B. (2003). Trust in schools: A core resource for improvement. *Educational Leadership, 60*(6), 40–45.

Bryk, A. S., Sebring, P. B., Allensworth, E., Luppescu, S., & Easton, J. Q. (2010). *Organizing schools for improvement: Lessons from Chicago*. University of Chicago Press.

Bryson, J. M. (2018). *Strategic planning for public and nonprofit organizations: A guide to strengthening and sustaining organizational achievement* (5th ed.). Wiley.

Buchanan, R. (1992). Wicked problems in design thinking. *Design Issues, 8*(2), 5–21. https://doi.org/10.2307/1511637

Darling-Hammond, L. (2010). *The flat world and education: How America's commitment to equity will determine our future*. Teachers College Press.

Dweck, C. S. (2006). *Mindset: The new psychology of success*. Random House.

Fullan, M. (2020). *Leading in a culture of change* (2nd ed.). Jossey-Bass.

Garmston, R. J., & Wellman, B. M. (2016). *The adaptive school: A sourcebook for developing collaborative groups* (3rd ed.). Rowman & Littlefield.

Grissom, J. A., Loeb, S., & Master, B. (2013). Effective instructional time use for school leaders: Longitudinal evidence from observations of principals. *Educational Researcher, 42*(8), 433–444. https://doi.org/10.3102/0013189X13510020

Grubb, W. N., & Allen, R. (2011). Rethinking school funding, resources, incentives, and outcomes. *J Educ Change, 12*, 121–130. https://doi.org/10.1007/s10833-010-9146-6

Guskey, T. R. (2002). Professional development and teacher change. *Teachers and Teaching, 8*(3), 381–391.

Hargreaves, A., & Fullan, M. (2012). *Professional capital: Transforming teaching in every school*. Teachers College Press.

Heifetz, R., Grashow, A., & Linsky, M. (2009). *The practice of adaptive leadership: Tools and tactics for changing your organization and the world*. Harvard Business Review Press.

IDEO (2015). *The field guide to human-centered design*. IDEO.org.

Ingersoll, R. M., & Strong, M. (2011). The impact of induction and mentoring programs for beginning teachers: A critical review of the research. *Review of Educational Research, 81*(2), 201–233. https://doi.org/10.3102/0034654311403323

Kotter, J. P. (2012). *Leading change*. Harvard Business Review Press.

Kouzes, J. M., & Posner, B. Z. (2017). *The leadership challenge: How to make extraordinary things happen in organizations* (6th ed.). Wiley.

Kraft, M. A., & Dougherty, S. M. (2013). The effect of teacher–family communication on student engagement: Evidence from a randomized field experiment. *Journal of Research on Educational Effectiveness, 6*(3), 199–222.

Kraft, M. A., & Papay, J. P. (2014). Can professional environments in schools promote teacher development? Explaining heterogeneity in returns to teaching experience. *Educational Effectiveness and Policy Analysis, 36*(4), 476–500.

Lave, J., & Wenger, E. (1991). *Situated learning: Legitimate peripheral participation*. Cambridge University Press. https://doi.org/10.1017/CBO9780511815355

Leithwood, K., Harris, A., & Hopkins, D. (2020). Seven strong claims about successful school leadership revisited. *School Leadership & Management, 40*(1), 5–22.

Liedtka, J. (2015). Perspective: Linking design thinking with innovation outcomes through cognitive bias reduction. *Journal of Product Innovation Management, 32*(6), 925–938. https://doi.org/10.1111/jpim.12163

Liedtka, J. (2018). Why design thinking works. *Harvard Business Review, 96*(5), 72–79.

Martin, R. (2009). *The design of business: Why design thinking is the next competitive advantage*. Harvard Business Press.

Odden, A. R., & Picus, L. O. (2020). *School finance: A policy perspective* (6th ed.). McGraw-Hill Higher Education.

Pfeffer, J., & Sutton, R. I. (2006). *Hard facts, dangerous half-truths, and total nonsense: Profiting from evidence-based management*. Harvard Business School Press.

Rock, D. (2008). SCARF: A brain-based model for collaborating with and influencing others. *NeuroLeadership Journal, 1*(1), 44–52.

Schein, E. H. (2017). *Organizational culture and leadership* (5th ed.). Wiley.

Senge, P. M. (2006). *The fifth discipline: The art and practice of the learning organization*. Doubleday.

Tschannen-Moran, M. (2014). *Trust matters: Leadership for successful schools* (2nd ed.). Jossey-Bass.

Warren, M. R., Hong, S., Rubin, C. L., & Sychitkokhong Uy, P. (2009). Beyond the bake sale: A community-based relational approach to parent engagement in schools. *Teachers College Record, 111*(9), 2209–2254. https://doi.org/10.1177/016146810911100901

Index

Note: *Italicized* and **bold** page numbers refer to figures and tables.

academic excellence 169
academic outcomes 167–168
acceleration: barriers to, removing 214–216; conditions for 211–214; skills 210–211
accountability 5, 40, 82, 104, 122, 127, 138, 193, 195, 199; external 110–111; internal 111
actions 113, **114**, **117**
adaptability 1, 5, 6, 17, 19, 22, 84, 107, 134, 141, 177, 208, 221
adaptation to growth 138–139
ADKAR model 129, 131
adolescent predicament 36–37
adults–young people engagement 34–36
Advanced Placement (AP) 168
agility 221–222
agreements over policy 154–155, **155**
Agyapong, B. 67
AI *see* artificial intelligence (AI)
Allen, R. 2
American International School of Budapest 72
American School in Japan (ASIJ): human-centered model 16; KVC 17–18; Strategic Design Framework (SDF) 16–17; Vision 2030 17, 20–22; vision-centered approach to strategy 16–17

American School of Budapest 75
Anderson, L. W. 159–160
antagonist 161
AP *see* Advanced Placement (AP)
Approaches to Learning (ATLs) 70
artifacts 114, **115**, **117**
artificial intelligence (AI) 11–12, 19
Ashkenas, R. 157, 159
ASIJ *see* American School in Japan (ASIJ)
ATLs *see* Approaches to Learning (ATLs)
authentic equity 2
authenticity 184–185, 187–188
authentic leadership 188–190
authentic learning 167–168; assessment practices with, aligning 171; structural support for 171; through professional development 170
autonomy 4, 6, 23, 47, 219

Balanced Assessment System, A (BAS) 61
BAS *see* Balanced Assessment System, A (BAS)
Bathon, J.: *Leadership for Deeper Learning* 140–141
Beevor, A.: *D-Day – The Battle for Normandy* 155–156
belonging: community contract for 30–31; in learning 172–173; to life, bringing 31–33

225

Index

better schools, becoming 58–59
big data 50–51
Bjork, E. L.: *Psychology of Everyday Life* 145
Bjork, R. A.: *Psychology of Everyday Life* 145
board of international school: balance 100–101; building 87; chair, choosing 92; composition of 91–92; dysfunctional 93; evaluation of 90; governance training 90; head evaluation, protocols for 98–100; institutional memory 88–89; leading during crisis 95–97; meeting 97–98; member behavior, addressing 91; member removal 91; new members, inviting 90; orientation of 90; partnerships 93–94; politics of change 94–95; pool of prospects 89; potential candidates, assessment of 89; strategic *versus* operational focus 92–93
Boerner, R. 2
Brown, D. J.: *Boys in the Boat, The* 22
Bunnell, T. 104–106

Canale, T. 72
Canali, T. 75
Cartesian-Newtonian worldview 6–7
CASEL *see* Collaborative for Academic, Social, and Emotional Learning (CASEL)
CGC *see* Common Ground Collaborative, The (CGC)
CGS *see* Collective Growth System, The (CGS)
Chadwell, D. 73, 79
change management 128–135; ability phase 132–133; awareness phase 129–130; desire phase 130–131; knowledge phase 131–132; reinforce phase 133–135; strategic 136
Ch-Ch-Ch-Changes 2024 163, *163*
Chohan, K. 2

CIS *see* Council of International Schools (CIS)
'CIS Paradigms' 49
cognition: distributed 12; embodied 11; situated 12
cognitive entrenchment 151
collaboration 2, 82, 202
Collaborative for Academic, Social, and Emotional Learning (CASEL) 191
Collective Growth System, The (CGS) 60
Committee on Trustees 92
Common Ground Collaborative, The (CGC) 49, 52, 53, 59, 61; learning process 54–58, **54**
community contract for belonging 30–31
community engagement 6, 23, 82
community partnerships, strengthening 176–177
complexity 166–167
contentious issue conversation starters 152, *153*
Council of International Schools (CIS) 5
COVID-19 pandemic 4, 9, 10, 18, 96
creativity 6, 7, 12, 18, 19, 33, 104, 187, 195, 196, 199, 208
credibility 206–207
critical thinking 6, 18, 26, 33, 35, 104, 169, 175
current landscape of international education 5–6
curriculum, streamlining 64–86; call to action 66; definition of 68–69; editorial criteria 75–77, *77–79*; editorial criteria review and actions 79–80; editorial stance 71; external alignment to standards 70–71; Five-Step Streamlining Curriculum Review Process 72–77, *75*; innovation 67–68; internal coherence 70; knowledge 64; learn from colleagues 80–85; need of 66–68; process credibility 71–72; proficiencies 65; program planning 68; projects 65–66; space 80; stage, setting 69–72

Dawkins-Jackson, P. 2
decisio-making: students' voice in 33
Deep Learning 18–19
Deming, W. E. 54–55
Denmark, V. 2
design thinking 208–209
dignity 25–48
'Disagree and Commit' 155–157
distributed cognition 12
DNA of learning 54–55
DPS International (DPSI) 81
DPSI *see* DPS International (DPSI)
Dreyfuss, H. 69–70
Drucker, P. 60

Early Supporters (ES) 147–148, 150
education, as force for good 180–181
educational equity 19
educational orientations *14*
educational systems' contradictions, acknowledgement of 33
Eighty Percent Rule 145
embodied cognition 11
emotional intelligence 184–185
empathy 5, 11, 19, 48, 172, 174, 175, 176, 178, 180, 183, 184, 188, 189–193, 195, 203, 205–206
empowerment 40
equity 15, 20, 21, 58, 59, 178, 189–190; authentic 2; educational 19; trust 121, 122, 125, 145–147
Erikson, E. 35
ES *see* Early Supporters (ES)
Essential Agreements 25, 28, 40–41; language 44–46; principles to design 41
ethical leadership 136
exam 29

faculty's acceptance of potential change, identification of 126–128
feedback 194–195
Fertig, M. 106

Freire, P.: *Pedagogy of the Oppressed* 19
Fullan, M.: *Coherence Framework* 19; *Leading in a Culture of Change* 192

global citizenship 1, 2, 6, 16, 18, 83
Goleman, D. 184
governance 2
Grading Smarter Not Harder (Dueck) 152, *153*
Grashow, A.: *Principles of Adaptive Leadership, The* 19
Gray-Smith, A. 67–68
group learning 41–42
guiding teachers through change 140–164; agreements over policy 154–155, **155**; contentious issue conversation starters 152, *153*; dialogue 145–147; difficulties in 145; 'Disagree and Commit' 155–157; minds through experiences, shifting 151–152; need for change, feeling 159–163, *160*, *162*; paradigm shift, four stages of 142–144; pilot 156–159, *157–159*; preparation for challenge *163*, 163–164; relationships 145–147; responding to unique mindsets 150–151; strategies 147–150; trust equity 145–147
Guskey, T. 155; *Engaging Parents and Families in Grading Reforms* 151–152, 156

head evaluation, protocols for 98–100
Heifetz, R. A.: *Principles of Adaptive Leadership, The* 19
hemispheres of the brain 8–9
Hiatt, J. 129, 134
HIL *see* human-centered/liberatory (HIL)
holistic-indigenous worldview 7
human-centered approach 14–16
human-centered/liberatory (HIL) 14, 15
human development 12–13
humanity 192–193

Index

human learning ecosystem 49–62; better schools, becoming 58–59; big data 50–51; defining 53–55; delivery 59–61; demonstration 61–62; design 55–58; diversification 58

inclusion 1, 2, 19–21, 58, 180
innovation 1–3, 6, 12, 20, 21, 47, 61, 79–85, 140, 155–157, 195–197, 199, 203, 208, 211, 214, 220, 221; curriculum 67–68; long-term 209; sustainable 217
institutional legitimacy, building blocks of: cultural-cognitive pillar 107–108; normative pillar 107; regulative pillar 106–107
institutional primary task: definition of 103–105; identification of 103–106
institutional wisdom 217–218
integrity: in organizational culture 137–138; value of 121–123
intention 221–222; and leadership 209

James, C. 104–105
Johnston, M. 2, 65

Krathwohl, D. R. 159–160
Kuhn, T. 142
KVC (Know, Value, Care) 17–19

leader emeritus 218–219
leadership framework 135–136
leadership growth 193–194
leadership self-assessment 136–137
learning: agility 10; cultures, building 59–61; definition of 53–55; evidence of 61–62; experts, building 53; worth of 55–58
Linsky, M.: *Principles of Adaptive Leadership, The* 19
Littleford, J. 2
Love Rwanda initiative 83

Matta, N. 157, 159
McBain, L. 2
McLeod, S.: *Leadership for Deeper Learning* 140–141
McTighe, J. 57
Meyrink, C. 71
Middle of the Roaders (MR) 148, 150
Middle Years Programme (MYP) 81
Milligan, E. 80
mindset shift, guiding staff through 168–172; academic excellence 169; assessment practices with authentic learning, aligning 171; authentic learning through professional development 170; impact with research and data 170–171; rigor 169; structural support for authentic learning 171–172
Mission Statement 60
Mollick, E. 11
Moran, C. 2
motivation 187–188
MR *see* Middle of the Roaders (MR)
MYP *see* Middle Years Programme (MYP)

NAIS *see* National Association of Independent Schools (NAIS)
National Association of Independent Schools (NAIS): Principles of Good Practice 93
NEASC *see* New England Association of Schools and Colleges (NEASC)
need for change, feeling 159–163, *160, 162*
New England Association of Schools and Colleges (NEASC) 5
New Pedagogies for Deep Learning (NPDL) 18
Nominating Committee 92
NPDL *see* New Pedagogies for Deep Learning (NPDL)

O'Reilly, L. 159
organizational culture 102–118; actions 113, **114**, **117**; artifacts 114, **115**, **117**; institutional legitimacy, building blocks of 106–109; institutional primary task, identification of 103–106; relational systems 110–112, **112**, **116**; symbolic systems 109–110, **110**, **116**
organizational readiness 219
ownership 43–44

paradigm shift, four stages of 142–144
Parker, P.: Art of Gathering 41
PBL *see* project-based learning (PBL)
personal development 193–194
pilot 156–159, *157–159*
PLCs *see* professional learning communities (PLCs)
politics of change 94–95
'Portrait of a Learner' 56, **56**
prefrontal cortex impairment 37–38
preparation for challenge 163–164, *163*
presence, power of 207
professional development: authentic learning through 170
professional learning communities (PLCs) 172
project-based learning (PBL) 168
psychologically safe school 28
psychological safety 195–197; practical strategies for fostering 199

Queen Bees & Wannabes (Wiseman) 36
Quinn, J.: *Coherence Framework* 19

Raz, A. 2
relational systems 110–112, **112**, **116**
relevance of education 32
resilience 1, 2, 5, 26, 97, 102, 145, 173, 177, 180, 183–203; authenticity and 184–185, 187–188; community 202; definition of 183; emotional 174; impact of 202–203; motivation and 187–188; over long time, sustaining 199–201; psychological safety 195–197, 199
resilient leadership 184–185
respect 38–41
Revised Bloom's Taxonomy 159
Richardson, J. W.: *Leadership for Deeper Learning* 140–141
rigor 169
Rosefsky, F.: *Knowledge in Action Efficacy Study* 168
Rules of Order 97

SALT International School: SALT Problem/Project-Based Learning (SPBL) course 83–84
SDGs *see* Sustainable Development Goals (SDGs)
SEI *see* social and emotional intelligence (SEI)
SEL *see* social-emotional learning (SEL)
self-awareness 184, 188, 192, 193, 210
self-knowledge 10
self-reflection 193–194
service 173–174; lifelong impact of 177–178; into school culture, integrating 174; systemic impact of 178–179
service learning: into curriculum, embedding 175–176; trip 28–29
shadowing 210–211
SIA *see* Students in Action (SIA)
situated cognition 12
social and emotional intelligence (SEI) 190–192
social contract 30
social-emotional learning (SEL) 6, 18
staff, knowing 125–126
Stanford University School of Education: "ChallengeSuccess" survey 26–27
Students in Action (SIA) 83, 84
success measurement 138–139
sustainable change strategy 137

Index

Sustainable Development Goals (SDGs) 81–83
symbolic systems 109–110, **110**, **116**
systems thinking, for adaptive change 19–20

teachers: on generation of students 33
transformational leadership 209
transparency, in leadership 198–199
trust 2, 33–34, 121–139; building 121–122, 136; equity 121, 122, 125, 145–147
turnover rate 31–32

UbD *see* Understanding by Design (UbD)
UDL *see* Universal Design for Learning (UDL)
Understanding by Design (UbD) 61
Universal Design for Learning (UDL) 20

validation 43
vision 51–52
vision-centered approach to strategy 16–17

VUCA (volatility, uncertainty, complexity, and ambiguity) 1, 4, 5, 9–11, 12, 18, 23, 183, 190

Walker, A. 104–105
WASC *see* Western Association for Schools and Colleges (WASC)
Western Association for Schools and Colleges (WASC) 5
Wheatley, M. J. 60
Wiggins, G. 57
Wiliam, D.: *Embedded Formative Assessment* 152
Wilson, R. C. 145
World Economic Forum: Future of Work 65; Global Risks Report 2024 102

xenophobia 27

Yeager, D.: *10–25: The Science of Motivating Young People* 34–35; on adolescent predicament 36
young people: engagement with adults 34–36; prefrontal cortex impairment 37–38

For Product Safety Concerns and Information please contact our EU representative GPSR@taylorandfrancis.com
Taylor & Francis Verlag GmbH, Kaufingerstraße 24, 80331 München, Germany